北京大学中国经济研究中心研究系列

Competitive Advantage
Anatomy and Constellation

■ Hao Ma

PEKING UNIVERSITY PRESS

First Edition 2004

Copyright © by Peking University Press. Beijing, China
All rights reserved. No part of this book may be reproduced in any form or by any means without permission in writing from the publisher.

ISBN 7-301-07774-2/F · 0919
Competitive Advantage: Anatomy and Constellation
by Hao Ma

Published by
Peking University Press
Peking University, Beijing
100871, China

Printed in the People's Republic of China

To My Wife
With Love

Preface to the Research Series of Peking University China Center for Economic Research

The publication of Adam Smith's seminal treatise on The Wealth of Nations in 1776 witnessed the separation of economics from philosophy and its inception as an independent field of scholarly inquiry among social sciences. Ever since, economics has attracted many students and gained tremendous impact, and has become a shinning star in the crown jewel of all social sciences. Economic theory is a simplified logical system that is advanced to explain human behavior and social phenomena. Like any theories in social sciences, economic theories arise from the observation, interpretation, and conceptualization of social economic phenomena, and have to be constantly re-invented with the evolution of the human society. Economic theories also have to constantly subject themselves to the verification and refutation by actual economic events and phenomena, old and new, so as to tell the wheat from the chaff and inform on what could be temporarily accepted and what should be suspected and abandoned.

From this perspective, China's economic reform and open door practice since the 1970s provide many a challenge to the modern day mainstream economic theories: from household responsibility system in the rural area to the privatization of previously state-owned enterprises, from the un-ambiguity of property rights and transition to modern corporation system to the dual track systems in resource allocation and product distribution. Such are the achievements of the reform effort and the ensuing problems, and many of them were unexpected by existing economic theories and hence could not be appropriately explained. However, underlying any economic phenomenon, there must be a certain logic or rationale. When existing theories cannot explain an economic phenomenon, new theories are called for. As such, China's reform and open door policies promise to be a goldmine for economic inquiries, rendering a great opportunity for innovation in economic theories.

Since the reform and opening up, with the incremental establishment and refinement of the market economic system, modern economics also has found its increasing impact in China. Whether international or domestic, the purposes of economic inquiries are to better understand social economic phenomena, and promote the progress of human society through the applications of economic theories and policy formulations. With the advancement and deepening of the market-oriented reform, many interests conflict each other, contradictions abound, making economic phenomena increasingly more complex. Facing a specific problem, what are the causes, what are the effects? Contemplating on a particular reform policy, what could be the impact it will exert, in part or in whole, on the incentive mechanism, resource allocation, and income distribution? Absent appropriate theoretical and methodological guidance, an economic problem could be difficult to dissect and a hasty policy could trigger even more new problems. Therefore, innovative effort in theory-building based on the new phenomena observed during the course of China's economic reform will not only contribute to the development of modern economic theories, but also further help provide impetus to the smooth sailing of China's reform cause. Such effort should be honorable duty mighty unavoidable to every serious Chinese economist.

Ten years ago, several young scholars and I, all fully trained overseas in modern economics, founded China Center for Economic Research (CCER) at Peking University, under the auspices of the

Peking University administration and support of various circles of society. Although the research environment, working conditions, and financial reward were much more superior overseas than they were in China then, the opportunity of witnessing and participating in history-making proved to be fascinating and the opportunity of making monumental contributions to modern economic theories irresistible. We hoped that, with CCER's new organizing system, and through conglomeration of a critical mass of aspiring, passionate, dedicated, and well-trained economic experts, we could make our contribution to China's economic education, its economic theories, and policy formulation, and, eventually its modernization.

In the first ten years of CCER, research faculty has increased to 24 from its original 6. CCER has become an important base for theoretical research and policy study in China. During the 10 years, many CCER faculty members have gone to the frontline and grassroots, conducting field research in rural areas and urban enterprises, and some have also participated in high-ranking policy consultation and decision process. Such efforts helped generate research publications and policy reports that boast penetrating analysis, unique insights, and convincing impact. They also offered practical help to the reform efforts of rural areas, state-owned enterprises, financial sector, fiscal policy, foreign trade, and telecommunications, etc. During the last 10 years, CCER has taken good advantage of its frequent communications and exchanges with leading economic research institutions in the world, hosting leading economists, many Nobel Laureats included, through conferences and short visits. These conferences and visits helped generate valuable discussions and research articles, reports, and briefings on China's financial system and its reform, the mobility of the rural labor force, income inequality between urban and urban areas, land policy, social security systems, and a host of other important issues encountered during China's reform. Now, in celebrating the 10 year anniversary of

CCER, Peking University Press takes the initiative and offers to publish a CCER research series showcasing the research results and achievement of the CCER faculty that include the above mentioned research output as well as output from other scholarly endeavors. On the one hand, this series provides a report card to all the leaders in various circles who have supported CCER in the past 10 years. On the other hand, it begs for the attention of experts and scholars, domestic and abroad, and hopes to generate further discussions and debates and induce more research effort on China's reform and development.

In the long history of China, 10 years are but a fleeting and transient moment; in terms of the research opportunity furnished by China's economic reform and the many theoretical questions that have to be addressed, the effort of CCER in the last 10 years is also but a straw in a haystack. Looking into the future, the CCER scholars will honor the initial charge of the original founding members, and, together with all concerned economic researchers and friends worldwide, attempt their very best in advancing China's economic education, theoretical development, and policy studies. I believe, with our collective effort, we will soon embrace the renaissance of China in the 21st century and witness the parade of grand masters in economic science sailing from the great land of China.

Justin Yifu Lin, Ph.D.
Professor and Director
China Center for Economic Research
Peking University
September 2004

Contents

Preface \ i

Acknowledgement \ vii

Introduction \ 1

PART ONE
Anatomy of Competitive Advantage

Chapter 1   What is Competitive Advantage \ 17

Chapter 2   SELECT: An Integrative Framework \ 37

Chapter 3   Dynamic Advantage and Positional Advantage \ 60

Chapter 4   Locale and Appropriability \ 88

Chapter 5   Luck and Competitive Advantage \ 115

Chapter 6   Managerial Initiative, Strategic Maneuver, and Strategic Co-option \ 144

Chapter 7   The Sustainability Challenge \ 167

Chapter 8   Competitive Advantage and Firm Performance \ 182

PART TWO

Constellation of Competitive Advantages

Chapter 9   ARTS: An Integrative Framework \ 207

Chapter 10   Advantage-Based View of the Firm \ 221

Epilogue \ 259

Bibliography \ 270

Preface

Business firms are important economic and social agents in the modern society. If the game of business can be construed as the competition for limited resources in business eco-sphere and in society at large, then winners of the game, by definition, are able to command a large share of the scarce social and economic resources and exert their impact on society. For any firms, winners in particular, their existence then can be justified by their competitive advantages over other firms or other types of social or economic agents. That is, they exist because they are in a better position to deliver customer value and contribute to the needs of society. And for that, they are duly rewarded through their superior performance. In one word, to win the game and to even survive, a firm needs competitive advantage.

This book attempts to advance an integrative and systematic framework on the nature and causes of competitive advantage. In order to enjoy persistent superior performance, a firm has to gain, enhance, and renew its competitive advantages over other firms on a constant basis. Where does competitive advantage come from? How do we detect them? How long can an advantage sustain? How do a firm's advantages interact and effect through time? Addressing these questions is of paramount importance for strategy research and practice, as the ultimate goal of strategy is indeed to achieve persistent superior performance. The framework offered in this book is advanced precisely for this purpose.

I shall emphasize that this book is written primarily for practitioners. For pure research purpose, one has to work in more narrowly defined areas using specific and often discipline-based tools or approaches so as to gain deeper understanding of a particular strategic issue. Business reality, however, is not necessarily organized around elegant theoretical lines. As such, strategy practitioners need multiple weapons in their tool-kit to tackle different strategy issues and situations. A strategist is necessarily a generalist, seeking practical help and guidance from a whole range of theories and frameworks. For this reason, this book is an eclectic endeavor. Taking a holistic approach, it does not work within any extant perspectives or research paradigms. Rather, it is issue-driven. And the issue here is competitive advantage.

To better understand competitive advantage, this book draws on all the resources hitherto available (any prior theories, models, frameworks, and evidence on competitive advantage) in the strategy and related fields. It attempts to embrace the strategy literature on competitive advantage in its totality. Using the SELECT framework (Substance, Expression, Locale, Effect, Cause, and Time-horizon of competitive advantage) and the ARTS framework (Amplification, Renewal, Trade-Off, and Sustaining of competitive advantages), it coalesces major research streams in strategy and presents them in a comprehensive and coherent way, more readily accessible to strategic management practitioners. So my role will be the architect, now let's review some of the major building blocks.

In the past four decades or so, we have witnessed a parade of important treatises on strategy. In the groundbreaking work on The Concept of Corporate Strategy (1971), Kenneth Andrews established the strategy concept as the cornerstone of the field, then known as Business Policy. He and his colleagues at Harvard championed the idea of fit between internal working of the organization and the external requirement of the environment, an idea that is central to the now famous SWOT framework.

Richard Rumelt, in 1974, published his work on Strategy, Structure, and Economic Performance, calling our attention to the advantage of firms pursuing related diversification that exploited synergy across businesses, and also the advantage of matching organizational structure with strategy, a theme first explored by Alfred Chandler, Jr. in Strategy and Structure (1962).

Charles Hofer and Dan Schendel's book Strategy Formulation: Analytical Concepts (1978) helped formalize the conceptual framework and advance the discipline status of Strategic Management, that guided research in the field for almost two decades. Their treatment of levels of strategy has been of particular value in understanding firm's pursuit of advantage at various levels of the diversified firm in contemporary business.

Raymond Miles and Charles Snow, in Organizational Strategy, Structure, and Process (1978), popularized their typology of generic strategies, emphasizing the notions of configuration, ideal type, and equi-finality in firm's search for competitive advantage and superior performance.

In the 1980s, Michael Porter's Competitive Strategy (1980) and Competitive Advantage (1985) propelled to prominence the industry positioning or structural approach. The five-force model, three generic strategies, and the value chain became standard language for strategy researchers, consultants, and practitioners alike.

Richard Nelson and Sydney Winter's work on An Evolutionary Theory of Economic Change (1982) helped us understand how organizational routine form and change as well as its implication for organizational learning, adaptation, and firm's search for advantage.

Pankaj Ghemawat's book on Commitment (1991) articulated the importance of persistence in strategy for sustainable advantage, which could arise out of a series of investment decisions that require irrevocable commitment of resources.

The great economist Joseph Schumpeter's seminal work on the process of capitalist economy has found its tremendous impact in the strategy field. Inspired largely by Schumpeter's theory of innovation, C. K Prahalad and Gary Hamel advocate Competing for the Future (1994), making strategic intent and core competence a staple in daily business conversation.

Schumpeter would also find its influence in Richard D'Aveni, who brings to our attention the phenomenon of Hypercompetition (1994), where archrivals engage in cutthroat battle through four escalating arenas; where only the paranoid survive; and where no sustainable advantage is possible.

In the mean time, we've also received the coroner's report, The Death of Competition (1996), in which James Moore convincingly argues that the traditional way of competition as we know it, i.e., product or market based bilateral competition, is no longer of much relevance. Instead, the focus of competition, which is indeed more intense than ever before, has been placed on leadership in business ecosystems rather than on product dominance or even industry dominance. So the competitive landscape is changing.

From game theory with a newly invented word, comes Co-opetition (1996), where Brandenburger and Nalebuff demonstrate the power of pursuing a strategy that explores the benefits of both competition and cooperation, a strategy that is mean to change the game.

Recently, Jay Barney's Gaining and Sustaining Competitive Advantage (2002) systematically expounds the resource-based view of the firm, a perspective emerged in the mid-1980s which is currently gaining the strongest momentum. He advises strategists to base a firm's strategy on its valuable, rare, and inimitable resources, providing a valuable approach for understanding sustainable competitive advantage.

Why do we need another book in strategy? What is this book about? My mission in this book is to cut across the important milestones in the field and integrate the various research streams in strategy into an integrative whole. The organizing theme of this book is competitive advantage. And the integrative whole is the proposed SELECT ARTS framework. My inspiration for undertaking such a work can be found in Schumpeter that an innovation is often a creative combination of existing ideas, approaches, or materials. I intend to make the SELECT ARTS framework more complete than its building blocks but will in no way claim to replace them.

One simply has to know when to use these extant theories and in what context. This framework helps strategy practitioners better apply them. True to the spirit of strategic decisions that depend on the quality of managerial choice, it's the general managers' task to select from the tool-kit what is needed for a particular strategic task. My mission will be complete if this book helps you gain some value-added understanding of the whole range of options when it comes to the art of creating and sustaining competitive advantage. Treating the firm as an evolving constellation of competitive advantage, this book offers a first cut on an advantage-based view of the firm.

Acknowledgement

This book culminates from my research and teaching in the field of strategic management and related areas in the past 8 years or so. But the intellectual journey that led to this important moment in my academic life spans more than two decades. It was at the Beijing Institute of Technology in 1984, I first encountered, as a young, aspiring sophomore, Daniel Wren's The Evolution of Management Thought. I was so fascinated by the classical management theories Professor Wren had so masterfully presented, I dreamed that one day I would write such a book, a book on management. Since then that dream has lived with me. And five years later it turned dead serious when I enrolled in the doctoral program in Strategic Management at The University of Texas at Austin.

I was fortunate enough to meet there my mentor and dissertation adviser Dave Jemison, who would go on to win the Outstanding Educator's Award of the Business Policy and Strategy Division of the Academy of Management as well as the Academy's George Terry Book Award. Dave introduced me to the conceptual foundations of Strategic Management and helped instill in me a genuine appreciation for management practice and hence a practical perspective to management research and teaching. He's perhaps the one most responsible for reinforcing my bias toward integrative thinking. I guess that's what strategic thinking is really about. So there goes the intellectual debt to Dave.

This book will not be possible without the help and inspiration from many people. My deepest gratitude goes to each and every one of them. My heavy intellectual debt goes to all the pioneers and major contributors to our field who have paved the way for my current attempt at a theoretical synthesis. I wish I could acknowledge all of them individually. In addition to the authors whose work I already mentioned earlier, I would also like to acknowledge in particular the following scholars and writers whose work has strongly influenced my thinking on the topics directly related to this book: Igor Ansoff, Chester Barnard, David Collis, Mary Parker Follett, Robert Grant, Bruce Henderson, Harold Koontz, Henry Mintzberg, James Brian Quinn, Herbert Simon, David Teece, Birger Wernerfelt, Jeffery Williams, and Oliver Williamson.

I would also like to thank my professors at Texas for their contribution to my doctoral training: Tim Ruefli, who introduced me to strategy content research; Reuben McDaniel, for showing me the power of policy analysis and, as a scholar, how to make sense of the world in which we live; Jim Fredrickson, for his contribution to my understanding of strategy process and top management team; George Huber, for sharing his insights on strategic decision making in complex organizations; and Brian Golden, who co-authored with me my first ever academic paper and remains a collaborator. Thanks also go to Jay Barney, who had graciously served as an off-campus expert member on my dissertation committee.

At Bryant College, now Bryant university, I am blessed with a very collegial faculty environment in the last decade. Special thanks go to my former colleagues in the strategy group, Tom Powell and Kumar Chittipeddi. Through numerous discussions, Tom had succeeded in convincing me that the most meaningful measure of the success of strategy is indeed superior performance. Kumar had been a good friend, collaborator, and a good department chair. I thank him and Ron DiBattista, my subsequent department chair, for their support and encouragement. I also thank Collen Anderson, our able reference librarian at Bryant's Hodgson Memorial Library, for her research assistance. Special thanks go to Ranjan Karri, who has been a valuable colleague and collaborator at Bryant since 2000. I have benefited from his insights and comments a great deal on a host of strategy issues and perspectives. Moreover, as a collaborator and co-author, he has made significant contribution to the research and writing presented in Chapter 6.

I would also like to thank all the students at Bryant and Texas, and most recently at Peking University, who took their strategy courses with me, for their influence on my thinking about many strategy issues. In particular, I thank my MBA students for sharing their experience and insights and for their input and response to my ideas. Most of these students are working professionals, many of whom hold key managerial positions. The reward of interacting with them is the sense of validation of what I have ventured on the research side. I must say this is indeed a very positive reinforcement. I also thank numerous managers whom I talked to in my various research projects related to this book for generously sharing their time, experience, and wisdom. I sincerely hope that, through this book, my work could reach and help many and more practicing managers in their work.

I would like to extend my gratitude to my colleagues at Beijing International MBA (BiMBA) program at China Center For Economic Research (CCER), Peking University, for their assistance and support. Special thanks go to Dr. Justin Yifu Lin, Director of CCER, for inviting me to join CCER and including my manuscript as part of CCER's 10-year anniversary celebration book series, and to Dr. Dayuan Hu, who has helped make my stay at BiMBA a most enjoyable experience.

I also thank Ms. Lin Junxiu and her editorial team at Peking University Press for handling my manuscript, especially my editor Zhang Yan for her thoughtful suggestions and able assistance that helped improved the manuscript.

This book was originally conceptualized in the Fall of 1996, based on a paper on competitive advantage by the author that was to be presented at the 1997 Academy of Management Annual Meetings in Boston. All major chapters had been drafted in the Fall of 1997 and constantly refined in the years to follow. For various reasons, the extensive research and rich output for this research program have not been in print in a book format as originally envisioned. Due to time sensitivity of the materials and the mighty pressure for publication placed on a budding scholar, major chunks of the planned book were revised, updated, and then submitted to peer-reviewed journals and had been subsequently published in various outlets, primarily in Management Decision, and also in Business Horizons, Competitiveness Review, as well as Advances in Competitiveness Research.

In order to be faithful to the original conception and design of the book, which I believe are sound and solid, I have tried to use primarily the original writings and source materials developed for the purpose of the book, in conjunction with the versions actually published in the various journals. Credits for the related journal articles are listed and acknowledged in bibliography. Effort is carefully taken to update the materials presented in this book, to minimize repetition and redundancy, and to ensure a uniform style in presentation. In order to preserve the original flow, historical context, and integrity of the materials and the entire book, the revision of the materials for the concerns of time-sensitivity and similar interventions as such are, however, intentionally kept at minimal.

Although many people have helped influence and shape the research and writing of this book and its eventual publication, all errors, inaccuracies, and omissions, however, remain mine alone.

On a personal note, during the 8 plus years while this book was conceived and researched, I have been constantly blessed by the life awakening and reassuring music of the immortal great Gustav Mahler, whose life and music remain an up-lifting revelation and intellectual inspiration. To Mahler, a true musician and a martyr, music is life. His music embraces life in its totality and helps make it better. The late

Leonard Bernstein would so comment: "Life without music is dreadful; music without life is academic." Thank you maestro, for reminding me why I do what I do, for strategy research needs to have its earthly impact!

This book cannot bear fruit without the solid support of my family, to whom I express my profoundest gratitude. My loving parents have always made my educational advancement their top priority and remained a lasting inspiration in my life, personal and professional. My dear sister and brother back in China generously shouldered my part of the family responsibility while I study and work in the United States. Finally, I want to thank my dearest wife Ashley, and her family, from the bottom of my heart. Her love and care light up my world and provide a constant source of joy. Her parents also offered much appreciated assistance that helped free me from domestic chores while I work on this project in the last two years. Emily, our 19-month baby daughter, cheerfully helps daddy put the final touch on this 8-year endeavor with her most lovely angel-like smile and the sweetest voice calling daddy.

Hao Ma
Lincoln, Rhode Island
Langrun Yuan, Beijing
August 31, 2004

Introduction

The essence of strategy is about winning. In business terms then, the ultimate goal of strategy is superior performance on a persistent basis. A well-conceived and successfully implemented strategy helps a firm achieve such persistent superior performance. And it does so by providing the firm with advantages over other players in the field, current or potential. To create and benefit from these advantages requires that a firm, or more precisely its strategists, think in winner's terms. Winning is a mentality, a built-in and active frame of mind. Winning is a perspective, a systematic and persistent view of the world. Winning is strategy! After all that is said and done, winners go down history as heroes. Not only do they exert immediate impacts on business and society, but also usually sustain their glory and fame through posterity. Think in winner's terms and strategize to win. That is what makes business exciting!

You must rule and win, or serve and lose, suffer or triumph, be the anvil or the hammer.

Johann Wolfgang von Goethe

To be winners, it is not enough that you view your firm as merely a collection of product-market activities or as a bundle of resources. You must also view your firm as a host or constellation of competitive advantages. You must be somehow better than other players. This winning mentality fuels the burning desire to be the best. This winning perspective facilitates the definition of your mission, the fundamental reason of your firm's very existence in business; and its identity, your firm's institutional image in society. You are in business precisely because you can deliver customer value better than others can. Your firm's image and identity derive from your unique contribution to the society in economic and non-economic ways that makes yours a winning team. In one word, you need to view your firm as a vehicle for winning, a constellation of advantages. Consider the following examples.

JUST DO IT!

Nike, Goddess of victory. The namesake firm is nothing short of a victory and legend in modern day business. In 1962, in a term paper while at the Stanford MBA program, Philip Knight proposed a business plan to produce premium quality athletic shoes using overseas cheap labor. Inspiration: cheaper Japanese-made cameras were able to compete with high-quality and more expensive German cameras. Lesson: Germany—home of the industry leader, Adidas—was simply not the best place in the world to put shoe machines due to its higher wage. Mission: crush Adidas. Strategy: high quality, low cost, and brand image. Strategist: vision, ambition, passion, and keen knowledge of sports. Implementation: dedicated and knowledgeable management team, flexible corporate structure, creative organizational culture, and competitive spirit. Results: victory, winning, and persistent superior performance.

The fact that the firm was founded based on low-cost manufacturing suggests the very idea of basing a firm's strategy on where its potential advantage lies, where it could possibly win. Ever since, Nike has consistently pursued and perfected its three-pronged strategy. Strong R&D insures better quality and design. Shifting manufacturing progressively to lower wage countries helps control manufacturing cost to the lowest possible, leaving higher margins for maneuvering in marketing. Effective advertising campaign, carefully orchestrated promotion effort, and celebrity endorsement facilitate the building and strengthening of the Nike image.

And image is exactly what Nike is selling. When people think of Nike, they think of the best in sports; and most importantly, they think of a wining attitude, both in sports and in life. On the office door of Phil Knight hangs a dartboard, the center of which occupies a picture of the Chairman of Reebok, Nike's long-time eyeball-to-eyeball nemesis.

"We are in this business to win," claimed Knight. And win they did. For decades, Nike has reminded us to win. In competitive business where rivalry becomes rather personal, either eat lunch or be lunch. It's the enormous competitive hype that makes the shoe business a glamour business. Thanks in no small part to Reebok's challenging Nike, the game of athletic footwear further becomes the battle for high image. When the elephants start dancing, it's the grass that suffers. The battle confers both players competitive advantage, consolidating their joint lead over the rest of the field. Smart as they fight, the war is rarely if ever on price. Hard as they fight, there is only one first place. When it comes down to the ultimate winning, Phil Knight believes that the winner could only be Nike. As the Nike commercial stated during the 1996 Olympic Games: You don't win Silver, you lose the Gold.

ALWAYS LOW PRICE, ALWAYS!

Check out the following numbers. 1945: Operating a Ben and Franklin franchise, Sam Walton's first formal experience in retailing; 1962: opening of the first 4 Wal-Mart stores; 1971: Wal-Mart went public; 1985: Sam Walton named by Forbes as the richest man in America; 1996: Wal-Mart surpassed General Motors as the biggest private employer in the US; 2003: with $ 256 billion of sales, Wal-Mart sits firmly atop as the number one on the Fortune 500.

What makes Wal-Mart tick? What is their secret for winning?

What have been Wal-Mart's advantages? It was their choice of location, one may say. Or it's their inventory management; their efficient transportation and distribution system; their bargaining power over and good relationship with suppliers. Or it's their advanced information system and technology. Or it's the frugal-oriented management style and corporate culture, the dedication of their employees, the team spirit.

Obviously, it's all of them. Their initial choice of location gave them almost monopoly advantage where the small rural towns were big enough for one Wal-Mart store yet small enough for another discount retailer. They effectively eliminated competition (if it existed at all) from the local mom and pop stores and exploited their scale advantage in these markets. Industry leaders then like Kmart basically ignored Wal-Mart's strategy and wrote off the possibility of large-scale discount retailing in rural areas. None so blind as those who won't see. And quickly Wal-Mart grew. As they preempted essentially all the ideal target locations across the country, their advantage on location became essentially inimitable by rivals.

Luckily it was for Wal-Mart, while they accumulated their strengths and learned their craft, there's hardly any competitive pressure or retaliation from industry incumbents against its entry and growth. They were able to develop numerous advantages while they learned how to best serve their customers. Their effective transportation and inventory management system enabled them to replenish the shelves store wide in about 3 days. Their early adoption of advanced information technology allowed for, among other things, better tracking of their merchandise, effective communication within the firm and with partners, and even advanced joint planning with suppliers on future inventory.

Most importantly perhaps was their overall culture and management style, which reinforced the low price mentality. "I am cheap," prided Sam Walton, a frugal multibillionaire, who in the early years encouraged executives to share rooms on buying trips, walk instead of riding a cab while traveling, and call suppliers collect. Such was the deep commitment to low cost and hence low price. One strategy, multiple advantages. It could only be the whole package!

When later Wal-Mart had to face rivals more directly in more urban markets, armed with its constellation of advantages—notably about 6% of cost advantage over rivals, it was almost winning without much of a fight. When you don't have advantage, don't fight; when you do have advantage, you don't have to fight. Things just come your way. It is like a generation effect. New, better, and more efficient competitors replace old, stagnant, and inefficient ones. Nothing succeeds like a success. In the last decade or so, every Wal-Mart store opening was perhaps bitterly witnessed by a Kmart closing, often in the same town! Now that is what winning is about in business wars.

WE BRING GOOD THINGS TO LIFE!

Size matters. Big is beautiful. Winning is sweet. Not only do large firms provide more employment, but they also form the backbone of a national economy, determining its livelihood. GE, number five of the Fortune 500 list in 2003, has long been one of the top most companies in terms of stock market capitalization. It has been paying a dividend to its shareholders every quarter since 1899, and the dividend has increased every year since 1975. In terms of value creation, GE is a sure winner.

Funded to exploit Thomas Edison's inventions and initially dedicated to the generation, distribution, and use of electrical power, the company that we came to know as GE has been a classic conglomerate and a fixture of the top echelon in the Fortune 500 list. Throughout the years, GE has been constantly watched and analyzed, its management and performance hailed and criticized. The conglomerate which brought you textbook concepts like Strategic Business Units and GE Business Screen and which, to many people, is often being associated with only light bulbs, is not exactly your typical trendy new-age firm like Microsoft, Intel, or Cisco. Yet the century-old firm is showing no sign of slowing down. Instead it is going steady and strong. And the fact of being the highest valued firm in the US itself makes it a winner, even in the league of the best and the largest.

At times, GE might have bitten more than it could chew; but it went on to chew more than it had bitten. Since Welch's rein in 1981, the company had reinvented itself all over again. Welch's famous three-circle rendition of the future shape of GE in 1984 categorized its business in three major groups: core (33% of profit); high tech (30% and rising); and services (29%). While GE divested underperforming and low-growth businesses, they went on shopping for more high-growth businesses that would increasingly represent its future. The changing business composition shifted GE's historic revenue base from domestic based traditional manufacturing and natural resource businesses to globally oriented services and high technology. That is, business in the latter two circles, the would-be core for the 21st century.

Welch's vision for the future of GE: the most profitable, highly diversified company on earth. This vision hinges on "integrated diversity" and winning in every business. In one word, "a boundaryless firm for a boundaryless future." Although GE's businesses are highly diversified in their scope, they are also highly related in terms of management logic. Variety is pleasing. Unity is strength. The simple theme that ties all businesses together is winning, a common concern for quality and excellence, to be better than the best. If a business cannot stay as one of its industry's top two players, it has no reason to justify its existence, in GE that is. Refusing to participate in losing businesses requires tremendous discipline, in addition to a keen winning attitude. This logic and criterion insure that every business GE owns is a winner, and the whole firm a system of winning teams. In this sense, GE might well be the perfect textbook example of a constellation of advantage. Under their new CEO Jeffrey Immelt, they are re-energizing the constellation again.

So what do we learn from the above examples? Plenty! But foremost, the determination to win. Nike perfectly exemplifies the winning attitude and spirit. Wal-Mart aims at being the best in merchandising. GE insists on every business in its portfolio being in the top two spots of their respective business. These firms are winners because they have the heart of a champion. Also, winning firms don't just do one thing well; they excel on multiple frontiers. Instead of banking solely on any particular advantages, they nurture an advantage system where various advantages complement and enhance each other. This makes their strategy effective, because it is just difficult or even irrational for rivals to imitate them and catch up in many areas simultaneously.

Furthermore, winning firms are good at managing the dynamics of their advantage constellation. Advantages evolve. Before old advantages getting eroded or obsolete, these firms are able to renew the constellation with new ones. Through time, they also change their focus and reliance on different advantages according to changes in the environment or competition. For instance, Nike's cost advantage became rather relative and diminishing when competitors imitated its outsourcing strategy. No problem. As the cost advantage weakened its effect, Nike had already successfully shifted its emphasis and further strengthened its differentiation advantage, advantage based on quality, image, and reputation. Wal-Mart's initial advantage in its locations also diminished when the pool of small rural towns ideal for Wal-Mart began to dry up. Don't worry. By the time they had to compete directly with Kmart and Target alike in more urban areas, Wal-Mart had already created a whole new host of advantages as they tried to better serve their initial locations. GE is essentially an evolving constellation of advantage in action. It purposefully screens and replenishes its portfolio and shifts to businesses where they would have advantage, dominance, and high chance to win.

To summarize, in the game of business, there are winners and there are losers. Any winner is necessarily a survivor; a mere survivor not necessarily a winner. A firm's *raison detre* lies in its advantage over rivals in serving customers. At least for successful firms it is so. To be a winner, you must have the winning mentality and perspective. Winning firms often win because they know best how to create and renew a constellation of advantages: how to excel in doing many things well and how to change and adapt to new competitive situations. As such, viewing the firm as an evolving constellation of advantages is to say that a firm is a vehicle for winning.

AN ADVANTAGE-BASED VIEW OF THE FIRM

I propose an advantage-based view of the firm. Such a view or framework can be sketched based on two interconnected components: dissecting the anatomy of firm advantage and outlining the dynamics of the firm's advantage as a system or constellation. Advantages come in various shapes and sizes, analyzing the anatomy of firm advantage cross sectionally helps us better understand its nature and cause, i.e., how individual advantages are configured and how they function. Advantages evolve through time, analyzing the constellation of a firm's advantages longitudinally allows us to observe firm advantages in action, i.e., how individual advantages emerge, interact, and vanish; and how the constellation changes and renews itself.

Fundamental questions that have guided the research reported in this book are as follows. They address the basic elements of an advantage-based view of the firm.

I. Questions regarding the Anatomy of Competitive Advantage:

What are the *substances* of competitive advantage?
What are the *expressions* of competitive advantage?
In what *locale* do competitive advantages reside?

How do we observe the *effects* of competitive advantages?
What are the *causes* of competitive advantages?
What determine the *time horizon* of competitive advantages?

II. Questions about the Constellation of Competitive Advantages:

What are the major *components* of a constellation?
How do different advantages *interact* among each other?
How does the constellation of advantage *evolve* over time?
How to *guide* the evolution of constellation of advantages?

The defining characteristic of the advantage-based view of the firm is that it treats the firm as a multidimensional, evolving system of advantages, a constellation. Such a constellation consists of various types of advantages that are simultaneously at work, where different advantages may reinforce, augment, and even derive from each other; temporal advantages might be sustained; obsolete advantages get to be replaced by new ones. Moreover, it treats the firm not only as a constellation of advantages, but also as a system that constantly and deliberately renews itself.

As will be elaborated in Chapter One, for the purpose of this book, *competitive advantage* is formally defined as the asymmetry or differential in any firm attribute or dimension that allows one firm to better serve the customers than others and hence create better customer value. *Constellation of advantage* is defined as a host or system of advantages which are of various types of anatomical configuration in terms of source, content, form, locale, effect, and time-horizon, that a firm possesses and/or has actual or potential access to, due to its individual traits, endowments, strategy, luck; its participation in certain groups, arrangements, and events; as well as due to changes in its environment which the firm has no control of.

Constellation of advantage is an evolving system. For any individual advantage in the constellation, the evolution process moves through multiple stages including its searching or emerging; capturing or realizing; enhancing, sustaining, or terminating. For constellation of advantage as a whole system, its composition evolves as existing advantages are eroded and new advantages arise. At any moment then, the constellation may host simultaneously emerging or potential advantages, temporal advantages, as well as sustainable advantages.

The major thesis of this book states that a well-balanced constellation of competitive advantages is the fundamental determinant of a firm's persistent superior performance, defined as consistent and sustained above-normal performance through time. And the central activity of strategic management is to create and maintain a healthy dynamics for its evolving constellation of competitive advantages, by constantly searching, realizing, sustaining, and amplifying individual advantages as well as renewing the constellation with new advantages, in adaptation to changes in its environment, competitors, customers, and the firm itself.

ADVANTAGE-BASED VIEW AS A MANAGEMENT PHILOSOPHY

The advantage-based view of the firm is both a management philosophy and an analytical framework. Being a management philosophy, it is useful in funneling a firm's strategic attention to its core value, distinctive competence, and unique capabilities. The advantage-based view prompts a firm to focus on what it does best. It mandates that a firm should engage in activities where it enjoys the most advantage over others; where it has a chance to win.

Better be the head of a dog than the tail of a lion.

At the individual firm level, in following this philosophy, a firm is more likely to achieve superior performance, because it is at a position to provide its best value for the customers. The moral is to work smart, not just harder. And this is perhaps what winning is about in business. Do what you love to do and what you do best. Make known your name. Earn your profit.

Pigs might fly, but they are unlikely birds.

At the economy or society level, should more firms adopt the advantage-based view of the firm, it is more likely that the scarce economic resources will be allocated and utilized more effectively and efficiently. This is so because that wastes could be reduced through minimizing the possibility where incompetent firms unnecessarily consume societal resources undertaking tasks in which they have no competitive advantages whatsoever. Furthermore, if more firms subscribe to the advantage-based view, there will likely be more win-win situations as firms focus on their best chance of winning—where their advantages lie; where their value-added is the greatest.

One firm's winning, however, does not necessarily suggests that others must fail. Business is not necessarily always a zero-sum game. Win-win situation is possible. In their successful book, *Co-opetition*, Adam Brandenburger and Barry Nalebuff (1996) offered the following observation: "What matters is not whether others win—it's a fact of life that they sometimes will—but whether *you* win." This said, both competition and cooperation, or combination of both, are simply means; so is strategizing to win without the fight. Remember, the ultimate goal is to win—to achieve advantage and persistent superior performance, whatever it takes.

ADVANTAGE-BASED VIEW AS AN ANALYTICAL FRAMEWORK

As an analytical framework, the advantage-based view enables a firm to better understand and utilize its advantages and achieve superior performance. Specifically, the analytical framework allows for the systematic analysis of the anatomy of competitive advantage and the dynamics of the constellation of advantage. Dissecting the anatomy of advantage facilitates the understanding of its cause, content, form, locale, effect, as well as time sensitivity. Knowledge of competitive advantage's anatomical structure and its various facets should be valuable for its nurturing, sustaining, and strengthening. Analyzing the constellation of advantage enables strategists to observe the interaction as well as the combined effect of a firm's various advantages. It affords the strategists opportunities to evaluate the firm's advantage constellation through time and how its changing composition affects the firm's performance.

Based on the aforementioned research questions, I develop a general framework to help strategy researchers and practitioners analyze the anatomy of competitive advantage. The *SELECT* framework helps us analyze anatomy of advantage by dissecting it into six interrelated facets: Substance, Expression (form), Locale, Effect, Cause, and Time Horizon.

The *ARTS* framework helps us analyze a constellation of competitive advantages. Specifically, it analyzes the components of the constellation—the rise and change of its dominant advantage and supplementing advantages, as well as the dynamics of the constellation—the Amplification of an advantage, the timing and tactics in the Renewal of advantage, the Trade-off among different, or competing, advantages, and the Sustaining of extant advantages.

OVERVIEW OF THE BOOK

This book is organized as follows. This *introduction* chapter briefly expounds the advantage-based view and the analytical frameworks and forecasts the entire book. The core of the advantage-based view is then presented in two interrelated parts.

Part I consists of chapters 1 through 8. Chapter 1 provides a working definition of competitive advantage and offers an initial attempt at understanding the nature and cause of competitive advantage. Chapter 2 presents the *SELECT* framework. Chapter 3 further elaborates on the substance of competitive advantage, juxtaposing positional advantage and dynamic advantage. Chapter 4 examines the various locales of competitive advantage, within or outside the firm, with a particular focus on the appropriability issue, i.e., to what extent a firm could benefit from the advantages of different locales. Chapters 5 and 6 expound in more details the causes of competitive advantage, with the former focusing on more serendipitous causes and the latter more deliberate and purposeful acts. Chapter 7 tackles the challenges to the sustainability of competitive advantage and systematically identifies the triggers and forces that destroy competitive advantage. Wrapping up Part One, Chapter 8 examines the various possible patterns in the relationship between competitive advantage and firm performance.

Part II comprises chapters 9 and 10. Chapter 9 presents the *ARTS* framework on constellation of competitive advantages. Chapter 10 presents the theoretical underpinnings for interpreting the constellation of competitive advantages and the practical challenges in managing it.

The *Epilogue* addresses the fundamental question of "Why do firms exist?" It explains the usefulness of the advantage-based view in defining firm mission, identity, and strategy. It also briefly reflects on the implication of the advantage-based view for firm's social responsibility, public policy, and competition between nations.

The presentation of the book is based on one basic guiding principle. That is, the balance between theoretical rigor and practical relevance. As such, the presentation draws from both theoretically grounded, scholarly research work in strategy and relevant fields, and from examples representing the contemporary business reality. While the scholarly work provides solid conceptual foundations, business examples help illustrate the richness and complexity of firm's strategy and its constellation of advantage. To illustrate the generality of the *SELECT* and

ARTS frameworks, a conscious decision is made to strive a balance between examples of well known perennial winners and lesser known challengers; American firms and those from the rest of the world.

Viewing winning and advantage as the ultimate goal, prior theories and frameworks will likely seem to be more complementary than contradictory, for they are all means that wait to be selected to serve the goal. Obviously, it is managerial judgment that helps make sense of the competitive situation and choose appropriate tools that guide the evolution of a firm's advantage constellation. And that, is exactly the inspiration for the advantage-based view: to help the general managers better do their jobs. As optimistic as it is, the advantage-based view treats the firm as a vehicle for winning. Advantage in providing customer value justifies a firm's existence. Winning rewards it. So act now. Create your own constellation of competitive advantages. And win!

PART ONE
Anatomy of Competitive Advantage

Chapter 1   What is Competitive Advantage

Competitive advantage arises from the differential among firms along any dimension of firm attributes and characteristics that allow one firm to better create customer value than do others. Along three general categories of competitive dimensions, a typology of generic competitive advantages is advanced that classifies competitive advantages into three types: ownership-based, access-based, as well as proficiency-based. To achieve and sustain competitive advantage, a firm needs to creatively and proactively exploit the three competitive dimensions, preempt rivals' attempt, and/or pursue any combination of proactive and preemptive efforts. Juxtaposing creation and preemption as well as ownership-based, access-based, and proficiency-based advantages, this chapter offers an integrative framework that helps management practitioners systematically analyze the nature and causes of competitive advantage.

Strategic Management practitioners and researchers alike have long been preoccupied with the phenomenon of persistent superior performance demonstrated by highly successful firms. As such, a great deal of attention has been focused, and rightly so, on the nature and causes of competitive advantage. To date, various theoretical frameworks and perspectives have been advanced that attempt to explain competitive advantage. For instance, the traditional industry analysis approach emphasizes the importance of industry structure and market position (Porter, 1980). The newly emerged resource-based view points to a firm's unique resources, core competence, and dynamic capabilities in a rapidly changing global market (Barney, 1991; Prahalad and Hamel, 1990; Teece, Pisano, and Shuen, 1997). Time honored theory of creative destruction forces us to rethink the importance of innovation, competing against time and destroying the old equilibrium as well as established convention (Schumpeter, 1934, 1950). Recently, the knowledge-based view articulates that creating a learning organization and fostering knowledge generation and exploitation should be the fundamental basis for competitive advantage in an increasingly information-based economy (Senge, 1990; Nonaka, 1991).

With "newest best practice" and "state-of-the-art strategic tools" in the popular business literature changing more quickly than items on restaurant menus (Eccles and Nohria, 1992; Micklethwait and Wooldridge, 1996), management practitioners are constantly bombarded by contradicting views and often confused by fragmented theoretical understanding. What is competitive advantage? What are the bases of competitive advantage? How to make sense of the extant perspectives and frameworks on competitive advantage? How can Strategic Management research inform a firm's search for competitive advantage? It is the purpose of this chapter to synthesize extant theories and provide a systematic framework for practicing managers to better understand the generic competitive advantages.

COMPETITIVE ADVANTAGE: A WORKING DEFINITION

Porter (1985: 3) suggests that: "competitive advantage grows fundamentally out of value a firm is able to create for its buyers that exceeds the firm's cost of creating it. Value is what buyers are willing to pay, and superior value stems from offering lower prices than competitors for equivalent benefits or providing unique benefits that more than offset a higher price." Building on Porter's (1985) definition, for the purpose of this book, competitive advantage can be defined as the asymmetry or differential among firms along any comparable dimension that allows one firm to better create customer value than do rivals. My definition features three characteristics.

First, competitive advantage here is defined at the most basic level of analysis. That is, in an ongoing competition among a set of firms, if a particular firm attribute enables a firm to have an edge over rivals, then we say it has a competitive advantage in that aspect. A particular competitive advantage over rivals in one aspect of competition may help the firm better serve the customer in that particular aspect, e.g., product quality. Then again, the effect of this particular advantage may be overwhelmed by a rival's competitive advantage in a different competitive aspect, e.g., location of stores.

To achieve superior performance, especially persistent superior performance, a firm often needs multiple competitive advantages. Beating rivals on multiple strategically important vectors is essential for a winning firm. Not surprisingly, superior firms are often excellent in multiple aspects. Banking solely on any individual advantages, even highly sustainable ones, may carry the firm through temporarily. Creating a constellation of multiple evolving competitive advantages and renewing such a constellation in a timely fashion, however, will likely make persistent superior performance more readily attainable (Ma, 1997).

In this sense, to avoid being tautological, I don't automatically equate competitive advantage (an often adopted grand notion in the strategy literature) to superior firm performance. This also allows for equi-finality, as firms basing their strategies on different types of competitive advantage can all enjoy superior performance.

Second, the definition is relational, depending on the context of analysis. Instead of insisting on that a competitive advantage must be something that one firm does better than all other firms, it allows for pair-wise comparison. Extending the above example, among two larger firms in that market, one may be more flexible than the other, which indicates competitive advantage of the one with relatively more flexibility, although neither firm is the most flexible in the entire market.

Third, the definition is operational. We can actually compare the firms' scores on a particular dimension and see whether it possesses competitive advantage or disadvantage against a particular rival or a set of rivals. Such dimensions or attributes, for instance, could be a superior location, e.g., Wal-Mart's often monopolized location in rural areas in the U.S.; domination of shelf-space in retail, e.g., Coca-Cola's or Pepsi's dominance in supermarkets; exclusive or favorable access to supply, e.g., De Beers in the diamond market; a well-known brand name, e.g., *Cartier*; employee know-how, e.g., the experience and expertise of Lincoln Electric's well-trained technicians; efficiency in business operation, e.g., Toyota's just-in-time manufacturing and inventory system. Along any of these attributes, the higher a firm scores *vis-à-vis* its rivals, the greater its competitive advantage is.

In order to build a host of competitive advantages and achieve superior performance, a firm has to gain individual competitive advantages one at a time. Enhancing one's understanding of the generic bases of the various competitive advantages is expected to help in the endeavor of advantage building. This chapter helps general managers to do just that. It will focus primarily on gaining advantage in the business arena. More broadly speaking, however, the essence of competitive advantage in any human endeavors is indeed the differential along any comparable dimension from which people derive value or to which people attach value, real or perceived. Before I present my framework on generic competitive advantages in business settings, let's first take a detour in a different but relevant social context so as to warm up to the various factors discussed in the integrative framework.

COMPETITIVE ADVANTAGE IN THE SOCIAL ARENA: THE LICENSE NUMBER GAME

It is perhaps reasonable to say that to have the license number of one's automobile as low as possible is often regarded as a social advantage in America. The advantage, albeit a largely perceived one, — prestige, pride, and attention received—associated with a lower numbered license plate is often great enough for people to have endless thirst and obsession for it. Why is it an advantage? Scarcity, Distinction, Uniqueness. Small numbers easily differentiate themselves from the regular multi-digit-and-letter plates alike. How can one achieve such an advantage? Power, Merit, Resource, Luck, Lobbying, Coercion, or any combination of them.

In the State of Rhode Island and Providence Plantation,① the smallest continental state in the U.S., there would be 27 license plates that are Number One, in different vehicle categories respectively. The best chance to get a lower number is to work for the government, and in powerful positions, that is. In all the official categories, State Plates, City Plates, Police Plates, and so on, each has a Number One. The chief officer has the formal authority to sport Number One on their respective vehicles in each official category. Also, in mid-1990s, an outgoing governor would give a lower-numbered plate to her wife as a birthday gift. It's a power thing.

One could also earn a lower number by merits, e.g., the Number One plate for the Veterans category should usually belong to the most honorable and often famous veteran in the state or the region. Or

---

① The ensuing discussion draws from Landis, B. 1997. License-plate lowdown: R. I. has 27 No. 1's. *Providence Sunday Journal*, September 28: A1, A15.

should it be an auction by the Motor Vehicle Registration for the low numbers, the one with deep-pocket resources win. Should it be a lottery procedure for equity reasons, then luck determines. Better yet, you could change the rule of the game and write your own law. Campers unsatisfied with being "lumped over in the category with commercial trucks for tax purposes" would lobby for their own category. The champion for this cause earned the right of Number One for his RV motor home.

In the secondary market after a lower number has already been assigned, many underground dealings could happen. Some car dealers would be arrested for faking license transfer letters without the owners' permission. Other dealers would fight to buy a choice plate with a price as high as $ 25,000; and the ensuing battle would go all the way to the State Supreme Court. Furthermore, even some government officials would sometimes coerce lower-number plates holders and try to take them away by picking bones from within eggs, e.g., they say your plate might not be displayed correctly.

So what's the implication of this example for advantage of business firms? Arguably, the license plate game is of limited scope and more or less single-staged and the results of which often perpetually sustain. This, to a great extent, differentiates it from typical business games where competition is often ongoing through multiple iterations; where managers could have possibly more latitude for strategic choice in addition to environmental determination. Yet the sources of advantage in both types of games are actually very similar. In fact, to gain advantage in any kind of game, one needs knowledge, resources, capabilities, creativity, and luck. Moreover, in any socially construed game or interaction, it often depends on who you are, who you know, what you have, and what you can do. The game of business is no exception.

Prior research in Strategic Management has pointed out various potential sources for firm advantage. Market power (Porter, 1980), unique resources (Barney, 1991), innovation (Schumpeter, 1934,

1950), efficiency (Williamson, 1991), to name but a few. Building on prior research and observations regarding the rising of advantage in various business situations, I develop a framework that helps general managers systematically analyze the generic sources of competitive advantage. These sources could be either exploited through purposeful strategizing (Andrews, 1971) or be made available to a firm by luck (Barney, 1986a), or a combination of both luck and managerial action (Lieberman and Montgomery, 1988). The importance thing is, however, that managers should at least be aware of these generic sources and the relationship among them so that they can be better informed in their search for competitive advantage.

GENERIC COMPETITIVE ADVANTAGES

A firm's competitive advantage often arises along one or more of the following three competitive dimensions: *Ownership-Based*, *Proficiency-Based*, and *Access-Based*. That is, a firm can gain advantage by *ownership* or *possession* of certain valuable assets or factors, e.g., strong market position (Porter, 1980), unique resource endowment (Barney, 1991), or reputation (Hall, 1992); by opportunity or rights to gain superior *access* to inputs and markets (Lieberman and Montgomery, 1988), e.g., exclusive relationship with supplier or distribution channel; by superior *knowledge, competence, or capabilities* in conducting and managing its business processes (Nonaka, 1991; Prahalad and Hamel, 1990; Teece et al., 1997): producing quality products at lower costs and delivering the right products and/or service to its customers in the right place at the right price and time through the right channels. Simply put, to achieve any advantage in business, a firm has to look deeply and systematically into what it has, what it knows and does, and what it can get.

As advantage comes from the *differential* in any firm attributes, be it ownership, access, or knowledge based, which allows one firm to better provide customer value than others can, any factor that contributes to the existence and/or enlargement of such a differential could serve as a source of firm advantage. That is, to gain competitive advantage, a firm could focus on raising its own level of playing; it could also proactively constrain or belittle rivals. The former approach exploits the above three dimensions of advantages by positively enhancing a focal firm's ability to create value better than others can. I term this approach *Creation-Oriented*. The latter approach exploits the three types of advantages for the focal firm by eliminating or reducing rivals' option space; by limiting, reducing, or neutralizing other players' ability to create customer value in comparison to that of the focal firm (cf. Wind, 1997). I define this approach *Preemption-Oriented*.

OWNERSHIP-BASED COMPETITIVE ADVANTAGE

Ownership-based competitive advantage refers to any assets or factors under a firm's possession from which a firm could gain an upper hand *vis-à-vis* its rivals in better serving customers. That is, by possessing certain characteristics or by being in a certain status, a firm enjoys advantage over others. The ownership-based competitive advantage lies within the firm. This includes, among others, strong market power, e.g., Microsoft's power in the computer-related business arising from its large installed base in PC operating system; unique resource endowments, e.g., Caterpillar's extensive world-wide dealer and maintenance system; exceptional managerial talents, e.g., Jack Welch at GE; superior organizational culture, e.g., the 3M culture that facilitates innovation; and admirable corporate reputation, e.g., Procter & Gamble or Gillette in personal care products.

Figure 1.1 Generic Competitive Advantages

	Creation-Oriented	Preemption-Oriented
Ownership-Based	Actively Acquire Valuable Assets	Constrain Rivals' Options in Acquiring Valuable Assets
Access-Based	Build Gateway for Access	Deny or Limit Rivals' Access
Proficiency-Based	Foster Organizational Learning and Refine Routine	Discourage Rivals' Learning and Imitating

Acquire Valuable Assets

Proactively acquiring and accumulating valuable resources and gaining market positions in a systematic way contributes to a firm's gaining and sustaining of ownership-based competitive advantage. Let's take the example of brand name, one of the most valuable assets a firm can own. To determine how rich a person or family is, one can not simply examine the income they take on a yearly basis. One needs to look at the accumulated wealth. Similarly, to understand how advantageous a firm is, e.g., how valuable a brand name is, one cannot simply examine its annual spending on advertising/promotion and hope to well capture the firm's strategy through such *flow* variables. One needs to see the firm's endowment of resources and market positions. It is usually the *stock* variables that determine a firm's advantage in any moment: what positions you have, what resources you possess, and how much goodwill you have deposited in customers and suppliers, i.e., the strength of your name, your reputation. While it is relative easy to adjust the flow instantaneously, it is difficult to change the stock level quickly, which usually requires a consistent pattern of in-flow of resources (Dierickx and Cool, 1989).

For instance, it may be possible or perceivable for a firm in the soft drink business to match or even surpass the advertising expenditure of Coca-Cola on a specific year, it would be impossible to create the reservoir of customer goodwill that has been accumulated, preserved, and renewed through a hundred years' spending on advertising and promotion. Possession of a good reputation shall be the most valuable assets, especially in the era when people's attention span is getting increasingly shorter and narrower. Executives at Coca-Cola like to say that if the place was, God forbid, obliterated off the face from the earth they could walk right into the bank and borrow $100 billion and rebuild Coca-Cola in a matter of months, just on the strength of the brand (*Fortune*, 1996a).

Constrain Rivals' Options

A firm could gain advantage by sabotage or constrain rivals' options in acquiring valuable assets or positions. While Wal-Mart's rural town-focused location strategy helped them avoid direct competition from major rivals, e.g., Kmart and Target, and achieve explosive growth in the 1970s and 1980s (Ghemawat, 1991), Sam Walton the entrepreneur was, nonetheless, no stranger to competition. In his early days of running the variety store, a Ben and Franklin franchise in Newport, Arkansas, Sam had faced a strong competitor across the street, John Dunham's Sterling Store. Well wired in competitive intelligence in the small town commerce circle, Walton would come to know that John Dunham intended to buy up the lease of its neighbor, a grocery store, and expand his retailing business. That would have made his store much bigger than Sam's Ben and Franklin. And that didn't happen. Sam made sure that didn't happen, as he rushed to the landlord and convinced her to give him the lease instead (Walton, 1992).

Sam confessed later in his autobiography that he did not know what he's going to do with the new space before he got the lease, but he's dead sure that he did not want the rival store to have it. He ended up putting there a small department store called Eagle and opened for business within six days. Although Sam's Ben and Franklin franchise was becoming the number one Ben and Franklin store in both sales and profit in the region, the Eagle never made much money. What Eagle did, however, was not only preempted a major competitor, but also provided a ground for experiment and learning outside the strict rules he had to endure in managing the franchise. If a piece of merchandise did not work in one store, he would try it at the other. Running both stores also gave rise the need to hire his first assistant manager. As reflected by Bud Walton, younger brother of Sam (Walton, 1992: 28):

> *That Newport store was really the beginning of where Wal-Mart is today. We did everything. We would wash windows, sweep floors, trim windows. We did all the stockroom work, checked the freight in. Everything it took to run a store. We had to keep expenses at the minimum. That is where it started, years ago. Our money was made by controlling expenses.*

As such, a preemptive move to avoid potential disadvantage as well as the experience and knowledge accumulated in running the Eagle store sewed the seed for Wal-Mart's later advantage in its efficient merchandising process.

ACCESS-BASED COMPETITIVE ADVANTAGE

Access-based competitive advantage refers to the possibility that a firm enjoys advantages over rivals because it has more superior access to the factor markets, i.e., resource input (Barney, 1986a), and/or product market, i.e., customers (Porter, 1980) than do rivals or it has such access that is not at all available to rivals. Such access depends on a firm's ability to tap the resources and skills, knowledge and expertise, market reach, as well as power and authority of other business or non-business entities (Ghemawat, 1986; Bailey, 1997). That is, access-based competitive advantage lies in a firm's external relationship with other concerned parties in its operating environment. Examples include a firm's relationship with suppliers, partners, distributors, licensing authorities, governmental agencies in charge of sales or import/export quota, or agencies overseeing approvals for the introduction of certain products or services, e.g., the FDA.

Build Gateway to Access

A firm enjoys advantage if it can access resource inputs or customers in ways more convenient and/or efficient than those of rivals or in ways no other rivals can. Procter & Gamble's dominance in shelf space at retail stores, for instance, renders the firm superior access to customers, old and new. The sheer volume and variety of the P&G products displayed would guarantee to attract customers' attention. And whichever P&G brand or division wins, they all contribute to the bottom line of the overall P&G firm.

Similarly, superior access to factor inputs also helps provide firms with advantage. For instance, top management consulting firms, BCG and McKinsey alike, due to its investment in sound relationships with top MBA programs worldwide, usually have better access to and often skim the best candidates of a graduating class. This superior access to talents insures that they are on the frontier in the competition for knowledge accumulation and dissemination in advising business firms (O'Shea and Madigan, 1997).

Without proper access, a firm, even one with superior capability or endowed with uniquely valuable assets would be at competitive disadvantage. It is interesting to note that the Japanese firms were able to obtain better access to the affluent North America consumer markets than were the Germans, for whatever historical or political reasons. Industrialists like Mr. Matsushita who actively supplied to the Japanese military apparatus during the World War II were let return to run their old firms after the war (Kotter, 1997). And access to western technology and the world market gave them the chance to amass economic fortune and power (Vogel, 1985).

On the other hand, German firms' access to the world market was not as smooth as that of their Japanese counterparts. For instance, the Berlin Philharmonic's first concert tour to the US after the World War II, led by Herbert von Karajan, was heavily boycott due to Karajan's wartime involvement with the Nazi party. During Karajan's tenure as chief conductor and later artistic adviser, the Berlin Philharmonic's access to the American audience would have to be largely reduced to recordings only and Karajan was confined to Europe as his primary sphere of influence, where he himself would vigorously deny access by US-based rival conductors like Sir Georg Solti or Leonard Bernstein to influential venues in Berlin and Salzburg (Lebrecht, 1994).

Deny Rival Access

A firm could gain advantage by denying rivals access to a particular piece of potentially valuable resource (Brandenburger and Nalebuff, 1996; Wind, 1997). To be sure, this practice is not necessarily a pure defensive measure to avoid disadvantage. It is, in fact, often an offensive defense to proactively alter a firm's relative competitive position *vis-à-vis* that of rivals'. Take for example the *Seinfeld Show* with NBC. For the 1990s, the *Seinfeld Show* has been consistently ranked as the most watched prime time program on TV in the U.S. Jerry Seinfeld, the show's namesake star, was named by *Forbes* (1998) as the highest paid actor on TV, and top earner in the entertainment business, for that matter. In the war of TV ratings, the most important determinant of advertising incomes for network broadcasters, NBC certainly struck gold with this show. *Seinfeld* was the first sitcom ever to hit the $ 1 million mark of advertising draw-in per minute, next only to the record drawn by the Superbowl (*Business Week*, 1997).

But the relationship between a hit sitcom and a major network can be tricky. And the germination of the *Seinfeld Show* was nothing but a smooth ride. After a poor audience response to the pilot show, NBC ordered only 4 episodes. But, recognizing the potential of the star, NBC executives were smart enough not to pass up the show and its star. They simply did not want its network rivals, notably ABC and CBS, snatch up Jerry Seinfeld and fuel their fight in the rating war. Especially, they did not want to see Seinfeld in gigs that would rival NBC's *The Tonight Show*, a perennial winner in the late night talk show segment of the business (*Business Week*, 1997). So by denying others access to a star, NBC not only avoided a potential threat, but, lucky for them, they were able to see that the potential star was indeed real, real enough to be hailed as to have set the defining standard of sitcoms in the 1990s.

Nike also uses preemptive strategy to enhance its access to star athletes and eventually customers while discouraging rivals from such access. Nike has been known for its practice of using celebrity athletes' endorsement. Proven commodities not withstanding, it also closely watches out for potential stars. Its policy is clear. They want the best to be associated with Nike. Nike CEO Phil Knight likes to say to his associates, go sign that somebody and don't spend too much, but don't let others sign him either. Such a general direction from the boss might be ambiguous, confusing or even frustrating to associates who have to figure out ways to execute it. But denying rival access is the spirit and signing the stars "cheap" is the challenge. Nike associates would use various tactics to influence and disarm potential signees. For instance, they would show in your limousine ride to the Nike campus video clips of the greatest athletes in Nike's service. This serves two purposes:

to create an awe and intimidate the potential star so as to strengthen Nike's bargaining power; and show off its army of celebrities and lure the signee to aspire to being in such great company (*Fortune*, 1995b).

To constantly polish the Nike image, Nike could not afford to see a potential super star join rival's camp. To make sure such a scenario won't happen, Nike indeed has to pay the price. One win in the Master's game as a pro would prompt Nike to sign Golf wunderkind Tiger Woods with an $ 8 million a year contract (*Fortune*, 1997b). In return, Nike also gets star loyalty. In the 1992 Barcelona Olympics, all the Nike associated basketball super stars, Michael Jordan, Charles Barkely, and company, in The Dream Team, would drape themselves in US national flags to cover the logo of Nike's arch rival Reebok, the official sponsor of the outfit for award ceremonies. With such an effective yet loyal troop of stars in service, Nike enjoys unparalleled access to the customers who want to "be like Michael" and "just do it" (*Fortune*, 1995b).

PROFICIENCY-BASED COMPETITIVE ADVANTAGE

Proficiency-based competitive advantage refers to the knowledge (Winter, 1987; Nonaka, 1991), competence (Prahalad and Hamel, 1990), and capabilities (Stalk, et al., 1992; Teece, et al., 1997) of a firm that enable it to conduct its business processes more effectively and/or efficiently than do rivals. Different from access-based advantage, which is external to the firm, the proficiency-based advantage lies primarily within the firm. Different from ownership-based advantage, which lies in a firm's status or possession, the proficiency-based advantage depends on a firm's ability to actually *do* things-to undertake business activities in manufacturing, selling products and delivering services. Proficiency-based competitive advantage includes, for example, strengths in process R&D, technical know-how, intimate knowledge of customers, ability to identify market opportunities.

Foster Learning and Build Routine

Knowledge is power. The wealthiest individual in America, Bill Gates, is a knowledge worker. The firms that now dominate our attention are often knowledge-based firms. For example, Disney knows how to please customers and induce them spend lots of money willingly and happily. Wal-Mart knows how to move merchandise most efficiently. Intel, Microsoft, Cisco, and HP, firms that redefine the way we work, and perhaps also the way we live and play, are really in the intellectual property business. A firm that constantly learns, accumulates and expands its knowledge base, or intellectual capital (Stewart, 1997), enjoys competitive advantage.

At Canon, inventing the mini-copier's low-cost disposable drum brought Canon technical knowledge and capability that facilitated miniaturization. Such knowledge and capability could then be shared with the firm's other office automation businesses, e.g., laser printers (Prahalad and Hamel, 1990). While a firm focuses on learning, its emphasis necessarily shifts from market or products to the firm's knowledge and capabilities. As such, Canon was not confined as being a camera firm but a firm with superior knowledge and capability in imaging. In the same token, Sharp was not bound by the calculator business but built broad-spelled and widely applicable skills in LCD and semiconductor technologies (Nonaka, 1991).

While ownership-based advantage derives from a firm's stock of resources and market positions, proficiency-based advantage derives from a firm's routine in conducting its business (Nelson and Winter, 1982). In the business of professional sports, a lousy team may on a lucky day beat the world champion, but in a series of games, the winner would surely be the one which has the ability to win on a consistent basis and which can show off excellence rather routinely. It is what a firm is capable of doing day in and day out that determines its advantage, not any heroic one-day surge. Excellent firms are often excellent consistently.

In the music business, a great symphony orchestra often not only entertains a good reputation but also boast a superb yet unique sound. And the unique sound it is that distinguishes one from the other; the great from the mediocre. To produce the unique sound consistently requires years of practice, learning, tacit understanding, collaborating, as well as constant refining and habitual performing during rehearsals and in concerts. And it is the ability to produce a great unique sound that gives rise to the orchestra its comparative advantage among competitors and its identity among patrons and audiences.

The late conductor Karajan would fondly reflect as such on the consummate playing of the Berlin Philharmonic which he presided over for more than three decades: It's like the English lawn which has to be cut and watered twice daily—and for three hundred years. Similarly, with Sir Georg Solti, the Chicago Symphony had the distinctive Chicago sound; with Eugene Ormandy, the legendary Philadelphia sound; with George Szell, the Cleveland Orchestra played in unison with the precision of a fine Swiss time piece. As organizational knowledge and capabilities remain in use, the legacies of excellence sustain. Legend has it that twenty years after the death of Otto Klemperer, critics could still feel his presence in the Philharmonia playing (Lebrecht, 1994).

Discourage Rival Learning and Imitating

A firm could gain advantage if it is able to effectively discourage rivals' learning of new knowledge and imitating in acquiring new capabilities. Preemptive measures against rival learning and imitating could be found way before the modern era of business. Let's continue on the subject of the music business. Music lovers worldwide now can literally enjoy any piece of music Beethoven had ever written due to ready availability and wide selections of recordings. And players would generally have no problems in getting hold of Beethoven scores, as they are now in public domain. But this was definitely not so in Beethoven's time. As both a composer and a celebrated concert pianist, Beethoven would often intentionally delay the publication of his stores, e.g., the delay in publishing a couple of his five piano concerti, so that rival pianist could not learn his scores and spoil the Beethoven magic. Similarly, wealthy patrons of Beethoven would often commission works from him and then maintain them in their private possession so as to prevent other nobles from stealing the wonder and prestige of owning and staging Beethoven works.

A classic example of preempting rivals' learning in modern day business can be found in Xerox and how it protected its technological know-how earlier in the business of photocopying. The Xerox technology would be guarded by 500 plus patents, which deter rival imitation and entering its market. While it lasted, the Xerox advantage was undisputed and helped establish and strengthen its near monopoly position in the photocopying business. Just because such advantage was later rendered largely obsolete by Canon's New Process technology, does not mean the initial practice in discouraging rival learning and imitation was unworthy. The point is, Xerox lost its advantage because it did not actively continue its own learning, at least not at the pace of hungrier contenders (Hamel and Prahalad, 1989). The same challenge now faces Microsoft. It can leverage its installed base in the operating system business and support its Internet browser, the Department of Justice's lawsuit notwithstanding. In the long run, however, Microsoft's competitive advantage must come out of its own innovation.

A firm can preempt rivals or destroy rivals' ownership-based advantages; it could deny rivals access-based advantages; it could discourage rivals' learning and imitating. But a firm cannot eliminate the rival's will to learn if the rival is so determined. To a great extent, preempting rivals' learning and imitating helps. But what really matters is whether you are learning, whether you are renewing and widening your knowledge-base, whether you are constantly sharpening your routine skills and capabilities. Creation and preemption. Both sources are important. Combined, they provide greater advantage.

CONCLUDING REMARKS

In this opening chapter, I propose a typology of generic competitive advantages. To get ahead in competition, a firm has to look deeply into what it has, what it can do, and what it can get. The framework advanced here integrates both proactive efforts in enhancing a firm's chances for the three generic types of competitive advantages—ownership, access, proficiency—and preemptive efforts in reducing the rivals' chances. It also integrates factors in the internal working of the organization, e.g., resources and capabilities, and factors in the external environment, e.g., market position and relationship with outside entities.

It must be noted, however, that the three generic competitive advantages may not necessarily always be independent of each other and may therefore work together simultaneously to provide a firm with competitive advantages. For instance, access to distribution or supply may be influenced by a firm's market positions. Proficiency and superior capability are often based on possession of unique resources. Learning and imitation are often dependent on appropriate access.

Wal-Mart provides a perfect example of all three generic competitive advantages at work. Its superior location provides easy access to consumers. Its market power enables better bargaining position against and favorable access to suppliers. Its advanced information technology, warehouse and transportation systems, and employee dedication and know-how all contribute to its overall capability in moving the largest quantity of merchandise most efficiently. In summary, to analyze a firm's competitive advantage, the three generic types should be consulted both individually and collectively.

Chapter 2   SELECT: An Integrative Framework

Competitive advantage is the basis for superior performance. Understanding the anatomy of competitive advantage is of paramount importance to general managers who bear the ultimate responsibility for a firm's long-term survival and success. This chapter advances an integrative framework called SELECT to help general managers systematically examine the various facets of the anatomy of competitive advantage: its substance, expression, locale, effect, cause, and time horizon. Analyzing the causes of competitive advantage helps a firm create and gain advantage. Studying the substance, expression, locale, and effect of competitive advantage allows the firm to better utilize the advantage. Examining the time horizon of competitive advantage enables the firm to fully exploit the advantage according to its potential and sustainability.

Why do firms exist? Why should a particular firm be in business? Call it mission. Call it vision. Call it strategic intent. Whatever it is, a firm needs such a rationale to justify its existence. And that rationale, I believe, is to create value and win. To create value better than rivals can; to contribute to the society in ways that are unique and indispensable. That, in the end, is what winning in business is really about. Just look at pioneering firms like GE, Wal-Mart, and Microsoft, which had in the 20th century fundamentally changed and shaped the way we live, work, learn, and play; or look at winning firms like Proctor & Gamble, Coca-Cola, or Merck that so many people find their daily lives depend on.

If the economics, the environment, or our abilities determine that we can't get there, we must take the same spirited action to disengage ourselves from that which we can't make better than the best.

Jack Welch
Former CEO, General Electric

For great business firms, winning is not a one time or now and then thing. Winning is a habit. To be a winner, a firm has to create, exploit, and sustain its competitive advantages against rivals. And it has to do so consistently if it wants to be a perennial winner. Where do competitive advantages come from? What are their contents and effects? Where do they reside inside or outside the firm? In what form can we observe them? How sustainable are they? These are all important questions concerning the multiple facets of the anatomy of competitive advantage. Competitive advantage comes in various shapes and sizes. Understanding the anatomy of competitive advantage helps general managers improve their firms' chance of gaining and sustaining of competitive advantage hence their chance of winning.

This paper advances an integrative framework to help general managers systematically analyze six facets of competitive advantage: its Substance, Expression, Locale, Effect, Cause, and Time-Horizon. Strategy is about winning. Strategy involves choice. It involves choice of a firm's scope of product-market activities (Porter, 1980) as well as the combination of its resources and capabilities (Barney, 1991; Prahalad and Hamel, 1990). It is ultimately about the choice of matching resource commitment with changing opportunities for gaining and sustaining competitive advantages. As such, it is only fitting that the framework we use to dissect the anatomy of competitive advantage should be termed in acronym as SELECT, a tool designed to help a firm choose the right configuration of its competitive advantages.

> *I've been in this business for 33 years, and it seems that every decade, we get reminded what this business is all about—providing better value to customers.*
>
> John Pepper
Former CEO, Procter & Gamble

In his now classic treatise on competitive advantage, Porter (1985:3) insightfully observes that: "Competitive advantage grows fundamentally out of value a firm is able to create for its buyers that exceeds the firm's cost of creating it. Value is what buyers are willing to pay, and superior value stems from offering lower prices than competitors for equivalent benefits or providing unique benefits that more than offset a higher price." Building on Porter's definition, I define *competitive advantage* as the asymmetry or differential in any firm attribute or dimension that allows one firm to better serve the customers than others and hence create better customer value.

Figure 2.1 Anatomy of Competitive Advantage: A SELECT Framework

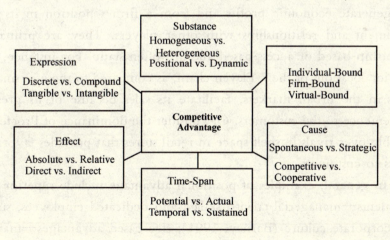

Now let's examine respectively the six facets of the anatomical

make-up of a competitive advantage. Although I attempt to be complete as well as parsimonious in advancing the SELECT framework, it is obvious that, due to the complex and often elusive nature of competitive advantage as a practical phenomenon and a theoretical concept, these six dimensions are not necessarily mutually exclusive and exhaustive.

THE REAL THING:
SUBSTANCE OF COMPETITIVE ADVANTAGE

What is the actual substance or content of competitive advantage? What is its nature and basic type? Two basic schemes can be used to categorize the substance of competitive advantage: the dichotomies between positional and dynamic and between homogeneous and heterogeneous.

Positional vs. Dynamic Advantages

Positional advantages derive from firm attributes and endowment that generate economic profits and from a firm's position in its environment and relationships with other players. They are primarily ownership-based or access-based and are often static. For instance, the superior locations of the 7-Eleven chain, as compared to those of smaller rivals in the urban markets, facilitate its sales because of its greater convenience to the customers. Or consider the dominance of Procter & Gamble over rivals in shelf space in retail stores that provides favorable access to customers.

In general, examples of positional advantage include superior endowments—managerial talents, skilled and dedicated employees, superior corporate culture (Barney, 1991); size-based advantages—market power, economy of scale, and economy of experience (Ghemawat, 1986); good relationship with complementor or collaborator (Brandenburger and Nalebuff, 1996); better control of supply and favorable access to distributors (Porter, 1980); and owning industry's technological standard, e.g. Wintel in PC (Hill, 1997).

Dynamic Advantages allow a firm to actually perform its business activities more effectively or efficiently than rivals. They are often knowledge and capability based, as competitive advantages in motion. For instance, Sony's superior capability in miniaturization helps strengthen its leadership in personal and portable electronics worldwide (Stalk, Evans, and Shulman, 1992). Toyota's flexible manufacturing capability allows it to respond to market changes more quickly than rivals. In the credit card business, MBNA America has the superior capability in identifying and serving large groups of customers who have great revenue and profit potential for MBNA (Reichheld, 1996).

Dynamic advantages often feature the following capabilities (and knowledge and competence): *entrepreneurial capabilities*—ability to locate valuable customers and to create or identify new market opportunities; *technical capabilities* that enhance creativity, efficiency, flexibility, speed, or quality in a firm's business process; *organizational capabilities* that help mobilize employees, foster organizational learning, and facilitate organizational changes; and *strategic capabilities* that enable the firm to create, integrate, coordinate its multiple streams of knowledge and competencies, and reconfigure and redeploy them along changing market opportunities.

Positional advantages and dynamic advantages often influence and derive from each other. On the one hand, dynamic advantages could stem from positional advantage, e.g., FedEx's endowment of vast and sophisticated air (and ground) transportation systems insure its capability in fast and reliable delivery of overnight packages. On the other hand, dynamic advantages can also help strengthen positional advantages, e.g., Canon's R&D and manufacturing capability helped secure its dominant positions and solid reputation worldwide in the office automation business (Ghoshal, 1992).

Homogeneous vs. Heterogeneous Advantages

A firm's advantage over a rival can be homogeneous or heterogeneous. When a firm and its rivals are competing in basically the same way using similar or homogeneous strengths and skills, the firm's advantage over rivals, if any, would likely be deriving from doing the same thing better. Such advantage is regarded as homogeneous advantage. For instance, Lincoln Electronic Company's cost advantage in electric arc welders derives from its long accumulated experience and its overall efficiency in operation and organization.

Recently, Porter (1996) argues that operational efficiency will be the only determinant of competitive advantage, if all firms have to play the same game without any opportunity to "be different." However, he further argues that such homogeneous advantage won't be strategic, for the essence of strategy is to do something different, not just doing the same thing better. On the other hand, on can also argue that strategizing is only pertinent for only a small subset of transactions or activities in business. And in most cases, doing things more efficiently than rivals, i.e., economizing, is all the necessary (Williamson, 1991). As such, homogeneous advantage is of vital yet practical importance for a firm's superior performance.

A firm can also enjoy heterogeneous advantage over rivals by playing the game differently or playing a totally different game: better serving the customers through different skills, resource combinations, or products from those of rivals. Canon's advantage in the copier business, for example, did not stem from their doing better than Xerox on what Xerox had traditionally been doing. Instead, it circumvented the advantage Xerox had built through its seemingly invincible fortress of sales and maintenance forces. Canon's New Process innovation allowed it to engage in the manufacturing of low cost and high quality copiers.

Its product advantage in small size and reliability helped make their products available to offices much smaller in size than the ones traditionally served by Xerox, thus preempting new market niches and expanding the overall scope of the copier market (Ghoshal, 1992). The resource-based view of the firm emphasizes the importance of heterogeneous advantages, as firm heterogeneity lies in the core argument of that view: unique, difficult-to-imitate, and firm-specific resources generate competitive advantage (Barney, 1991).

THE MYSTICAL APPEARANCE: EXPRESSION OF COMPETITIVE ADVANTAGE

What is the structural form of competitive advantage? How does competitive advantage express itself? How can we observe the presence of competitive advantage? We can capture the expression or form of competitive advantage using two categories. First, competitive advantage could be either tangible or intangible. Second, competitive advantage could be either discrete or compound.

Tangible vs. Intangible Advantages

A tangible competitive advantage is an advantage that can be readily observed by the focal firm and its rivals as presented in certain visible physical form or data. The location advantage of Wal-Mart (Ghemawat, 1991) would be an ideal example of a tangible advantage, so is the huge installed base of Microsoft's operating systems for PCs. Tangible advantages are often resulted from a firm's commitment of large amount of resources in certain areas that are not easily reversible, e.g., preemptive investment in capacity.

Ghemawat (1991) defines commitment as the tendency toward the persistence of a firm's strategy. And he regards commitment to be both sufficient and necessary to explain sustained firm advantage, as evidenced in a firm's persistent superior performance. The resultant tangible advantage from a firm's commitment, on the one hand, enables the firm to perform better than its existing rivals; on the other hand, helps intimidate and deter potential entrants, hence sustain the superior performance.

Intangible advantage refers to an advantage that is not easily observable in any physical form or is hidden behind certain factors which makes it difficult to detect and identify in any concrete fashion. Intangible advantage can be derived from a firm's trade secrets, brand name, reputation, employee know-how (Itami, 1987; Hall, 1992), organizational culture (Barney, 1991), or even certain level of organizational slack (Nohria and Gulati, 1996). For example, Ben & Jerry's enjoys tremendous reputation advantage due to its unique organizational culture and philosophy that emphasize the balance of a firm's social and economic missions. 3M's policy allowing its engineers 15% of company time to work on their own pet projects contributed significantly to its product innovation (Ghoshal and Bartlett, 1997).

Arguably, intangible advantage is perhaps more difficult to replicate or attack than tangible advantage, simply because intangible advantage is more likely to derive from firm traits, characteristics, and capabilities that are causally ambiguous and socially complex (Barney, 1991). As such, in many cases, intangible advantage often sustains for a long period of time. For example, the advantage derived from the *Cartier* name, a symbol for luxury, prestige, and status, lasts long after any tangible advantages reflected in its products disappear.

Discrete vs. Compound Advantages

Competitive advantage could function in either stand-alone, discrete fashion or it can be a compound of multiple individual advantages that work together as an integrative whole. In this sense, compound advantage can be regarded as a higher-order advantage to discrete advantage.

A discrete advantage can be found in the example of AT&T's ownership of a vast network of cable and optic fiber lines that support its long-distance calling service. This advantage *per se* contributes directly to the firm's performance. Discrete advantages are often positional as they derive from primarily ownership or access-based sources. Typical discrete advantages include superior real estate locations, unique physical assets, patent and other intellectual properties, exclusive contract, import or export license, or cash reserves.

On the other hand, Coca-Cola's persistent superior performance in the soft drink industry depends largely on its brand recognition, perhaps the best know brand in the entire world. Such an advantage in reputation is obviously an advantage of a higher order, a *compound advantage.* That is, it comprises, among other advantages, the secret formula for good taste, availability and prevalence due to its sophisticated distribution systems, and customer good will accumulated from a century's advertising and promotion.

Typical compound advantages can also be dynamic as they are often based primarily on firm knowledge and capabilities (Stalk, et al., 1992). Such compound advantages can be found in superior capabilities which mobilize and coordinate multiple assets and skills to build competitive advantages in differentiation, quality product or service, low cost, quick response to the market, or constant innovation. For instance, Canon's capability to harness multiple streams of competencies in image processing and leverage its manufacturing and marketing strengths has brought it competitive advantage in quickly introducing a wide range of innovative products of high quality with great efficiency and lower cost (Ghoshal, 1992).

THE SECRET SITE:
LOCALE OF COMPETITIVE ADVANTAGE

Since our concern is superior performance and winning of the *firm*, it is only appropriate to ask the questions "Does a competitive advantage actually reside and stick within the firm?" and "Can the firm benefit from such an advantage?" The locale of competitive advantage can be traced at three different levels: *individual-bound*, *firm-bound*, or *virtual-bound*.

Individual-Bound Advantages

An individual-bound advantage is one such that it is derived from particular individuals or certain mobile assets. For example, the core advantages of a talent agency or an LBO operation often lie in one or few individuals' personal networks and their knowledge about and contact with the clientele base. Should these individuals move or defect, the advantages of the firm could collapse all at once. Such individual-bound advantages are not easily sustainable because the resources underlying them are mobile. Furthermore, it is more likely that these individuals or assets holders rather than the firm capture bigger portion of the rewards and benefits of the competitive advantage, although such advantage is usually associated nominally with the firm.

On a good year, star performer Bill Cosby would earn more from his sitcom than the profits of the entire TV Network he associates with (Evans and Wurster, 1997). The Network may possess advantage over the ones without such super stars and super hits, but the rewards of the advantages are not easily appropriable to the Network. And the Network is also subject to hold up and the stars' fight for better compensation, e.g., the demand in 1997 by *Seinfeld* cast member for $ 1 million per person per episode from NBC to have the return for another season of *The Seinfeld Show*, the standard-defining sitcom of the 1990s (*Business Week*, 1997).

Firm-Bound Advantages

A firm-bound advantage is one based on attributes that are stored in and shared by, collectively, many people or the entire firm. Such advantage is by definition socially complex, less mobile, and difficult to duplicate (Barney, 1991). Superior corporate culture serves as a good illustration of firm-bound advantage. As a shared norm and value system, culture institutionalizes through time. A corporate culture that values innovation and creativity, e.g., that of 3M or Hewlett Packard, provides an advantage over more laggard firms.

With firm-bound competitive advantage, the firm is larger than the individuals. It is often the firm, not any individuals or assets holders, that stands to gain. Intangible advantages, especially those knowledge-based, e.g., technical know-how, are often firm-bound advantages. For example, the Kao corporation's philosophy and practice of shared learning through the entire firm provide it with advantage in innovation and flexibility (Ghoshal and Bartlett, 1997). Similarly, reputation advantage is also more firm-bound. For instance, the Discovery channel, a major brand name in cable TV, comparing to NBC and other major network broadcasters, could fare much better when dealing with its individual program providers (Evans and Wurster, 1997).

Virtual-Bound Advantages

A firm's competitive advantage could also be virtual-bound. That is, the advantage lies outside of the firm's boundary and resides in certain network, relationships, other entities that the firm has access to. When IBM launched its PC in the early 1980s, it quickly developed into a formidable force by assembling a superior team of vendors of various parts of PC. The problem with IBM, however, is that the core components of the PC were supplied by outsiders instead of being developed in house at IBM. As such, IBM's advantage in the PC business, e.g., advantage over Apple Macintosh computers in the corporate market, was largely virtual. As the former partners Microsoft and Intel grew stronger, they were able to break away and rival IBM. Because it is Intel and Microsoft, not IBM, that determined the PC standard (Chesbrough and Teece, 1996). As such, unless a firm has firm control of the virtual source of competitive advantage, the firm is less likely to either benefit the most from the competitive advantage or sustain such competitive advantage in the long run.

THE EARTHLY PRESENCE: EFFECT OF COMPETITIVE ADVANTAGE

How do we observe the effect of competitive advantage? In what ways does an advantage help a firm provide better customer value? The strength of an advantage's effect could be observed as being either *absolute* or *relative*. And the functioning of an advantage could be either *direct* or *indirect*.

Absolute vs. Relative Advantages

On a comparable scale, if a firm has an advantage over its rivals with an overwhelming magnitude that seems insurmountable by rivals, then we say that the firm has an absolute advantage. If a firm's advantage over rivals is merely in small differentials, then we say the firm has a relative advantage or comparative advantage *vis-à-vis* its rivals. For instance, IBM's advantage in its main frame computer business had been an absolute one because of its dominant market share and accumulated experience and expertise. IBM's advantage in the PC business, even in its heydays, was only marginal and relative as more firms were able to contest the market with clones and establish profitable positions.

Direct vs. Indirect Advantages

A direct advantage is one such that contributes to a firm's value creating and capturing in a direct manner. An indirect advantage is one that indirectly contributes to such a practice, in ways that support, amplify, or give rise to a direct advantage. Typically, a direct advantage is somewhat more tangible. A good example can be found in Honda's excellence in making quality engines. Honda's expertise on engines contributes directly to the quality and reputation of its products, enhancing sales and profit.

On the other hand, a firm often derives its indirect advantage from its supporting activities in the value chain (Porter, 1985) or from its broadly spelled strengths, e.g., R&D capability and corporate culture (Barney, 1991). Such a broad advantage, indirect as it is, must be translated into some specific advantages that contribute to performance directly, e.g., cost advantage or differentiation advantage in the market (Porter, 1985). For example, the competitive advantage Southwest Airlines derives from its efficiency-oriented culture contributes significantly to its overall low cost advantage.

THE MAGIC KEY:
CAUSE OF COMPETITIVE ADVANTAGE

Where does competitive advantage come from? Through what channels? By what means? Many factors can cause the rise of competitive advantage. Generally speaking, we can categorize the causes of competitive advantage as *spontaneous* vs. *strategic*. Spontaneous causes include shifts in environment as well as pure luck (Barney, 1986a). Strategic causes refer to competition (D'Aveni, 1994), cooperation (Contractor and Lorange, 1988), or combination of both (Brandenburger and Nalebuff, 1996), through deliberate strategy formulation and implementation.

Spontaneous Causes

Barney (1986a, 1991) suggests that, in imperfectly competitive factor markets, firms could enjoy competitive advantage over rivals simply because they are lucky. For instance, they could have acquired certain valuable resource in certain historical events and the path-dependency phenomenon would preclude other firms from acquiring the same resource at similar price or even acquiring it at all (1991). For instance, Caterpillar's extensive dealer and service network around the world largely stemmed from its roles in supplying to the allied forces during the Second World War. For competitors who didn't travel that particular path, matching Caterpillar's dealer and service network will be either prohibitively costly or not at all possible.

Environmental changes often give rise to or invalidate advantages of certain firms. For instance, the health craze in America has severely tarnished the brand-awareness advantage of Kentucky Fried Chicken (which was changed to KFC to downplay the word "fried") while helping make possible the promotional advantages of sports and fitness-related firms like Nike. Similarly, changes in government regulation also affect a firm's competitive advantage. For instance, the competitive advantages of the major tobacco makers were diminishing due to increasing governmental regulations (Miles, 1982). Or in another case, the deregulation of the banking industry might give rise of competitive advantage to those banks that had already well diversified geographically while other banks with limited scope of operation struggle against increasing competition.

Competitive Advantage vs. Cooperative Advantage

In the realm of strategy as the cause of competitive advantage, a firm can gain advantage from either competition or cooperation, or both, through its purposeful strategizing. First, a firm is able to sharpen its routine and skills (Nelson and Winter, 1982) in intense competition (D'Aveni, 1994). Porter (1990) suggests that intense competition at domestic market, due to small market size, demanding customers, and large number of competitors, has kept the Japanese automakers on their edge. Such intense competition helps hone their skills and leads to competitive advantage as they expand in international market. In context like the so-called hypercompetition, researchers argue that, basically, there is no such thing as a sustained competitive advantage. To be successful in hypercompetition, a firm has to constantly jockey for positions and create a series of temporal advantages through well-thought-out competitive moves and maneuvering (D'Aveni, 1994; Grove, 1996).

On the other hand, firms often gain advantages through cooperative strategies. Cooperation often provide cooperating firms with economies of scale and scope, and speed advantages that otherwise would not be available (Contractor and Lorange, 1988; Hamel, Doz, and Prahalad, 1989; Brandenburger and Nalebuff, 1996). Especially, firms participating in cooperative arrangements often enjoy advantages over those who choose to go alone. For instance, JVC's licensing strategy in pushing its VHS format as the industry standard is a classical example where cooperative efforts paid off, conferring JVC and its parent Matsushita tremendous advantage, while Sony's proprietary β system losing ground (Yoffie, 1990).

It is interesting to note that cooperative advantage can rise when archrivals choose to cooperate (Hamel, et al., 1989; Brandenburger and Nalebuff, 1996). Hamel and colleagues suggest that strategic alliance and other cooperative arrangements are essentially learning races. A participating firm could learn from its partners valuable know-how and skills while protecting its own advantage. Thus, a quick learner who has clear objectives and is better prepared for joining a cooperative arrangement will gain cooperative advantage.

Rivals can also enhance and amplify their advantage through cooperative arrangements. The now famous Three Tenor concerts coupled with the World Cup Soccer Games in 1990 and 1994 and the subsequent 10 city world tour have made Carreras, Domingo, and Pavarotti, each of them representing a huge business Kingdom, not only the most famous tenors of our time but also popular icons in entertainment (*Time*, 1994). These archrivals in opera theaters, popular concerts, and in business endorsements, by joining forces, created an ever glowing reputation for all of them and significantly increased their audience base and exposure, triggering increasing demand for their recordings and videos. The cooperative advantage they gained further distinguished them from the rest of the tenor specie, and, for that matter, popular entertainers.

THE TWILIGHT OF LIFE: TIME HORIZON OF COMPETITIVE ADVANTAGE

What is the life span of a competitive advantage? When does a potential advantage materialize? How sustainable is an advantage? An advantage could be either *actual* or *potential*; and it could be either *temporal* or *sustained*.

Potential vs. Actual Advantages

An actual competitive advantage is a competitive advantage that is currently in effect. A potential advantage could be one that is in reserve, yet untapped, underutilized, or misplaced. This may sound counter intuitive. For instance, Hughes Electronics had throughout the years amassed tremendous strengths in satellite technology from its service of defense contracts. However, such strengths only rendered Hughes a broad, potential, and hitherto underutilized advantage in the commercial market. Applying this strength to home satellite TV market brought into lights its potential technological advantage on a wider scope.

On the other hand, a potential advantage could fail to materialize. For instance, the excellent research done on the first personal computer with user-friendly Graphic User Interfaces (GUI) by the Palo Alto Research Center (PARC) at Xerox, a great potential advantage in the PC business, did not win top management's attention and failed to transform into any actual competitive advantage for Xerox in the PC business.

Temporal vs. Sustained Advantages

Temporal advantage refers to a competitive advantage that is short-term, transient, unsustained. Sustainable advantage refers to an advantage that is long lasting in time and that is not easily matched or surpassed by rivals. For example, American Airlines' SABRE computer reservation system, when it was first introduced, provided AA with advantage in capacity utilization and other areas of its operation. Its pioneer use of the system, however, was quickly imitated by its rivals. Computer reservation soon became the industry's standard practice.

Sustainable advantage, on the other hand, withstands the test of imitation and other threats of dissipation. For instance, the sustained advantage of Coca-Cola's brand image and reputation for more than a century remains an envy of all. Sustainable advantage could be a particular single advantage that is well sustained through time, e.g., De Beer's century-long near monopoly in the supply of diamond worldwide.

Sustainable advantage could also be accumulated through envelopment of a series of temporal advantages. Take Intel for example. Intel's rise to dominance in the computer chip business has been engineered largely through the establishment of a series of temporal advantages. Before any generation of its technology gets thoroughly imitated and its temporal advantage runs thin, it introduces a new generation, making imitators again playing catch-up. In such a hypercompetitive industry, Intel's overall advantage has been lasting for about two decades and running (Grove, 1996).

Eroding of an advantage is the opposite of its sustaining. An advantage could be eroded in different ways including, but not limited to, the threats of competitive imitation, substitution, a firm's own misapplication or negligence, unexpected environmental changes, e.g., governmental ruling, as well as invalidation by Schumpeterian type of shock (Hamel and Prahalad, 1989; Evans and Wurster, 1997).

The attempt to sustain an advantage is to fight the battle against its erosion. Yet, no matter what, fewer advantages are sustainable and many are eroded. As all advantages will eventually be eroded though time, instead of trying to desperately sustain and hold on to one disappearing advantage, it might be advisable for a firm to develop reserves of potential advantages and prepare for long term superior performance. That's exactly what Nike has been doing in the past three decades or so. Next, I will use the case of Nike to demonstrate the application of the SELECT framework.

SELECT IN ACTION:
THE NIKE CASE REVISITED

The major advantages Nike has enjoyed over rivals through out the years are based on cost and image. First, cost advantage. Phil Knight's vision of offshore manufacturing, a strategic move based on an original idea in the athletic footwear industry, was the major cause of the initial rise of such advantage. It was a smart ploy that allowed Nike to compete effectively against the industry's then worldwide leader,

Adidas. Such a cost advantage was largely discrete and tangible in *expression*. The advantage was no secrete, simply in the form of a single, tangible item: lower labor cost, given shoe manufacturing's labor intensive nature and not much use of technology.

The *substance* of the competitive advantage over rivals, e.g., Adidas, could be interpreted as homogeneous, because Nike did not fundamentally alter the nature of shoe manufacturing as its suppliers still used intensive labor as did Adidas, but only cheaper. Nike positioned itself in the value chain to focus on only the designing and marketing. Its cost advantage stemmed from its relationship with partners. As such, the cost advantage reflected its *position* in the value-adding activities rather than its actual capability in making shoes, notwithstanding its ability in managing supplier relationship. In this sense, the *locale* of the advantage was basically outside the firm, i.e., virtual-bound. Due to its tremendous bargaining power over the more scattered and small-scaled manufacturers, Nike was able to appropriate a greater share of the profit.

The *effect* of the cost advantage was no doubt a direct contributor to Nike's crushing Adidas. While it was more of an *absolute* advantage against Adidas in the early years, the cost advantage became increasingly *relative* in degree against rivals later, as these rivals, including the dethroned Adidas, imitated Nike's outsourcing practice. As of 1990, all but a couple of the more than 30 brands of athletic footwear sold in the US were made in lower-wage countries (Miller, 1993). Although the source of its cost advantage was imitable, it is rather unlikely that the imitators would actually outdo Nike on cost, beating it at its own game. Regarding the time sensitivity of Nike's cost advantage, albeit a relative one now, it has been fairly *sustainable*.

Table 2.1 Application of SELECT: The Nike Case

Competitive Advantage	Cost Advantage	Image Advantage
Substance	Positional Homogeneous	Positional Heterogeneous
Expression	Tangible Discrete	Tangible Compound
Locale	Virtual-Bound	Firm Bound
Effect	Direct Relative	Direct Absolute
Cause	Strategic Cooperative	Strategic
Time-Horizon	Fairly Sustainable	Largely Sustainable

Where did Nike's image advantage come from? Well, in a nutshell, demonstration effect of top athletes. The image has definitely been winning and high performance. It was nurtured through the world's best athletes associated with Nike. The original *cause* of Nike's advantage in image lay in the conception of its initial strategy, Knight's vision of being the best in sports. The direct cause was its knowledge-based capability in coordinating its marketing activities. First, they furnished their shoes to players in Olympic trials and the Olympic games. By 1982, every world record in men's mid to long distance running was set by players wearing Nike shoes. That brought tremendous publicity and brand identity. Second, advertising provided another weapon to build the Nike image. Since the early 1980s, all Nike advertising has been focusing on the Nike brand instead of any single line of products. That is, a simple, easy to remember logo "Swoosh" and a catchy, uplifting slogan "Just do it" (Klein, 1990). Third, promotion by sponsoring sports events as well as athletes at different levels, e.g., college varsity teams, brought the Nike brand excellent exposure and helped induce customer loyalty. Finally, and most importantly perhaps, Nike redefined celebrity endorsement in the sports business. Its huge army of all-star sports celebrities in basketball, football, tennis, and in essentially every area of sports, constantly bombarded the customers through TV commercials and other channels. These best of the best in sports help polish the Nike image on a daily basis, as we speak.

Regarding its *form*, the image advantage is a compound one

instead of being discrete, deriving from multiple activities and accumulating through time. It is *intangible* in the sense that it is in the form of social psychological and emotional appeal to the customers, enabling customers to value its products more than those of rivals. It is also somewhat *tangible* in the sense that the image is so vivid and specific and you can almost feel and touch it. For instance, a pair of shoes from the Air Jordan line may well cost over $ 100 a pair. Yet consumers, youngsters in particular, would easily identify with, Michael Jordan, the superstar whom they emulate and admire, who remains for over 10 years a perfect pitchman for Nike. Tangible as the image advantage is, rivals can not easily match. For Nike is not simply a brand name; it demands and creates social conformity, being often the sole "in" choice.

Unlike its cost advantage, Nike's advantage in image has its *locale* within the firm. Despite the individual appeal of the celebrity, the overall winner is still Nike the firm, for the advantage is firm bound, it is the *firm's* image. Regarding the *substance* of the image advantage, it is more positional due to the fact that the image is a status-defining endowment of the firm; and it is heterogeneous instead of homogeneous *vis-à-vis* rivals because of the distinctiveness of the Nike image. Nike's image, its biggest assets arguably, gives Nike a differentiated position high on the top of its industry. Image sells shoes. Nike sells image. The *effect* of Nike's image advantage seems to be, to many people, an absolute one, despite the challenge of Reebok in the 1980s and the new challenge of Fila in the 1990s. For three decades or so, Nike's image advantage has maintained great *sustainability*.

Clearly, Nike's two major competitive advantages are of different configurations. As the cause of cost advantage is much more imitable than that of image advantage, the latter is in reality of stronger effect and greater sustainability. While the cost advantage is derived from access to low-wage partners, image advantage builds on well-orchestrated marketing activities. While cost advantage features operating efficiency and remains largely homogeneous *vis-à-vis* rivals, image advantage strives for the uniqueness and heterogeneity. While cost advantage played rather dominant role in the early stage of Nike's growth, Nike's focus has been more and more placed on image advantage. While cost advantage builds on access to others' manufacturing strengths, image advantage must derive from Nike's own capability. It might be too strong an argument to say that Nike's cost advantage gave rise to its image advantage. It is, nonetheless, a fair statement that cost advantage provided an extremely high margin, making possible the expensive, star-laden, marketing and promotion activities, which conjure up the winning image. To win the game in the athletic gear industry, Nike obviously needs both advantages in its service, and much more.

As we can see from the Nike case, studying the anatomy of a competitive advantage helps us better understand how a particular advantage configures and effects. It also forms as a basis for understanding a particular competitive advantage's changing roles in a firm's evolving constellation of advantage. It helps a firm focus its commitment on activities that create greater value and, more importantly, capture the value within the firm.

CONCLUDING REMARKS

I have in this chapter dissected the anatomy of competitive advantage and advanced a framework named SELECT, within which different research streams on competitive advantage were juxtaposed. This framework contributes to the integration of the hitherto fragmented literature on competitive advantage and provides a practical guide for general managers to systematically analyze the substance, expression, locale, effect, cause, and time-horizon of competitive advantage.

It should be noted that the six facets of the anatomy of competitive advantage are interrelated to each other. For instance, sustainability of a competitive advantage is necessarily influenced by its specific substance (e.g., market or resource positions vs. capability and know-how), its form of expression (e.g., tangible discrete advantage like favorable access to distribution vs. intangible compound advantage like superior corporate culture), its locale (e.g., an individual-bound advantage like informal network and expertise in an intensive personal selling business vs. R&D-based core competence embedded in and shared across a large and diverse corporation), as well as its effect (e.g., a decisive and absolute advantage like a monopoly rights vs. one shoulder's advantage over rivals in customer goodwill and loyalty).

Obviously, the cause of competitive advantage also matters. Whether you gain an advantage in a spontaneous, untested manner or through a brutal battle with a resilient rival, makes a world of difference in the advantage's sustainability. So does the cause impact the other facets. Moreover, substance could not be separated from its form; effect derives from its substance; form of expression often associates with the locale; and locale also shapes the effect. In one word, these various facets of the anatomy need to be viewed together as a living organism. Understanding the six facets of the anatomy of competitive advantage individually as well as jointly is expected to help general managers better perform their fundamental task: achieving superior performance and win.

Chapter 3   Dynamic Advantage and Positional Advantage

This chapter addresses the theoretical underpinnings of positional advantage and dynamic advantage as well as the relationship between the two. Competitive advantage could be categorized as either a status-defining position that leads to better firm performance, a positional advantage, or an action-oriented capability that allows a firm to function more effectively and efficiently, a dynamic advantage. Positional advantages often form the basis of and can reinforce dynamic advantages while dynamic advantages may contribute to the gaining and sustaining of positional advantages. In an ongoing competition, the lack of positional advantages could overwhelm or diminish the effect of a firm's dynamic advantages while the lack of dynamic advantages could also jeopardize or make obsolete a firm's established positional advantages. Both types of competitive advantage are therefore essential for a firm's success, though the importance of each to a firm's performance depends on the varying environmental contexts.

What are the various possible types of competitive advantages? How to systematically analyze the substance of competitive advantages a firm could possibly possess so as to achieve persistent superior performance? This chapter attempts to advance a theoretical framework that draws on and integrates multiple streams of strategy research on competitive advantage. Specifically, it presents a dichotomy of competitive advantage—positional and dynamic—and addresses the relationships between the two types of competitive advantage and their implication for firm performance. The chapter is organized as follows. First, it examines the nature of positional advantage and dynamic advantage. Second, it advances a systematic framework on the specific content of the two types of advantage. Finally, it discusses the relationship between the two, followed by concluding remarks.

A DICHOTOMY OF COMPETITIVE ADVANTAGE

Based on an extensive search of literature, I categorize the various competitive advantages into a dichotomy according to their content. That is, competitive advantage is either a status-defining position which itself *per se* contributes to better firm performance, or it is an action-oriented ability that allows a firm to function more effectively and efficiently in its business activities. The former type can be termed as *positional advantage* and the latter *dynamic advantage*.

Positional advantage often derives from endowment (Barney, 1991) or market position or access (Porter, 1980; Ghemawat, 1986) while dynamic advantage typically arises from the firm's knowledge, expertise, competence, or capabilities (Winter, 1987; Prahalad and Hamel, 1990; Stalk, Evans, and Shulman, 1992; Teece, Pisano, and Shuen, 1997), although it is also possible for the firm to enjoy dynamic advantage by accessing or tapping other firms' knowledge and capabilities (Contractor and Lorange, 1988; Hamel, Doz, and Prahalad, 1989).

Specifically, positional advantage is based on a firm's unique endowment of resources (Rumelt, 1984; Barney, 1986a, 1991), dominant market positions (Porter, 1980, 1985), superior accesses to suppliers or distribution channels (Ghemawat, 1986), and other traits that are relatively static in nature. It relies on a firm's status, social or economical, actual or perceived, in the eyes of customers, competitors, partners, regulators, and other stakeholders. Positional advantages not only contributes directly to a firm's value creation but also serves as a cushion for the firm to experiment different ways of competing and operation. Rumelt (1984: 569) insightfully remarks that: "If opportunities for significant shifts in strategic position are infrequent, and if isolating mechanisms create defensible positions, it follows that many firms can ignore strategy for long periods of time and still appear profitable...If a strategic position is strong enough, even fools can churn out good results (for a while)." (*parenthesis original*).

Dynamic advantage is based on a firm's competence and capability in conducting business activities, including but not limited to, ability to identify market opportunities (Hamel and Prahalad, 1989), knowledge of customers (Hall, 1992), technical know-how and capabilities (Teece, et al., 1997), speed of action and response in the market (Stalk, 1990), efficiency (Williamson, 1991) and flexibility (Sanchez, 1995) of business or organizational processes. According to the dynamic capability approach to strategy (Teece, et al., 1997), it is perhaps a firm's managerial capability in constantly reconfiguring and redeploying its competencies along changing market opportunities that leads to superior performance. Different from positional advantage which are by definition more static, dynamic advantage is more process and action oriented, largely deriving from the continuous sharpening of routines (Nelson and Winter, 1982) and exercising of core competencies (Prahalad and Hamel, 1990).

Given this general dichotomy of types of competitive advantage, what are the specific content of positional advantage and dynamic advantage? The following two sections attempt to provide a systematic account of the two types of competitive advantage.

POSITIONAL ADVANTAGE

A firm operates in two basic types of market: product market and factor market (Barney, 1986a; Dierickx and Cool, 1989; Zajac, 1992). Players and entities in both product and factor markets consist of what can be called a business ecological system, where they interact and co-evolve and where the government is also often an important player that affects how a firm interacts with other players and how it creates value for its customers (Moore, 1996).

In a firm's striving for leadership within its focal business eco-system, its endowment and position or status *vis-à-vis* that of other players and entities in the business eco-system determine its positional advantage. In addition, a firm's focal business eco-system may also compete with other business eco-systems, often for the same set of customers, especially in situations where competing industry standards are of concern (Hill, 1997). As such, a firm's position against that of players in other business eco-systems also determines its competitive advantage.

As can be seen in Figure 3.1, different business eco-systems often overlap with each other. As such, it is possible that one firm can belong to multiple eco-systems at the same time. Also, within any particular business eco-system, a firm can play multiple roles simultaneously. For instance, Apple Computer and Microsoft on any day can be both competitors (in operating systems) and collaborators or complementors (in application software) in the business eco-system known as the personal computer business.

Furthermore, each of the two players also represents a sub business eco-system within the personal computer business eco-system. Within their respective sub eco-system, each serves as a keystone specie around which other players build and co-evolve. For instance, Microsoft, along with Intel, defines the Wintel format, while Apple and Motorola's microprocessors define the Macintosh format. As individual specie, Microsoft straddles both sub-business-eco-systems. So are those third party players, e.g., software writers, who may choose to serve both the Apple and Wintel systems.

Figure 3.1 Firm Positions in Business Eco-Systems

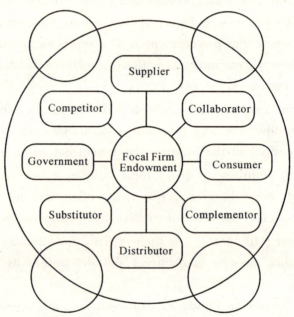

Note: *The big circle represents the focal business eco-systems. Smaller circles overlapping the big circle represent other business eco-systems. Please note that the sizes of the circles are for illustration purpose only.*

Based on extant literature, I discuss the various positional advantages in two general categories: market position (Porter, 1980) and access (Ghemawat, 1986); and resource endowment (Barney, 1991). Notice that, generally speaking, in the terms developed in chapter one, positional advantages are often *ownership-based* or *access-based* while dynamic advantages are often *proficiency-based*.

Position Against Competitors

Size often confers advantage. A firm with larger size relative to its rivals in the same business typically indicates its strong market position *vis-à-vis* rivals. At least three types of factors underlie positional advantages with reference to rivals: market power, scale economy, and experience economy.

First, a big firm often has deep pockets to outlast rivals in battle (D'Aveni, 1994). It therefore has clout among rivals as being able to issue and implement credible threats (Ghemawat, 1986). It also has a greater margin of error in its action and more bargaining power against suppliers and buyers. Size often suggests credibility and dependability in the eyes of customers. Moreover, big firms often enjoy competitive or anti-competitive practice unavailable to smaller rivals, e.g., price leadership, product bundling, easier access to external capital, etc. Second, firms don't just become big simply because of good fortune. There is often deep-seated economics that enables a firm to become big and keep being big. Economy of scale is a major element of size advantage. Third, a firm can also gain advantage because of accumulated volumes in production and service independent of its absolute size. The cost reduction comes from experience or learning that has accrued while producing the products or delivering the services repeatedly, which increases efficiency and productivity (BCG, 1972).

Positions with Complementors, Collaborators, and Substitutors

First, a firm can enjoy positional advantage over rivals if it boast a better relationship to their complementors, the presence of whose products makes the focal firm's products more valuable to the customers (Brandenburger and Nalebuff, 1996). The reason why Microsoft won the war of PC operating systems in the early 1980s was largely due to Microsoft's aggressive co-option of complementors. It persuaded software writers to write application softwares for the MS-DOS instead of rival systems, hence enlarging MS-DOS' installed base. Similar is the case of its defining the Wintel format in PC in tandem with complementor Intel.

Second, firms of smaller scales can offset big firms' size advantage and enhance their advantage over other smaller firms by joining forces together or participate in certain trade alliances (Contractor and Lorange, 1988). In the retailing industry, smaller firms often join purchasing alliances where they can pool their orders together to increase volume and bargain with manufacturers for better deals. Such aggregate strengths provide competitive advantages over those firms which have to go alone.

Third, consider the following sound bites. *Got milk? Beef, it's what's for dinner. Pork, the other white meat. Cotton, the fabric of life. Plastics makes it possible.* Sounds familiar? These well-known catchy phrases in various commercials in the US promote the collective interests of the respective trade and industries which are rather fragmented and whose products are generic commodities difficult to differentiate. Yet by joining forces through trade associations or business councils, firms in these industries are able to better position themselves and hopefully derive some advantages from the "perceived" uniqueness and indispensability of their products over substitute products (Porter, 1980).

Access to Suppliers and Distributors

A firm enjoys advantage if it has better relationships with suppliers than do rivals (Porter, 1980). That is, a firm's positional advantages over rivals can be found in its access to suppliers in ways that are more convenient, cheap, or complete. For instance, a bottled water firm will have cost advantage due to convenient access to supply if it is located closer to the source of spring waters. A firm with long-term contract with a supplier will have advantage over latecomers if they have to pay the supplier more for the same supply deal. Or in the case of retailing, a retailer that can cherry-pick or has access to the full range of a supplier's product will have advantages over retailers that have to settled for undesirable products by the same supplier. A first mover in a business could lock up critical supply for its products and/or maintain favorable treatment from suppliers even when new entrants jump in (Lieberman and Montgomery, 1988; Brandenburger and Nalebuff, 1996).

Firms possessing favorable access to distributors enjoy positional advantage over rivals. Proven brands are often staples of what's on retailers' shelves. As such, firms with established brand names often have advantages over challenging firms in their respective relationships with and hence access to distributors. Foot Locker, a major retailer of athletic footwear would often provide differential treatment against different brands that it carries. For instance, with famous names like Nike and Reebok, they may have to order and even pay in advance to have the latest models of their shoes. Foot Locker needs them as its major draw to attract customers and generate the bulk of its revenues (Miller, 1993). Smaller or newer brands have to deal with Footlocker on consignment basis, incurring competitive disadvantage.

Position with Customers and the Government

A firm possesses advantage over rivals if its brands could be more easily recalled by the customers or are more respected by the customers than are rival brands (Aaker, 1991). A firm can also possess positional advantage over rivals if it enjoys a unique rapport with the customers and its brand name is one of a kind that, in the mind of customers, has no substitutes for its distinctiveness. NutraSweet's aggressive campaign promotes its famous "Swirl" logo (Brandenburger and Nalebuff, 1996) and the "Intel Inside" campaign has been so effective in promoting brand awareness that customers, computer literate or not, would now often insist on having Intel Inside when they buy their PCs (Aaker, 1996). Government policy can also confer a firm positional advantage. It comes as more favorable treatment to the focal firm than to rival firms, in aspects like quota or license for import and export, tax credit or relief, go- vernmental subsidy, less regulation, etc. (D'Aveni, 1994; Bailey, 1997).

Overall Position: Dominant Industry Standard

The overall positional advantage a firm has over rivals is often reflected in its dominance in technological or industry standard, which indicates its strong position relative to various players in its operating environment (Hill, 1997). For a firm to enjoy positional advantage from dominance in industry standard, it often has to have met multiple conditions. First, a firm needs a unique and quality product *vis-à-vis* those of rivals', e.g., Intel, x86 series in computer chips (Grove, 1996). Second, it needs a larger installed base of customers, e.g., MS-DOS against CP/M and later against Macintosh in PC operating systems. Third, it needs to have collaborators who are willing to follow the standard, e.g., firms which licensed JVC's VHS system in the home VCR market (Yoffie, 1990). Fourth, it needs trusting complementors, e.g., CD player producers needed the backing of record companies to promote the new format when it first came out (McGahan, 1991). Finally, government also often becomes a determining factor. In countries where the governments heavily control and regulate the telecommunication industry, the choice of industry standards for cellular phones and pagers by the concerned governmental agencies could also make or break a firm (*Forbes*, 1997a).

Firm Endowment As Positional Advantage

The above discussion of positional advantage focuses on a firm's external relationship with players in its environment. Positional advantage also derives from firm endowments, possession of strengths within the firm itself. In general, we can categorize a firm's endowment in the following areas: financial capital, physical assets, intellectual property, human resources, organizational capital, and managerial talents (cf. Barney, 1991).

A firm's financial endowment affects a firm's position and ability to act in the market. Firms with strong financial capital endowment possess positional advantage over rivals with weaker financial endowment. Major tobacco firms, Philips Morris for instance, were able to diversify relatively easily and hold on to new opportunities for growth. Firms without strong financial endowment often endure disadvantage over rivals or substitutors. For instance, typewriter manufacturers were unable to effectively respond to the computer-based word processing introduced by Wang Computers.

The physical endowment of a firm includes all fixed assets, e.g., plants and equipment, and real estate locations, which a firm possesses. A firm can have advantage over rivals if it possesses superior physical assets than do rivals. For instance, Wal-Mart's preemption of premier locations in the rural areas provided them advantages over rivals in customer access (Ghemawat, 1991). Beyond locations, a firm's physical technology assets can also provide a firm with positional advantages, e.g., AT&T's extensive assets in cables and optical fiber lines for international long-distance phone calls. Similarly, more advanced and sophisticated computer systems and information technology could also provide a firm with competitive advantages.

A firm can also enjoy positional advantage if it possesses superior intellectual property rights, e.g., trade secrets, patents, and copyrights (Hall, 1992). For instance, Disney's vault of classic cartoon movies and MGM's collection of classic black and white movies provide the firms with positional advantages unmatched by their respective rivals.

Although most of the patented technologies are often quickly imitated through reverse engineering within a couple of years, patents, while they last, guarantee the firms advantage over rivals, especially when government strictly reinforce such patents.

Human resources provide competitive advantage if a firm's employees are better trained with sound skills and knowledge who are also highly motivated and loyal (Pfeffer, 1994). USAA spends 2.7% of its annual budget on employee training and education, doubling the industry's average, which helps enhance its service quality (Reichheld, 1996). The skills, knowledge, commitment, and enthusiasm of employees at Southwest Airlines play an integral part of its overall strategy and contribute greatly to its on-time performance, baggage handling, and overall customer satisfaction (Pfeffer, 1994).

Organizational capital refers to a firm's collective human capital and its form of being and deployment within the organization (Barney, 1991). It includes the firm's organizational structure, systems, processes, as well as culture (Barney, 1986b). A firm will have positional advantage over rivals if it possesses unique organizational capital that allows it to function more effectively and/or efficiently. Also, an often time derived advantage is that well managed firms with superior organizational capital attract more superior human capital.

General managers bear the ultimate responsibility for a firm's performance. Creating competitive advantage and win are their fundamental task. In this sense, a firm's managerial resources might well be the most important human capital that a firm possesses. Superior managerial talents create better value to customers and shareholders. Poor management ruins and destroys value. The supply of elite managerial talents—those with vision, experience, courage, and proven track records—is limited. And there is no substitute for managerial talents. Based on the resource-based reasoning (Barney, 1991; Dierickx and Cool, 1989), firms possessing such rare talents therefore enjoys a positional advantage over those that have to settle with the second best.

DYNAMIC ADVANTAGE

A firm can derive competitive advantage from its proficiency—knowledge, skills, competence, and capabilities—in conducting business activities and processes, in addition to its positional advantage. While positional advantage is based on owning valuable assets (Barney, 1991), occupying strong market positions (Porter, 1980), and possessing superior access (Ghemawat, 1986), dynamic advantages provide the firm an edge in what it actually *does*. Such dynamic advantage allows the firm to perform its value adding activities more effectively and/or efficiently than do its rivals.

Based on prior strategy literature, four major aspects of a firm's capabilities can be identified that confer dynamic advantages: entrepreneurial, organizational, technical, and managerial.

A firm's entrepreneurial capability refers to its ability to forecast environmental changes, locate customers, and identify new market opportunities (Stalk, Pecaut, and Burnett, 1996). Organizational capability is the firm's ability to lead and motivate its people (Pfeffer, 1994), foster learning (Senge, 1990), and facilitate necessary organizational changes. Technical capability refers to the technical skills a firm has in R&D, which include both the product design and development and process knowledge, its core competence and business-specific capabilities, and manufacturing strengths (Prahalad and Hamel, 1990). Managerial capability refers to a firm's ability to coordinate, integrate, reconfigure, and deployment of multiple streams of knowledge, skills, and capabilities along market opportunities, which Teece and colleagues (1997) refer to as dynamic capability.

Also, several major indicators can be used to characterize the different aspects of firm capabilities that underlie dynamic advantage: creativity (Schumpeter, 1934), efficiency (Williamson, 1991), speed (Stalk, 1990), flexibility (Sanchez, 1995), and quality (Powell, 1995).

That is, a firm enjoys dynamic advantage if its knowledge and capabilities allow its business activities and processes to be more creative, efficient, and flexible. A firm also enjoys advantage if it could respond to the customers and the markets quickly. From a quality management perspective, quality applies not only to the end product but also the business process. A firm with a quality-focused process could command competitive advantage (Powell, 1995). Based on the above aspects and indicators (see Figure 3.2), content of a firm's specific dynamic advantages can be outlined.

Figure 3.2 Dynamic Advantage: Firm Knowledge and Capabilities

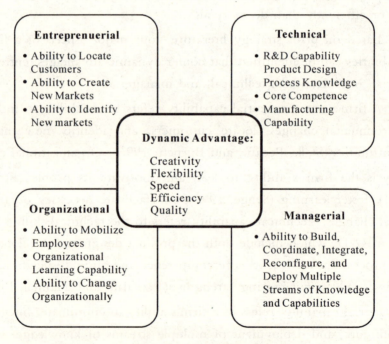

Advantage through Entrepreneurial Capability

A firm's entrepreneurial capability is needed to effectively align the firm with its environment and to broaden and enlarge its business space (Miles and Snow, 1978). A firm enjoys advantage over rivals if it can more accurately forecast trends and changes in its environment, possesses superior intimate knowledge of its customer base and is good at targeting and selecting customers, or has keen sense of how to identify new market opportunities from environmental stimuli.

Knowledge of customers is essential for the success of a firm's business. The fundamental idea of superior performance lies in creating superior customer value. The ability to locate customers, especially those who form the backbone of the customer base—loyal, predictable, and with high profit-generating potential—and intimate knowledge about them afford a firm competitive advantage. You got to know whom you are delivering super value to. Serving the right customers and providing them with what they really need are a service to both the firm and the customers in the long run (Reichheld, 1996).

As certain environmental changes unwind, some firms see threats, some see opportunities, while others tend not to see. A firm gains advantage if it has superior capability in forecasting trends in its industry and the general environment and creating new markets. Sony, for instance, has benefited greatly from its excellent capability in creating new market opportunities. Twice in its cooperation with Philips (in audio cassette and Compact Disc respectively), Sony was able to quickly formulate a marketing concept and flood the market with its products before Philips and other firms even had a clear vision of the market (McGahan, 1991).

Advantage through Technical Capability

While entrepreneurial capability helps a firm identify its core customers and market opportunities, technical capability deals with how a firm serves the customers through its technologies and operating processes. A firm gains advantage if its technical capability allows it to be more efficient, flexible, and high quality in its operation and quicker in response to customers' needs (Bower and Hout, 1988; Stalk, 1990; Stalk and Hout, 1990). Specifically, technical capabilities include basic R&D strengths, core competence and business specific capabilities, and manufacturing strengths.

Basic R&D strengths provides a sound technical foundation for the entire firm, e.g., Sony's strengths in basic R&D in many areas of consumer electronics. Core competence, as a firm's unique and often signature skills and capabilities, allows the firm to excel in multiple product markets (Prahalad and Hamel, 1990). For instance, Sony's capability in miniaturization enabled it to lead in portable electronics ranging from Walkman, Discman, to Watchman. Business-specific capability, skills and expertise required to excel at a specific business, adds special strengths to a particular product or product line. For instance, Sony's Trinitron technology provided it with an edge in picture quality for color TV. Finally, superior manufacturing capability enables a firm to produce quality pro- ducts, often quickly and efficiently. Sony's manufacturing strengths, for example, played major roles in establishing its strong market position in the CD player business (McGahan, 1991).

Advantage through Organizational Capability

Organizational capability helps mobilize a firm's employees toward the common goal of creating customer value, foster organizational learning, and facilitate organizational change when needed. It complements technical capability in carrying out a firm's business processes and activities. In fact, technical capabilities are often built in certain organizational routines, a firm's set way and pattern of conducting business activities (Nelson and Winter, 1982; Winter, 1987).

In modern day firms, innovation is less likely to be an individual effort but instead a collective process. And creativity is not just a technical phenomenon, but involves organizational process and skills.

Organizational capability helps put a firm's technical creativity into perspective and insures that the firm will benefit from such technical innovation. For instance, 3M's organizational capability to persistently encourage and systematically explore technical innovation has been a major factor that helps insure its continued success through innovation and creativity (Bartlett and Mohammed, 1995). Similarly, a firm's efficiency in its operation often arises from both its technical process and organizational process, and often simultaneously, e.g., Lincoln Electric's technical efficiency comes primarily from its experience-based learning and continuous improvement (Fast and Berg, 1983).

To respond to the market quickly is not only a technical task, it requires organizational routines that facilitate the flexibility and speed of the firm's technical activities. For instance, USAA organizes its business activities in such a way that the centralized operation will provide customers flexibility and quick response. As a major auto insurance provider, USAA has created a loyal customer base among military personnel, who frequently move. With its centralized database and telephone sales representatives, it provides service that can be accessed from almost anywhere in the world. Comparing to traditional organizational set-up and practice of many insurance companies, USAA's technical and organizational capability in centralizing its operation gives it a competitive edge (Reichheld, 1996).

Advantage through Managerial Capability

Managerial capability enables the firm to build, coordinate, integrate, and reconfigure multiple streams of competencies and deploy them strategically to exploit changing market opportunities. It is a higher order capability that helps generate other capabilities and put them into productive use (Collis, 1994; Teece, et al., 1997).

A firm's core competencies can also be applied to multiple product markets. In order to do so, a firm needs appropriate managerial capability to leverage its core competencies in the technical aspect, as well as capabilities in organizational and entrepreneurial aspects. For instance, Canon's superior managerial capability affords it competitive advantage in a whole range of product markets. Due to its superior managerial capability, Canon is able to integrate its various streams of knowledge and expertise in image processing, e.g., micro-electronics, precision mechanics, and fine optics, and apply it to multiple products, ranging from cameras to camcorders, fax machines to printers, and copiers to scanners (Prahalad and Hamel, 1990; Nonaka, 1991; Ghoshal, 1992). Similarly, the superior managerial capability of Honda allows it to leverage its competence in engine building to multiple businesses that include automobile, motorcycle, lawn mower, and outdoor generator (Prahalad and Hamel, 1990; Stalk, et al., 1992).

Such managerial capability deals with all of the other three capabilities. For cross-market leveraging to begin with, a firm should have built the multiple core competencies. The accumulation of such core competencies often requires organizational capabilities that facilitate shared learning across divisions and units. To deploy these competencies, market opportunities and customer groups and needs must be properly identified. Finally, they have to be deployed selectively using sound managerial judgment. So it's the integrated capabilities from all four aspects that often underlie a firm's dynamic advantage.

A firm's technical capabilities often need to be reconfigured and redeployed to capitalize on emerging market opportunities or neutralize competitive threats. It requires superb managerial skills and capabilities to effectively handle such reconfiguration (Teece, et al., 1997).

Consider the changes Bill Gates made at Microsoft in 1996. Knowing fully well how they themselves, as a once small company, fundamentally changed the competitive landscape in the computer industry, Microsoft is much alert to and open-minded about any new phenomenon in the business. It was not about to sitting on its laurels.

Gates and associates at Microsoft were quick to perceive the threats of Netscape and the Internet to their vision of PC-based future for the computer industry. And its excellent managerial capability allowed Microsoft to quickly adapt to the new competitive situation (*Wall Street Journal*, 1997).

In the same token, Microsoft's ability to locate and create new areas of business that feature network externality can also provide new opportunities for it to leverage its competence in the software business and its expertise in exploiting network externality.

Finally, a firm with superior managerial capability is expected to survive and thrive through multiple rounds of technological trajectories or changes of its core businesses. For instance, 3M had changed its core business from mining, to sandpapers and related abrasive and adhesive products, to today's multiple areas and variety of high-tech businesses (Bartlett and Mohammed, 1995). What has remained consistent is the superior managerial capability that weaves together technical, organizational, and entrepreneurial capabilities and skills. Such managerial capability helps sustain an organization that persistently thrives on institutionalized innovation.

Next, I first compare and contrast the general characteristics of positional advantage and dynamic advantage. Then I discuss the different patterns of their relationship and implications for firm performance.

POSITIONAL ADVANTAGE AND DYNAMIC ADVANTAGE: A COMPARISON

Knowing the rival and knowing oneself helps a firm better approach its competition in the market. This requires that a firm understand in what areas its rivals may possess competitive advantage, be it positional or dynamic. While some types of competitive advantage are easily discernible, other types are difficult to grasp. Comparing and contrasting positional advantage with dynamic advantage help enhance our understanding of the characteristics of each type of competitive advantage.

First, positional advantage is often discrete while dynamic advantage is often more compound. A particular item of resource endowment, e.g., a superior real estate location, certain market position or status, e.g., the largest installed base, or established access, e.g., Coca-Cola's dominance of retail shelf space, can in themselves contribute to a firm's performance. Such positional advantage is often based on certain stand-alone attributes of the firm. Dynamic competitive advantage, on the other hand is often based on a compound of a host of factors. For instance, core competence is often a marriage between technical strengths and organizational capabilities (Prahalad and Hamel, 1990).

Second, relatedly, positional advantage is often more tangible than dynamic advantage. While it is relative easy to identify the underlying attributes of positional advantage, it is often difficult to locate the exact source of a dynamic advantage, e.g., the quickness of response of Toyota to market changes. Especially, when such dynamic advantage entails human expertise and unquantifiable factors, it obscures the source even more. Furthermore, in certain cases, dynamic advantage may not even be discernible to rivals. For instance, a firm's unique ability in identifying market opportunities could be concealed from rivals more easily than the apparent positional advantage, e.g., location.

Third, positional advantage is more context-specific while dynamic advantage is more broadly applicable. A firm's position *vis-à-vis* particular rivals defines the context of positional advantage. For instance, a firm's market share dominance in a particular market does not necessarily translate into leadership in other markets. Dynamic advantage, on the other hand, building on core competencies and more leverageable capabilities, may be applied to various end product markets. For instance, IBM's dominance in the mainframe business did not lead to its dominance in the PC business. Instead, it is the overall technical and organizational capabilities of IBM to provide an integrated solution to the business computing needs that carry its day.

Fourth, dynamic advantage is process-oriented while positional advantage is more status-oriented. Dynamic advantage enables a firm to function more effectively or efficiently in business operations. Positional advantage at any specific point of time defines a firm's actual competitiveness *vis-à-vis* rivals. In this sense, positional advantage indicates current competitive status of the firm, while dynamic advantage helps insure a firm is competitive in the ongoing competition. That is, positional advantage reflects a firm's current fit with the environment and dynamic advantage aims at long-term fit.

As the strategy literature pays increasingly more attention to the importance of dynamic competitive advantage (Stalk, et al., 1992; D'Aveni, 1994; Teece et al., 1997), however, it does not mean that positional advantage (Porter, 1980; Wernerfelt, 1984; Barney, 1991) is no longer important in our current competitive reality. A careful examination of the relationship between positional advantage and dynamic advantage would reveal that both types of advantage are indispensable for a firm's superior performance.

Positional advantages and dynamic advantages often reinforce each other. On the one hand, positional advantages often form the basis of or give rise to dynamic advantages. On the other hand, dynamic advantages could lead to and strengthen a firm's positional advantages. In this sense, positional advantages could be interpreted as fossilized dynamic advantages, as the current position may reflect a firm's capabilities and actions taken in a prior period of time. However, lacking dynamic advantages, a firm's future positional advantages will likely be at peril. Also, without positional advantages, a firm's dynamic advantages would unlikely to fully reach their potential.

FROM POSITIONAL ADVANTAGE TO DYNAMIC ADVANTAGE

Positional Advantages as a Basis for Dynamic Advantages

What a firm can do in the market depends largely on what it possesses and what it can access (Ghemawat, 1986). For instance, the dynamic advantage of Toyota in efficient, flexible, and quality manufacturing has been based on its positional advantages in ownership of advanced technological systems, good relationships with suppliers, and its knowledgeable workers. Similarly, Microsoft's dynamic advantage lies in its speed in response to competitive threat, e.g., its quick introduction of its Internet browsers. Such dynamic advantage it enjoys, however, is also largely based on its ownership of the operating system standard and the huge installed base for its software products, i.e., positional advantage.

Positional Advantages Give Rise to and Enhance Dynamic Advantages

A firm with strong market positions could further strengthen its dynamic advantage by attracting more superior resources and renewing its capabilities. For instance, Microsoft's market position and reputation would attract the most talented engineers fresh out of the school to replenish its knowledge base and creative force. Such superior access to critical supply of talents for its software development, an intellectual property-based business, enables Microsoft to maintain strong technical capability to create new innovative products (*Fortune*, 1997).

FROM DYNAMIC ADVANTAGE TO POSITIONAL ADVANTAGE

Dynamic Advantages Lead to Positional Advantages

Positional advantages are often the reward of a firm's dynamic advantages. A firm that is creative, efficient, flexible, quick in response to customers, and quality-focused will likely enjoy better access to customers and resource providers, possess better relationship with collaborators and complementors, and win stronger market positions against competitors and substitutors. For example, Nike's current market power and reputation have been carefully built through its various dynamic advantages in its business over rivals. Its designing capability, its marketing strengths, and its ability to manage the entire network of various players in its empire all contribute to its gaining and strengthening of its market positions (Miller, 1993; Katz, 1994).

Dynamic Advantages Strengthen Positional Advantages

Dynamic advantages not only help a firm to gain positional advantages but also help strengthen its positional advantages. For instance, Intel's dominant position in the microprocessor business is not maintained merely through erecting barriers to imitation or using other anti-competitive practice. Instead, it consolidates its position through a host of dynamic advantages in developing a series of new products through innovation (D'Aveni, 1994; Grove, 1996). Similarly, Disney's dynamic advantages in creating new animated characters and in spanning the boundary of people's imagination constantly help polish the Disney image and strengthen its market position.

DYNAMIC ADVANTAGE AND POSITIONAL ADVANTAGE: POTENTIAL PITFALLS

Dynamic Advantages without Positional Advantages

A firm may have certain dynamic advantages yet lack endowment to further pursue and establish its positional advantages. Consider the classic example of EMI in the CT scanner business. It possessed dynamic advantage in developing innovative products with great commercial potential. Yet, due to lacking of manufacturing strengths and marketing muscles, it could not translate its dynamic advantage into positional advantages in the form of market leadership. Instead, later-comers with strong endowment, like GE, were able to dominate the CT scanner market. And the Sony flop in its VCR business also illustrates this point (Yoffie, 1990). With dynamic advantage in developing a superior product, yet lacking support from collaborators and/or complementors, the positional advantages in market dominance Sony expected did not materialize.

Positional Advantages without Dynamic Advantage

A firm's positional advantages are often indicators of its past glories. Without ongoing dynamic advantages to enhance its positions and create new positional advantages, the firm is likely to experience downward spiral, for extant positional advantages are subject to erosion due to competitive imitation or circumvention, environmental shift or other combination of factors.

For instance, Kmart is still a company whose size puts it in the upper echelons of the Fortune 500 firms. However, it is not able to match the superior capabilities of Wal-Mart alike in efficiently moving merchandises (Stalk, et al., 1992; Moore, 1996). With its dynamic advantages diminishing against Wal-Mart and category killers like Home Depot and Toys R Us, its once enviable positional advantages in discount retailing become shaky: laying off employees, closing stores, and facing down-graded credit ratings.

DYNAMIC ADVANTAGE, POSITIONAL ADVANTAGE, AND PERFORMANCE

While both positional advantage and dynamic advantage contribute to a firm's performance, the importance of the two types of competitive advantage varies in different types of competitive environment. Consistent with our discussion of business eco-system presented earlier, I categorize a firm's environment using both product market (Porter, 1980) and resource factor market (Barney, 1996a; Zajac, 1992) dimensions. In product market, we could capture the market dynamism by the rate of market growth (Wernerfelt and Montgomery, 1989) and shift in industry standard (Schumpeter, 1934; Rumelt, 1984; Hill, 1997). In the resource market, we could use the rate of resource mobility or imitability (Rumelt, 1984, 1987; Williams, 1992) to categorize the environment.

Product Market Environment

Wernerfelt and Montgomery (1989) demonstrate that "what is an attractive industry" depends on a particular firm's competence, or in the term of this paper, the types of competitive advantage. For instance, a low-cost positioned firm may be more profitable in a stable industry than in a high growth industry, because the high growth rate is likely to shield inefficient firms from cut-throat cost pressure, rendering the cost effective firm's cost advantage relatively unimportant. Similarly, we could argue that the rate of growth of an industry will dictate the importance of positional advantage and dynamic advantage in terms of their contribution to firm performance.

First, I expect that positional advantage may contribute more to a firm's performance in low growth industries than in high-growth industries. In high growth industries, weaker firms may have a better chance challenging the well-positioned leaders than in low-growth industries where dominant market position often has long-term ramifications.

Second, I expect that dynamic advantage will be more important to firm performance in high-growth industries than in low-growth industries. In low growth industries where market shifts occur rather infrequently, positional advantage alone would likely sustain a firm's superior performance (Rumelt, 1984). While in high growth industries, positional advantage is less likely sustainable, and dynamic advantage is more important for a firm's performance because it allows the firm to better exploit the market opportunities furnished by the high growth.

Moreover, in "winner take it all" industries (Hill, 1997) where Schumpeterian shocks occur infrequently and where industry standard has long term impact on the industry's structure and competition, I expect that positional advantage will have more influence on firm performance than dynamic advantage, at least within a particular round of technological trajectory (Teece, et al., 1997). For in such industries, despite a firm's superior capability in R&D, manufacturing, or marketing, if it fails to capture the dominant industry standard, it will have to play second fiddle to the one that sets the standard.

Resource Factor Environment

Williams (1992) identified three types of competitive environment based on resource sustainability: slow cycle, standard cycle, and fast cycle. The slow cycle features stickiness of resource position where isolating mechanisms are durable (Rumelt, 1987) and businesses are managed in a "guild-like" manner (Williams, 1992). The standard cycle features high resource-imitation pressures where standardized production for high volume is the key of competition, e.g., auto and fast food. Finally, the fast cycle faces the highest resource-imitation pressure, similar to D'Aveni's (1994) description of hypercompetition.

We expect that positional advantage would be the most important in slow cycle environment, important in standard cycle environment, and least important in fast cycle environment. As the resource mobility increases from the slow cycle to fast cycle, a firm's resource endowment becomes less important. While a firm still enjoys positional advantage by possessing stronger resource endowment, due to its easy mobility and imitation pressure, its earning potential diminishes.

For instance, De Beers, during the early part of the century could simply rely on its positional advantage, i.e., monopoly of supply, to generate persistent profit. Later when more locations of diamond mine were found around the globe, competitive pressure mounted. De Beer had to increasingly rely on more dynamic advantages to sustain its profits. It has to pay more attention to its capability in maintaining the image of exclusiveness of diamond in the minds of consumers and in identifying potential threats, co-opting other suppliers, etc.

On the other hand, dynamic advantage is expected to have more impact on performance in fast cycle environment than in standard cycle and slow cycle environments. In fast cycle environment where resource mobility is the greatest, positional advantage are often only transient while the ability to constantly innovate—basis of dynamic advantage—becomes especially pertinent. Here resource endowment changes and market position changes. What really matters is the ability to identify market opportunity and quickly assemble a critical mass of needed resources and execute a strategic decision in timely manner.

For instance, Intel's market share in the memory device business once dropped significantly from a dominant presence to almost elimination in a matter of several years due to the entrance of the more efficient Japanese manufacturers, which led to Intel's exit from that very market which it helped create. But fortunately, Intel had nurtured a host of organizational, technological, and managerial capability that provided them with dynamic advantages in the microprocessor business, which had constantly renewed their temporal positional advantages over rivals (Grove, 1996).

Finally, a firm may operate simultaneously in all three cycles that makes the relationship between position advantage, dynamic advantage, and performance complicated. For instance, for the moment at least, the PC operating system of Microsoft may be considered a slow cycle environment while the Internet browser a fast cycle business. As explained earlier, both types of competitive advantage are hard at work in enhancing Microsoft's performance, with positional advantage providing the necessary springboard for better creating and exploiting its dynamic advantages.

CONCLUDING REMARKS

Positional and dynamic advantages are two basic types of competitive advantages. While positional advantages allow the firm to exploit its endowment, position, or status, dynamic advantages enable a firm to conduct its business activities more effectively and/or efficiently. Obviously, a firm needs to have both to achieve persistent superior performance. Examples of Nike and Wal-Mart drive home the point. Wal-Mart has shifted its dominant advantages from location based (Ghemawat, 1991) to knowledge and capability-based (Stalk et al., 1992). Similarly, Nike's dominant advantage has shifted from low-cost outsourcing to image and differentiation-based advantage that relies primarily on Nike's in-house capability (Miller, 1993; *Fortune*,

1995b). As both firms shifted their dominant advantages from more positional advantages, e.g., outsourcing or location, to more knowledge or capability-based dynamic advantages, e.g., ability to coordinate multiple strengths in multiple aspects of their respective businesses, both firms, however, further strengthened their positional advantages, instead of downplaying them. A business firm needs positional advantages, e.g., market power, to preserve the achievement brought by the dynamic advantages. But more importantly, a firm needs to leverage its positional advantages and further gain and exercise its dynamic advantages.

In conclusion, putting both positional and dynamic advantages in use and carefully attending to their timely renewal stand as the fundamental task of general managers in their striving for persistent superior performance. The framework developed in this chapter regarding the various positional and dynamic advantages as well as their relationships, I hope, will help general managers better perform such a task and help strategy researchers better understand the relationship between competitive advantage and firm performance.

Chapter 4   Locale and Appropriability

The locales of a firm's competitive advantages vary and they have different implications on which party will appropriate the economic rents generated by the firm's competitive advantage. This chapter dissects the locales of competitive advantages and discusses the respective appropriability regime in an integrative framework comprising two systems of categorization: levels of strategy within the firm and hierarchy of ownership of assets and factors underpinning the firm's competitive advantages. It profiles some general categories of possible locales of competitive advantages and comments on how the firm could benefit from these competitive advantages with different locales. The major challenges for general managers in attending advantages at different locales are then outlined. Some general propositions are offered in the concluding remarks, which emphasize the firm's performance as the key concern when we study competitive advantages.

A fox strolling in the mountain forest was caught by a tiger, which was about to have the fox eaten. The ever-sly fox said to the tiger: "You dare not eat me, for I am the King of all beasts." The tiger asked: "How can you prove that?" "You only need to walk behind me and see how the other animals and beasts behave and treat me," the fox replied. The tiger and fox then made rounds in the forests with the fox leading the way and the tiger trailing immediately behind. When all the animals and beasts saw the tiger, they show fear or respect. The tiger, wrongfully thought that the fear and respect were shown to the fox instead of him, set the fox free. This story eventually culminates into an idiom in Chinese: the fox leverages the might and prestige of the tiger.

In the jungle, might (read raw power) may appear a useful and often decisive competitive advantage, vital for fortune and survival. When you have might yourself, then you have competitive advantage, competitive advantage based on what you *own*. When you don't have might, you can borrow, exploit, make use of, or literally, take advantage of other party's competitive advantage, competitive advantage based on what you can *access*. You can access other party's competitive advantage based on certain relationship with that party, e.g., friendship, acquaintance, family or blood tie, etc. or pure happenstance. You can also have competitive advantage based on your own knowledge, wisdom, and your capability, i.e., *proficiency* based competitive advantage. Such advantage can also help you access other party's competitive advantage, as demonstrated in the fox and tiger case where the fox resorts to a cunning ploy.

So, generally speaking, competitive advantage could be based on what you have, what you can get, and what you know and can do, as explained in detail in Chapter 1. However, the above case of tiger and fox should help push our thinking beyond our understanding of ownership-based, access-based, and proficiency-based advantages, and really force us to penetrate a step further and probe the question of "locale" of a firm's competitive advantages: Where could a firm's competitive advantages possibly reside? In the tiger and fox case, clearly, the fox leverages a "virtual" competitive advantage. The advantage *per se* resides with the tiger, yet the primary beneficiary turns out to be the fox, which, through its manipulation of the perception of the tiger, accesses and leverages the tiger's advantage. As such, it is also meaningful to ask: How does the locale of competitive advantage affect the appropriability of economic rents it generates?

The purposes of this chapter are to categorize and profile the possible locales of a firm's competitive advantages and examine the appropriability regime of competitive advantages that reside at the different locales. This endeavor will help us better understand when and where the firm will enjoy the greatest benefits from its various competitive advantages, actual or virtual. The chapter is organized as follows. It first discusses two categorization systems that track the locales of a firm's competitive advantages: levels of strategy and hierarchy of ownership, based on which an integrative framework is then advanced that addresses the various possible locales and their respective appropriability implications, followed by a discussion of the challenges in managing competitive advantages at different locales and some concluding remarks.

LEVELS OF STRATEGY AND LOCALES OF COMPETITIVE ADVANTAGE

It has long been established in the strategic management literature that the purpose of strategy is to create competitive advantage and generate superior firm performance (Chandler, 1962; Ansoff, 1965; Andrews, 1971; Porter, 1985; Barney, 1991; Powell, 2001). As the typical modern business firm features diversified operations often managed with a multidivisional structure (Chandler, 1962, Rumelt, 1974), strategic management has permeated into multiple levels of a firm's operation. Chandler (1962) was among the first to differentiate between a firm's corporate level strategy and business level strategy. Hofer and Schendel (1978) further categorize four levels of strategy, from institutional, corporate, business, to functional or operational.

Institutional Level

The institutional level strategy, above and beyond the inter-firm competition in the economic arena, deals with the firm's institutional value, public image, and social legitimacy in the community and society where it operates (Selznick, 1957; Miles, 1982; Freeman, 1984). Firms that are better at stakeholder management (Freeman, 1984) and project positive public image and social identity (Miles, 1982) will have competitive advantages over those who are weak in this aspect. When organizations are infused with value, they become institutionalized and take on unique identities (Selznick, 1957). Work, in such organizations, is not just a job; it has meanings, meanings in helping people, advancing people's well being, and improving the world in which we live.

Corporate Level

Chandler (1962), Ansoff (1965), and Andrews (1971) are among the pioneers that expound the essence of corporate strategy, emphasizing the importance of domain selection (Hofer and Schendel, 1978) and the distinctive competence (Selznick, 1957). Later contributions on portfolio planning (BCG, 1972), performance implication (Rumelt, 1974), dominant logics (Bettis and Prahalad, 1986), merger and acquisition (Porter, 1987; Haspeslag and Jemison, 1991), core competence (Prahalad and Hamel, 1990), resource and capabilities (Haspeslag and Jemison, 1991; Collis and Montgomery, 1997, Teece, Pisano, and Shuen, 1997) and parenting advantages (Goold, Campbell, and Alexander, 1995) help enrich tremendously our understanding of the management of diversification strategy and competitive advantages at the corporate level.

Business Level

At the business strategy level, the tenor for competitive advantage is at its strongest and loudest. From Miles and Snow's (1978) typology of generic competitive postures to Porter's (1980) generic strategies; from Porter's (1985) value chain to Kim and Mauborgne's (1997, 2005) value innovation; from industry positioning (Porter, 1980) to resource endowment (Barney, 1991; Peteraf, 1993); from competitive dynamics (Chen, 1996) to organizational factors (Hansen and Wernerfelt, 1989), studies of various business level strategies have advanced our understanding of competitive advantages at the business level: differentiation, cost leadership, focus, (Porter, 1980), resource-based (Barney, 1991; Peteraf, 1993), time-based (Stalk, 1990), efficiency-based (Williamson, 1991), capability based (Stalk a, 1992; Teece et al, 1997), or knowledge-based (Nonaka, 1991; Winter, 1997; Grant, 2004).

Functional Level

At the functional level (or operational level) strategy, research studies focus their attention on the specific functional areas and the operational details that support the strategy in a particular business. For instance, Biggadike (1981) and Aaker (1996) expound the nature and techniques of marketing strategy, examines how effective marketing strategy could create competitive advantage and help a firm win in a line of business. Hayes, Pisano, Upton, and Wheelwright (2004) provide an excellent account of operational and technological strategy and explain how quality manufacturing could contribute to product advantage and hence contribute to a business's bottom line. Of course, appropriate human resource strategy, financial strategy, and strategies in other functional areas will all help contribute to a business's competitive advantages.

OWNERSHIP HIERARCHY AND LOCALES OF COMPETITIVE ADVANTAGE

The locales of a firm's competitive advantages could also be examined using the hierarchy of ownership of the assets and factors underpinning these advantages. The ownership ranges from individuals, firms, to virtual (other firms and institutions outside the focal firm's boundary).

Individual-Bound

As mentioned in Chapter 2, in an auspicious year during the prime of Bill Cosby's illustrious career, it was reported that the famed American comedian's annual earnings would easily dwarf the total profits of the entire CBS network, the comedian's employer which aired his sitcoms (Evans and Wurster, 1997). People watch Cosby, not CBS. The star power shines over and above the carrier. The CBS network might possess competitive advantages over rivals in terms of higher ratings. Yet, as a business firm, CBS failed in benefiting much from Cosby's spectacular sitcoms, because the basis (actual ownership) of its competitive advantages (ratings) lies in the comedian, an individual, who is mobile and can easily jump ship to a competing network. This mobility gives the concerned individuals bargaining power in the appropriability game as the firm cannot enjoy and sustain the advantage without the concerned individuals (Barney, 1991; Grant, 1991).

In essence, individual-bound competitive advantages rely primarily on assets and factors owned by individuals or group of individuals, not necessarily the firms that employ them. Although the firm does on surface "possess" these advantages nominally, it is subject to the hold up of the actual individual owners. Obviously, the economic rents generated by such individual-bound competitive advantage are largely claimed by the actual owners of the resources and factors that underpin the competitive advantages.

Firm-Bound

The relationship between Discovery Channel, the premium Cable TV station featuring scientific topics, and its content providers and program contributors fitting illustrate what could be called firm-bound competitive advantage. It could easily dictate the programming and boast sizable bargaining power over its content providers and program contributors (Evans and Wurster, 1997). In this case, people habitually watch the Discovery Channel, not necessarily the individual program. The Channel (firm) itself is more reputable and larger than any individual programs and their providers who have to fight for spots on the channel and consider it a prestige and privilege for having their programs shown. Discovery Channel overshadows individual programs in earnings, because the competitive advantage (and its ownership) largely remains with the Channel, e.g., its interesting programming themes, consistency and credibility, quality control, and the resulting brand equity, etc.

Firm-bound competitive advantages rely on resources, capabilities, and other factors that feature ownership by the firm and they are often embedded within the firm's routine and permeate in many activities the firm engages in (Nelson and Winter, 1982). No individuals could (easily) claim rights to the advantages and the advantages *per se* are generally thought to be the firm's property. Such advantages would not easily be eroded because of the defection of certain individuals or loss of certain assets of the firm. Moreover, such firm-bound competitive advantages, sustainable ones in particular, are often causally ambiguous and socially complex, hence less duplicable and imitable, and also less tradable (Barney, 1991; Grant, 1991), e.g., a superior organizational culture (Barney, 1986), excellence in organizational learning

(Nonaka, 1991), and organizational routines (Nelson and Winter, 1982) and programs and standard operating procedures (March and Simon, 1958).

Virtual-Bound

Now, let's revisit our opening story about the fox and the tiger and examine the case of virtual competitive advantage, which could be defined as competitive advantages whose underpinning assets and factors are (actually) owned by other firms or institutions and hence reside outside of the focal firm's boundary. In the year end of 1997, all athletic footwear products made in China and shipped to the US ready to be distributed in the US market stood at $ 12 a pair. The average retail was around $ 65. The low cost manufacturing done in China lent Nike tremendous cost advantage and plenty of latitude for lavish spending on high-powered marketing campaigns. Nike does not make shoes. The Chinese do. Nike's competitive advantage in cost is indeed virtual-bound, as it leverages the cat's paws from afar. So long as Nike retains bargaining power against the still fragmented and much smaller scaled manufacturers, its virtual-bound advantage in cost savings will likely sustain (Chesbrough and Teece, 1996).

In summary, based on the ownership hierarchy, the locale of a firm's competitive advantage could be individual-bound, firm-bound, or virtual-bound. In terms of appropriability, firm-bound advantages are the ones, by definition, that benefit the firm the most. The individual-bound advantages will contribute to the firm's performance more in partnership-based firms than in other forms of business ownership. Virtual competitive advantages could be a great enhancer for a firm's performance so long as the firm could maintain upper hand in bargaining with the actual owner of the virtual advantage.

LOCALES OF COMPETITIVE ADVANTAGE AND APPROPRIABILITY

Given the above two categorization systems, we could now form an integrative framework that helps catalog the inventory of various possible locales of a firm's competitive advantages and examine their respective appropriability. See Figure 4.1 for a graphic account. For illustrative purpose, I choose three items to describe each of the 12 possible locales.

Figure 4.1   Locales of Competitive Advantage: An Integrative Account

Levels of Strategy	Hierarchy of Ownership		
	Individual-Bound	*Firm-Bound*	*Virtual-Bound*
Institutional	**Goodwill Ambassador** Role Model Spokesperson Philanthropist	**Institutional Image** Care for People Social Concern Concern for Environment	**Social Contribution** Charity Organizations Social Institutions Medical Research
Corporate	**Commanding Generals** Visionary Leadership General Mgmt Skills Financial Acumen	**Corporate Routine** Dynamic Capability Core Competence Parenting Skills	**Relational Capital** Rival-Partners Credit Community Government
Business	**Elite Managers** Business-Specific Skills Clientele Network Outside Contacts	**Business Position** Market Position Brand Image Process Efficiency	**Useful Partners** R&D Consortium Strategic Alliance Network
Function	**Star Employees** Star Buyer Technical Wizard Super Salesperson	**Operational Process** Supply Chain Manufacturing Marketing Prowess	**Superior Access** Supplier Relationship Outsourcing Partners Distributor Relation

INSTITUTIONAL ADVANTAGES

Goodwill Ambassador

A firm possesses competitive advantage over rivals if it enjoys the service of Goodwill Ambassadors, who will promote the positive social image and identity of the firm and hence enhance the social legitimacy of the firm in the eyes if the general public. The ambassador could be a famous employee or a manager, or a group of individuals, who goes above and beyond the call of duty, exemplifies the spirit and behavior that are socially desirable and valuable. Sometimes, it could take just one publicly well-know figure to do the trick. Better yet, the CEO or top leader of a firm herself might just suffice the requirement of such a role that brings enormous positive publicity and customer goodwill. Consider Anita Roddick (1991) of Body Shop. Her deep concern for environmental issues and insistence on no-animal testing earns broad praises and applauses for her initiative as well as her products.

Similarly, Ben&Jerry's namesake founders, in their advocating of social mission, personify their ideals in promoting egalitarianism, caring for the socially disadvantaged, and being environmentally conscious and responsible. The late Dave Thomas of Wendy's Hamburgers, himself an orphan, spent his whole life and fortune to promote the care for and the wellbeing of the unfortunate children. These are individuals who shoulder unusually large banners, with even larger dreams and ideals in their minds. They appear as *spokespersons* for certain social causes, they act as *philanthropists* to help protect the environment, and they serve as *role models* to help enlighten the thoughts and behavior of the general public. The ensuing competitive advantages these leaders bring to their firms at the institutional level, unless the social commitment become an institutionalized organizational behavior, will remain individual-bound advantages.

Institutional Image

A good institutional image is a firm-bound competitive advantage. It exemplifies a firm's commitment to its social responsibility, in addition to its mission as an economic entity. Many firms attempt to project an image of good corporate citizen in the community and society that they operate. They do so systematically through institutionalized rules and procedures, not necessarily according to some individuals' wills. The ensuing advantage is therefore often firm-bound. A firm that enjoys this kind of institutional advantage will also likely enjoy customer goodwill and positive recognition in the competitive arena. Broadly speaking, institutional image could be based on good corporate deeds on three fronts: care for people (Pfeffer, 1994), being socially responsible (Miles, 1982), and concern for the environment (Shrivastava, 1996).

First, people are the only righteous source of power. Honor their dignity. Encourage their creativity. People will make wonder. For a long period of time, Southwest Airlines in the U.S. has been high on the list of *Fortune* magazine's Companies American Most Want to Work for and the Most Admired Companies list. Its people-centered organizational culture easily draws enthusiastic followings in the recruiting market for Southwest Airlines. People come here not only for the money, but for fun, love, and pride.

Second, being socially sensitive and acting in socially responsible manners are welcome deeds by the community and the public. For instance, Johnson & Johnson's commitment to the best interests of its customers and its corporate integrity has earned the trust of consumers and doctors alike around the world. Similarly, GE, for years, carefully nurtures the image that "GE, We bring good things to life."

Third, with increasing population pressure, energy shortage, pollution of all kinds, we are taxing the environment to support the standard we are living. For sustainable growth and development, firms need to attend to environment issues and concerns much more than what they are currently accustomed to. Firms committed to bring people non-polluting and environmental friendly products and services will certainly enjoy an edge over those that grow at the cost of the environment, grossly sacrificing the current and long term interests of the community and society at large.

Social Contribution

Many firms directly involve in various social causes and engagement, e.g., Ben&Jerry's sets up a foundation to save the Brazilian forest, hires inner city workers, uses only locally produced dairy products, etc. Other firms build their virtue advantage at the institutional level through their association with and contribution to certain entities and institutions that are directly involved in various social causes and environmental causes. Typical institutions of these kinds are *charities* that help the poor, e.g., the Salvage Army; *social institutions* that help advance the interests and causes of various social groups, e.g., victims of domestic violence or the Public Television, and *medical research institutions*, e.g., AIDS research foundations. Contribution to and support of these institutions will help enhance customer goodwill as well as generate and reinforce positive publicity and institutional image. As the firms themselves do not directly engage in the various social causes, the potential advantages that they derive from their associations with these institutions are indeed virtual ones.

CORPORATE ADVANTAGES

Commanding Generals

The task of corporate strategy is to define the scope of a firm's business portfolio, build core competence, and managing external relations (Chandler, 1962; Ansoff, 1965; Andrews, 1971; Prahalad and Hamel, 1990). At the corporate level, individual-bound competitive advantages come from the commanding corporate generals whose vision, skills, experience, and judgment have vital impact on the performance of the corporation. Such advantages are individual-bound, specific to these corporate generals and independent of the firm and its environment, and often come from at least three types of individuals: the *entrepreneurs and their visionary leadership*; *the empire builder and their general management skills*; *the financier with their financial acumen who excels in the market for corporate control*, or any combinations of *entrepreneurial, managerial, and financial talents*. Walt Disney exemplified an entrepreneur with vision and conviction. He believed that his theme parks would fly. Steve Jobs' running of Apple for the second time vindicates his vision and leadership. Take away the founders of a firm, you take away its heart and soul. These founder-owners are themselves the firm. Both Disney and Apple faltered immediately after the departure of their founders. Consider Alfred P. Sloan, the consummate general manager, who helped make GM the mark of excellence for a long while and the largest auto-making empire on earth. Or consider the later day Jack Welch of GE and Andy Grove of Intel, who epitomize the best general managers and empire builders of modern day corporations. Consider Warren Buffet the super invester, Sumner Redstone the consummate deal maker, and Kirk Kerkorian the shrew financier. Who could deny the personal impacts these corporate generals made on their firms though their unique traits and personal touches?

Corporate Routine

Unlike many firms that wavered after the death of the founder or the departure of a strong leader, Wal-Mart went on unabatedly after Walton's passing and quickly beat the $ 125 billion sales target set by

Walton before the century-end deadline and now actually double that figure in just 5 years! Not to deny Walton's personal genius and hands on impact on Wal-Mart, his greatest achievement might well be his being able to build firm-bound advantages (sustainable after his departure) stronger and greater than do most, if not all, mortals that ever set foot in a corporate executive suites. Wal-Mart's spectacular success relies on a host of competitive advantages that are based on the firm's unique resources and capabilities, which are more powerful than any talented individuals. Generally speaking, at the corporate level, firm-bound competitive advantages typically reflect three areas of corporate routine (Nelson and Winter, 1982): *core competence* that supports a series of product markets (Prahalad and Hamel, 1990), *dynamic capabilities* that renew and/or redeploy the core competence (Teece, Pisano, and Shuen, 1997), as well as *parenting skills* that add value to strategic business units within the corporate portfolio (Goold, et. al, 1995).

Related diversifiers achieve synergies through sharing similar resources and capabilities, e.g. R&D capacity, distribution channels, among its SBUs (Chanlder, 1962; Rumelt, 1974). Exploring such synergies, building and exploiting core competences require sophisticated administrative coordination and integration (Gupta and Govindarajan, 2002). Firms that boast fine routines in nurturing and utilizing core competences will have competitive advantages at the corporate level (Prahalad and Hamel, 1990). As core competence could also turn into core rigidity (Leonard-Barton, 1994), a firm needs to attend to the dynamic fit between a firm's resources and capabilities and the requirement of the changing environment and new opportunities. Dynamic capabilities (Teece, et al, 1997) in renewing a firm's competence pool, reconfiguring a firm's portfolio are built-in routines within the firm that will help ensure its long term viability. From the perspective of headquarter and SBU relationship, Goold, et. al, (1995) focus on parenting skills as essential for corporate success. Parenting skills are those that help the headquarters identify the potential business subsidiaries that best suit its style of parentage whose market standing and performance could be enhanced from such parentage. In summary, as the core competence, dynamic capabilities, and parenting skills are all routines built within the firm, the ensuing competitive advantages are therefore clearly firm-bound advantages, hard to copy and imitate by rivals (Barney, 1991), whose benefits belong primarily to the firm, not to any individuals or groups.

Relational Capital

At the corporate level, virtual-bound advantages often arise with the relationship the firm has with and the credit it enjoys from other entities and institutions in its environment that could potentially afford the firm certain resources when needed. Such relationship and credit could be interpreted as relational capitals the firm could call on but do not unilaterally own (Dyer and Singh, 1999). These relationship could be forged with rivals and substitutors, collaborators and complementors, customers, interest groups, the general public, and, the government (Porter, 1980; Brandenburger and Nalebuff, 1996). More specifically, three sets of relationship are generally the most important and substantive ones at the corporate level: *major rivals/partners*, *credit community*, and *the government*. First, major firms often have mutual forbearance understanding or arrangements, and they respect each others' interests in their respective spheres of influence (D'Aveni, 2004). They are often buyers and suppliers to each other, and encounter in multiple markets. As such, they typically treat each other with mutual respect and engage in live and let live (Axelrod, 1984). If a firm enjoys tacit mutual understanding and mains good relationship with rivals, partners, and other parties in the market, it will enjoy the general benefits derived from such understanding and relationship, e.g., other firms' respect in terms of consultation before action, refraining from overtly aggressive behavior, honoring price leadership, following de factor standard, etc.

Second, good relationship with the credit communities, e. g., financial institutions, credit-rating agencies, certifying bodies, and other stakeholders that may extend resources and favor in case of need and difficulties is another virtual advantage at the corporate level. It's the overall firm's credit, not necessarily a particular line's credit, that carries more weight in the communities that extend you credit or honor your credit. Of course, such credit is eventually determined by a firm's ongoing performance. However, the current credit often takes into consideration of past good will and good deeds. So, in emergency, such credit will help the firm weather the storm better than do a firm with an inferior credit standing.

Third, maintaining good government relationship is another essential task the corporate level management must actively engage in (D'Aveni, 1994; Bailey, 1997). Porter (1990) documents the essential role government play in business competition. Although not an active participant of the business game, the government, as enforcer of the game rule and often the judge of the game, also makes available to or with hold from different players in the game resources or policies that will make or break a firm (Bailey, 1997). Globally dominant firms are often good at governmental relations, from GE to Microsoft, from HP to Motorola, from Anheuser-Busch to PepsiCola, government relation help win contracts and gain business. Hong Kong tycoon Li Kai Shing's plan to build Oriental Plaza in the 1990s, with the backing of the Chinese government, once forced McDonald's 3-sotry restaurant out of the choicest business locations in Beijing. Enough said about government relationship as competitive advantage. However, bear in mind that no firm can take government relationship and its favor for granted. The government has no obligation in honoring any of its favors. The firm, however, must constantly service this relationship.

BUSINESS ADVANTAGES

Elite Managers

Competitive advantages are especially germane at the business level, as competition typically happens at this level where different players compete in a particular business line. Putting to an extreme, corporations don't compete against each other. Their business units do (Porter, 1987). Managers at the business level are the ones responsible for creating competitive advantages and win in specific businesses. Elite managers with sound professional reputation, excellent track record, and expert skills are often themselves sources of competitive advantage. Such individual-bound competitive advantages could be derived from elite managers in at least three forms: *Business-Specific Skills*, *Clientele Network*, and *Outside Contacts*. First, these elite managers in a profession are not only business executives; they are actually doers in their business who have intimate understanding of the fundamentals of their business and possess business specific skills to realize their ideas, dreams and visions. Bill Gates' original trade was programming and he has life long love for it, the core of the Microsoft business. Sam Walton of Wal-Mart was a salesman by heart and he knew how to best run merchandizing. Phil Knight was himself a long distance runner, who understands how Nike could better cater to the needs of athletes. Although these elite managers went on to build bigger and more diverse empire and become corporate generals, they were essential to the success of their firms when they were single-business firms. Their knowledge and expertise rank them as elites at the pinnacle of their trade. And such expertise and skills help their respective business win competition.

Second, in many professional businesses, e.g., accounting, attorney, advertising, talent agencies, etc., the elite managers represent the firm. Inter-firm relations are often forged at personal level between these elite managers and elite managers of the client firms. Such valuable *clientele network* could prove to be competitive advantages over rivals when it comes to accessing supply or distribution. Because of the intense personal nature of such relationship, the clientele networks are often more relevant at the individual level than at the firm level. If a well respected elite manager jumps ship, it is likely that his clientele will shift business dealings to his new firm instead of remaining with the former firm. So the advantage is more mobile and its benefits more appropriable by the elite managers.

Third, outside contacts of the elite managers could also be competitive advantages. Contacts with political parties, legal bodies, governmental agencies, interest groups, community leaders, and the competitive intelligence community (Baron, 1995; Bailey, 1997), among others, will help the firm access information and resources. This will further help the firm better understand the future trends in business ahead of competition.

Business Position

At the firm level, we observe the most salient competitive advantage a firm could possess, that is, its actual position in the competitive landscape, and how good it is that the firm is at conducting its business activities. Three factors could be enlisted to describe a firm's competitive advantage at the business level: *Market Position*, *Brand Image*, and *Process Efficiency*. Market position could be observed by a firm's market share, its relative size to the next largest competitor, and its growth potential. It reflects the firm's credibility in the market place and a strong position could help deter rivals' challenges (Caves and Ghemawat, 1992). When attacking a firm with solid and strong market position, a rival often has to think twice before action. A strong market position also makes it easier for the firm to access the distribution and the supply of resource factors, including human resources. Porter's (1980) differentiation and cost leadership are two classic examples of firms achieving defensible market positions against other stakeholders in the market.

Brand image is the firm's ultimate position in people's mind. A firm with a good brand image possesses competitive advantage over other brands because it contributes to the firm's sales and profits directly. People are willing to pay price premiums to such differentiated products that boast strong brands (Aaker, 1996; Porter, 1980).

Whether a firm pursues a differentiation or cost leadership strategy at the business level, the quality and efficiency of the business activities it engages in will prove to be great competitive advantages. For instance, a firm's productivity, efficiency in transaction, and overall cost structure will have essential impact on a firm's success as a cost leader. Similarly, design quality and manufacturing quality will have major impact on a firm's success as a differentiated player. Moreover, creativity (Schumpeter, 1934), flexibility (Sanchez, 1993), and speed of response to the market (Stalk, 1990) could also help a firm compete in the business level.

Useful Partners

At the business level, the competitive landscape is fast changing. The typical and bilateral (one on one) rivalry on certain limited dimension is dead (Moore, 1996). What comes now is often competition between groups of firms with shifting boundaries and membership of firms in the different groups (Gomes-Casseres, 1994). Participating in collaborative arrangement and leveraging other firms' resources are essential in the new game. They help the firm create virtual competitive advantages. So the challenge is to find useful partners in the new competitive landscape. Useful partners could come in various forms, through *R&D Consortium*, *Strategic Alliance*, and *Network*. First, R&D consortium is often used by a firm to leverage other partners' resources and capabilities when solving critical technical problems. It enhances the scale and scope of participating firms' strengths while helping spreading its risk. A firm does not have to do everything all by itself. It needs to know when and where to look for useful partners. Second, strategic alliance could be forged with partners to solve not only technological problems but also address competitive concerns, e.g., to compete with a common rival or other strategic alliance. For instance, a small firm joining strategic alliances with stronger leaders will likely reduce the competitive pressure it faces from other players. Third, a firm could also leverage other partners' resources and skills in the same network, e.g., the complementary skills of a marketing firm and an R&D firm, to jointly promote the network's technology as the de facto industry standard (Hill, 1997).

FUNCTIONAL ADVANTAGES

Star Employees

The various functions at the operational level directly deal with the value-adding activities of the firm's business in its value chain that consists of input, throughput, and output (Porter, 1985). At the functional level or the operational level, individuals possessing extraordinary gifts and talents, skills and expertise, experience and contacts could offer the firm competitive advantages. These individual-bound competitive advantages could derive from those *star buyers*, *technical wizards*, and *super salespersons*, among other talents.

Star buyers are experienced people in the purchasing and logistics department of the firm that guarantee the firm superior access to supplies with excellent quality and/or low cost. They are experts in their trade and are well connected with the supplier community. They may also hold managerial titles, such as purchasing manager, but they are at a lower rank than elite managers at the business level. As such, they hold relatively little bargaining power against their employer when it comes to the appropriability concern. Their professional standing and reputation within the supplier community also depends on the firm's power and reputation.

Similarly, at the output end, super salespersons are also valuable assets of the firm that help insure distribution and sales of the firm's products or services in the most expedient and economic way, affording the firm competitive advantage in the market place. Similar to star buyers, the experience and skills of these stars are largely developed within (or co-developed with) the firm and their efforts would become sunk costs should they choose to defect from the firm. As such, the competitive advantages based on these super salespersons are largely appropriable by the firm.

At the throughput or manufacturing process, technical wizard, those operational experts with superior technical talents could bring the firm competitive advantage, in terms of their contribution to quality and efficiency in production as well as to product and process innovation. This is especially true for start-up companies in the high-tech arena where technical wizards as star-employees indicate technical strengths, potential, and credibility.

Operational Process

While star employees help firms function well, the firm's process, programs, and routines in its daily operation represent the firm's actual capability and its competitiveness (Peters, 1984) and, as firm-bound characteristics, are often more reliable and appropriable from the firm's point of view. Such operational level advantages could range from excellence in *supply chain management (SCM)*, *manufacturing* and *operation*, *to marketing prowess*, that help a firm better create value at the input, throughput, and output stages of the business process.

Superior supply chain management integrates the suppliers' strengths into a focal firm's value chain and maximizes both parties' expertise and benefits. For instance, the Kanban system used in the Japanese auto industry helps automakers successfully managing inventory and supply, insuring timeliness, quality, and reliability. The operational effectiveness (Porter, 1996) of the Japanese automakers, e.g., technical know-how of the work force, further enhances the efficiency and quality level of their manufacturing process, allowing for dynamic competitive advantages such as speed and flexibility. Needless to say, marketing prowess of firms' such as Coca-Cola, Proctor and Gamble, Gillette, etc. help make their products available at the widest scope possible through many a point of sales in different variety. Such functional level advantages could be so salient, robust, and permeating, that they could well represent the core competence of the entire business organization.

Superior Access

At the functional level, a firm's competitive advantage reflects in its superior access: supplier relationship, outsourcing partners, and distributor relationship. A firm could boast fine skills in managing its access to other parties' resources, e.g., manufacturing capacity, however, it does not actually own such access. The competitive advantage arising from such superior success is therefore virtual in nature.

First, it takes time and effort to nurture a reliable and collaborative supplier mix. Wal-Mart's seamless relationship with major suppliers like P&G allow both parties to benefit from close collaboration, e.g., sharing of information through electronic data interchange, making Wal-Mart a virtual part of the P&G marketing machine and P&G a virtual part of Wal-Mart's manufacturing arm, allowing for speed, cost savings, and flexibility in Wal-Mart's operation and its earlier payment of accounts payable to P&G than industry average. Second, in many industries, vertical integration has given way to outsourcing, where cost savings could be achieved through virtual relationship with outsourcing partners. Nike's shoe making operation in Asia represents a classic example of leveraging a virtual competitive advantage by outsourcing a firm's manufacturing job to partners who could manage the job more efficiently. Finally, access to distributor proves to be perhaps the most critical virtual advantage a firm could enjoy at the operational level. It could make or break a firm. It gives the incumbents competitive advantage in terms of entry barriers. It also provides potential gateways for new entrants to attack the incumbent leaders. Building relationship with the distributors or the channels bears direct strategic implication for the firm's survival and success.

LOCALES OF ADVANTAGES AND MANAGERIAL CHALLENGES

In depicting the varying locales of competitive advantage, I hope to broaden the ken of the general management and remind them of the whole range of possibilities in building and harboring a firm's competitive advantage. In the following passages, I offer some general observations on the challenges in managing competitive advantages at different locales.

Sincere Pursuit, Lip Service, or Play As Needed?

Not all firm intend to or could be able to create competitive advantage at the institutional level. Some firms are better off if they just focus on what they do best at the competitive arena and explore competitive advantage at the business level, or corporate level. For instance, Philip Morris (now Altria), besieged by negative publicity of its cigarettes business, once tried to emphasize its good deeds as a corporate citizen by pointing out how Philip Morris' other divisions, e.g., Kraft, were bringing quality food to millions of Americans and offering socially responsible contributions to the communities they serve. Such a strategy aiming at mending its institutional image went backfire as it unintentionally exposed the relationship between Kraft and Philip Morris, causing negative publicity and damage to the Kraft brand.

Many firms claim in their company documents and slogans etc. that they care about the social image but do not do much to match that claim, while others sincerely believe that "doing good" will pay off economically and therefore actively and substantively engage in good deeds that are socially desirable. Still other firms will play the game when necessary but will not treat the institutional level of competitive advantage as their main fare.

Whether to exploit institutional level advantage and to what extent a firm should make a commitment to this cause are fundamental questions that challenge the general management at the institutional level.

A Branded House or House of Brands?

A firm also has to balance its competitive advantages at both the corporate and the business level. Porter claims that corporations don't compete, businesses do, and therefore competitive advantages at the business level are the more fundamental. Hamel and Prahalad believe that core competence at the corporate level is critical to a firm's success at the various businesses that share such competence and therefore corporate level advantages are the more fundamental. I believe that whether business level advantages are more important than corporate level advantages is an empirical issue that depends on competitive context. It is the general management's fundamental challenge to decide on the appropriate balance for a particular firm. Specifically, the challenge is to build a "branded house" like GE where the GE name and all that GE headquarters have to offer present its business units parenting advantage, or to build a "house of brands" where the house might not be famous or influential, yet the individual businesses boast strong brands and customer loyalty, e.g., Bell Helicopter and Cessna Jet in Textron.

A Committed Player or Project-Based Hit and Runner?

A firm also has to decide on its commitment to a particular line of business when it attempts to develop a host of competitive advantage. A committed player often relies more on its own investment and resource commitment that are largely irreversible, so as to preempt the market and create sustainable competitive advantage that will benefit the firm in the long-run. On the other hand, there are more and more virtual organizations that are more project-based than perpetual. For instance, an oil drilling company might specialize in locating and drilling small pockets of meager reserves, using leased equipment and mobile personnel, and quickly moves from one site to another. A hit-and-run kind of operation attempts to be as mobile and virtual as possible. It avoids any kind of long-term commitment. To what extent a firm is an actual entity and to what extent it is a shell, this is a key concern.

Elites or Routine?

A firm could be more powerful than any of its parts or contributors of resources. It could become competent in many business lines by establishing fine organizational and technological routines. The institution is larger than any individual. It could also choose to specialize in certain business niches and requesting the service of elite professionals with special training, expertise, and experience. The more specialized the business is, the more powerful the elite experts could be in its bargaining position with the firm. This is because that the competitive advantage of the firm is more likely to be individual-bound than firm bound.

For instance, a typical law firm (accounting firm, advertising agency, or consulting boutique, especially smaller ones) often counts its survival and success on the personal contacts and skills of some star employees, who could make or break the firm. If they decide to jump ship, due to the intense personal dealing nature of the business, their clientele base goes with them, hence the rocking of their former firm. No wonder that partnership is the most popular form of firm ownership in these businesses, where the star employees' interests could be accommodated in line with that of the firm, as they are themselves the owners of the firm. That is, star employees are the essence and indispensable equivalent of the firm. To what extent should the firm keep the balance between individual-bound and firm bound advantage is another key concern for a firm.

Make or Buy?

Similar to the commitment vs. hit-and-run scenario, the strategic decision of "make or buy", from a transaction cost perspective, not only affects the boundary of the firm, but also influences the locale of a firm's competitive advantage and its appropriability. Factors impacting the decision might include uncertainty and complexity of the transaction, potential of hold-up, concern for control, etc. IBM designed the open architecture of its IBM PC by leveraging the competence of Microsoft and Intel, which gave IBM decisive competitive advantages, allowing it to surpass the then No. one desktop computer maker Apple and garner 26% of market share merely three years after its launch (Chesbrough and Teece, 1996). Initially, this open architecture enables IBM to exploit virtual advantages of Microsoft and Intel and help quickly establish industry standard. Yet, when Microsoft and Intel grow too big to rival the dominant position of IBM in the PC business eco-system, IBM's virtual advantage became a deadly disadvantage, costing it the right of control in the PC universe it has help created. So a virtual advantage could benefit the firm that taps it, it could also burn the firm that lost its grip during the process. When the focal firm loses its grip, the virtual advantage it once enjoyed could turn into competitive disadvantage and work against the firm instead.

CONCLUDING REMARKS

In the discussion of the relationship between locale and appropriability of competitive advantage, the focal concern is how a firm could benefit most from the competitive advantages it could leverage that reside in different locales. While most prior discussion in the strategy literature focus on firm-bound competitive advantage at the corporate and business levels, the integrative account offered at this chapter examines advantages at all four levels of strategic management that could also be individual bound or virtual-bound, in addition to firm-bound. It paints a more complete picture about the locales of competitive advantage and also, as a first systematic endeavor, offers some initial observations on the appropriability regime.

Although the integrative account depicts as complete as possible the various locales of competitive advantage, it is unlikely that a firm will possess competitive advantages at all these levels, against all rivals. Hopefully, this chapter could help a firm achieve more advantages at more levels, through its useful description of the nature and characteristics of the varying locales of competitive advantages and their appropriability. Of course, some competitive advantages are likely to straddle multiple levels of the firm, e.g., reputation or brand recognition. Such a more complicated phenomenon requires further treatment in future work that goes beyond the framework presented here.

Chapter 5 Luck and Competitive Advantage

In addition to effective strategic maneuvering and well-run internal management, luck often plays a non-trivial role as a determinant of competitive advantage and firm performance. This chapter first presents a comprehensive framework on the various causes of competitive advantage and then, as a sub-framework, advances a typology of different scenarios of luck—Pure Luck, Prepared Luck, Useful Weeds, and Skunk Work—and expounds the strategic implications of these scenarios for the firm's gaining of competitive advantage. Taking a proactive approach, it untangles the typical environmental sources of luck as well as the intra-firm mechanisms and processes through which a firm could better induce, recognize, and exploit lucky incidents of innovations from useful weeds or skunk works.

Various forces and factors—environmental, organizational, or personal—could cause the rise of competitive advantages for a particular firm. These factors and forces, using the firm as the unit of analysis, can be *endogenous*, working primarily within the firm as a system, or *exogenous*, effecting primarily outside the firm's boundary. Also, these forces and factors could either be *spontaneous*, arising and disappearing without the conscious control of the firm; or *deliberate*, subject to purposeful *strategic* actions in competition, cooperation, or both, and/or *managerial* actions in managing a firm's organizational structure, system, process, culture, technology, and people.

Based on the two dimensions represented in Figure 5.1, the causes of competitive advantage can be classified into the following general categories: *Pure Luck*; *Prepared Luck*; *Useful Weed*; *Skunk Work*; *Managerial Initiative* (e. g. , *Creation and Innovation*) ; *Strategic Maneuver* (e. g. , *Competition and Cooperation*) and *Strategic Co-option*.

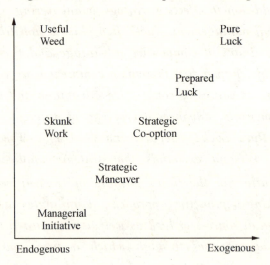

Figure 5.1 Causes of Competitive Advantage

Strategy is the linkage between the firm and its environment. That is, strategy deals with both external and internal factors of a firm. As such, both managerial initiative and strategic maneuver should be considered deliberate *strategic* actions. However, here I emphasize strategic maneuver as explicit and specific strategic moves—geared more toward external forces—to achieve firm advantage while I define managerial initiative as focusing on more broad-based organizational competence that is often needed for sound strategy implementation as well as conception. The above categories can also be further divided into sub-categories so as to better examine the various specific causes of competitive advantage.

As I will explore the more deliberate and purposeful actions taken by the firms in their search for competitive advantage in the next chapter, e.g. strategic maneuvers, let's first examine the effect of luck on competitive advantage.

It is no secret that scholars and practitioners in Strategic Management tend to believe that general managers do matter when it comes to creating competitive advantage and sustaining superior firm performance (Andrews, 1971). Such a view has long been a dominant and cherished assumption in this field where we believe that general managers' choices and actions, to a great extent, determine firm performance and results (Child, 1972; Rumelt, Schendel, and Teece, 1991). There also exist, however, from time to time, voices that help direct our attention to the aspect of stochastic nature of firm performance (Mancke, 1974; Jacobson, 1992) and the seemingly inexplicable term known simply as luck (Barney, 1986a), a sort of serendipitous happenings, often unfathomable even to its beneficiaries and unpredictable a priori.

Elusive as a theoretical concept yet certain in its earthly presence, luck, admit it or not, as a non-trivial determinant of performance, begs our further understanding and should perhaps neither be conveniently reduced to the "error term" in statistical analysis nor casually dismissed as being a-theoretical. To date, there's rarely any formal effort that systematically explains how luck impact the gaining of competitive advantage and firm performance. What do we mean by luck? How many different types of luck are there? Could a firm enhance its likelihood of getting lucky? Motivated by these questions, this chapter attempts to dissect the luck phenomenon in the context of business competition and provide an integrative framework expounding luck as a determinant of competitive advantage.

Therefore, any factor, action, or event that could enlarge the differential between rival firms on a particular dimension that allows a firm to better create customer value than others may be a potential cause of competitive advantage (Ma, 1999). Luck, by definition, discriminates against some players. It creates heterogeneity among firms along strategically meaningful dimensions, e.g., access to critical supply of certain unique resources, and causes differentials in firms' resource profiles and their abilities to exploit the opportunities in the product markets (Barney, 1986a, 1991). As such, it would be theoretically fruitful and practically relevant to examine the various ways in which luck creates differential treatment among competing firms and therefore confers competitive advantage to some while denying others.

LUCK AS COMPETITIVE ADVANTAGE: A TYPOLOGY OF SCENARIOS

Luck is also a two-way street. While some firms wait for the lucky break passively, others seek it proactively. Based on the two dimensions discussed in Figure 5.1, the various scenarios where luck confers competitive advantage can be classified into the following general categories: *Pure Luck*, *Prepared Luck*, *Useful Weed*, and *Skunk Work*.

To practicing general managers, however, it is perhaps more meaningful to focus on how they could, through their own efforts, improve their odds of getting struck by luck than merely knowing the fact that in most cases luck is totally serendipitous and beyond their control. As such, I shall first briefly explain in the following paragraphs each of the above four scenarios with case examples, and then elaborate respectively in the next two segments on what general managers should do to court luck, from either the external environment or within the firm. That is, this chapter takes an unequivocally proactive approach toward luck as a determinant of competitive advantage.

Pure Luck

Pure luck defies human intention and action. Pure luck in gaining advantage refers to the situation where factors exogenous to the firm give rise to competitive advantage spontaneously, not subjecting to the firm's purposeful control and/or intentional manipulation. For instance, a lucky farmer's land happens to be more fertile than that of its neighbors', thus conferring advantage in productivity. Or even better, owners of farmland may find oil underneath or reserves of other precious natural resources. Such pure luck provides firms with Richardian type of rents that cannot be created proactively (Rumelt, 1984, 1987). From the resource-based view of the firm, Barney (1986a) explains that luck, or path-dependence to use a more formal term, creates unique endowments for some firms that can be used to conceive and implement inimitable strategy, enabling sustained competitive advantage.

One person's loss is another's gain.

In an ongoing competition, chancy events could also spell luck for certain firms in the form of windfall gains. For instance, the recent September 11th terrorist attack against the US had spawned huge demand for American national flags for patriotic reasons. As such, one of the side effects of this terrible tragedy turned out to be that some Taiwanese flag makers were flooded with tons of orders of American flags that required around the clock shifts in making them, awarding them much needed business in a time of a local economic slump. In the same token, this tragedy also spelled lucky opportunities for many New York City street vendors who could now sell basically the same $ 2 T-shirts (in quality and style) for $ 5 apiece which now feature the American flag or some patriotic slogans such as "United We Stand" instead of those usual "I Love New York" ones.

Obviously, the strategic implication of such pure luck is perhaps for the firm's general managers to be keenly aware of the presence of luck and appropriately exploit it. The real challenge here, however, is perhaps not to become over confident or complacent in the face of luck, in addition to recognizing and exploiting it effectively.

Prepared Luck

In business context, luck often descends upon the firm from unique historical events, changes in social cultural trends, breakthroughs in technology, shift in customer tastes and demand, governmental regulation or deregulation, or private or asymmetric information. These factors affect different firms in asymmetrical fashion and create differentials among the firms along strategic dimensions, which dictate the firms' value creation and options for action. Beyond pure luck, which is not controllable by the firm at all, the above factors often present themselves to firms as mere opportunities or threats upon which firms can act. Whether a particular firm is lucky or not depends on its particular position, endowment, capabilities, as well as its action at the time.

Fate shuffles the cards and we play.

Arthur Schopenhauer

Touted by *Fortune* (1995c) as "the deal of the decade," it has been by now well known how luck blessed Microsoft with the biggest break in its history in 1980: its MS-DOS licensing agreement with IBM. It was a story of Microsoft buying an obscure operating system from Seattle Computer for $50000 and turned around licensing it to IBM. Seattle Computer apparently did not know much about the IBM call and why Microsoft wanted to buy its system. Interestingly, the Seattle Computer deal was finally nailed, not before, but rather 48 hours after Microsoft had already signed the contract with IBM to supply the operating system, which they then renamed as MS-DOS. And the rest is history.

Microsoft was lucky to have stumbled over the IBM opportunity and the Q-DOS deal. It was also lucky that Digital Research, the firm that developed the CP/M operating system—the most influential one at the time, did not treat very seriously the IBM launch of PC and

Microsoft as a rival. Also contacted by IBM, CP/M responded to the potential luck rather differently than Microsoft did, as the CP/M boss was largely turned off by IBM's secretive and arrogant manner. However, without the software expertise, Microsoft was unlikely to be closely contacted by IBM. If Gates and partners only thought about themselves as an application software maker, they won't have the foresight about the importance of the operating system in the future of the PC business. Foreseeing the potential of IBM clones, they were able to include a clause in the contract with IBM to allow them to also supply their DOS to other PC makers. Aggressively soliciting software written for their DOS, Microsoft won the war of operating system in the US PC market within a year.

As such, luck is usually nothing but opportunities knocking upon those who are looking for them, who will notice them, and who will act on them. Luck favors prepared mind. And luck favors those in action. In this sense, luck is really serendipitous opportunities seized and unique potential realized. The key challenge here for general managers is to be always on the alert for potential opportunities and act proactively.

Useful Weeds

A firm could also gain advantage from serendipity within the firm, from its often seemingly accidental innovation and creativity. A core element of creativity is spontaneity. To insure spontaneity, a firm has to maintain certain level of slack to allow for self-initiated actions, experimentations, and improvisations by individual employees. With these activities sometimes come unexpected gains for the firm in the form of inventions of commercial viability, discovery of new processes, or new product innovation. Needless to say, such activities often also result in waste, redundancy, and, failure. In reference to formal organizational agendas, these activities would be idle, irrelevant, or distracting.

> *What is weed? A plant whose virtues have not yet been discovered.*
>
> *Ralph Waldo Emerson*

Based on the insightful remarks of Emerson, I term the self-initiated activities by individuals within the firm—for whatever motives—as useful weeds, which may generate advantages for the firm in new product, process, knowledge, or capability. The innovation and/or invention from such activities may not be conforming to the firm's current business scope and strategy. The general managers have to take notice of them and proactively exploit their commercial potentials.

For instance, the NutraSweet sweetener, aspartame, was discovered by a chemist at G. D. Searle through personal activities that violated the formal organizational policies and standard operating procedures: he tasted the overspill liquid during an experiment for an antiulcer drug (Brandenburger and Nalebuff, 1996). That incident not only changed the course of the firm but also created a brand new product that would quickly be of global market reach. Also consider the institutionalized innovative environment at 3M which gave birth to the detachable adhesive and its star product the Post-it note. The product came from a "failed" project where an extremely week adhesive was developed by a scientist who was in fact trying to create the exact opposite properties (Bartlett and Mohammed, 1995). The above cited examples, along with the discovery of Penicillin and du Pont's Taflon, and a host of other lucky incidents all attest to the need to view "weeds" from unconventional perspectives.

The key challenge here is to commercialize innovations, unintended innovations that present themselves as opportunities for commercial viability. Until an innovation can be channeled toward the right customer markets and/or organizational activities, these spontaneous discovery or invention will remain weeds. When these weeds are appropriately appreciated and acted upon, they could often become useful and may provide the firm with unexpected competitive advantage. Open-mindedness and tolerance for errors are therefore also necessary.

Skunk Work

Skunk work happens when individuals or working groups—often temporary or informal ones—within an organization work voluntarily and secretively on their own initiative to tackle entrepreneurial, technical, or organizational challenges which will likely lead to innovative practice and beneficial results to the formal organization. The fundamental difference between skunk work and managerial initiative is that the latter is often organization-wide and explicitly endorsed and promoted by top management while the former often concerns a sub set or a special unit of the organization. Although it usually requires championing or tacit permission from the top management, skunk work basically works independently of or even against the entire organization's formal agenda. As such, it could be viewed as semi-grassroot effort in innovation, potentially seeking lucky breaks or courting disaster.

Consider the example of *Skunk Works* at Lockheed (Bennis and Biederman, 1997). In 1943, *Skunk Works* founder Clarence Johnson hand-picked about two dozen engineers and a supporting staff and started a project whose mission was to develop a jet fighter that could rival Luftwaffe. The *Skunk Works* was able to bypass the Lockheed bureaucracy and escape from the firm's pressing operational agenda in making military planes to support US's war effort. The group focused solely on their secret mission. To keep it secret, the group had used neither janitors nor secretaries; group members were dead silent about their mission even to their own families. Warren Bennis and Patricia Biederman observed that: "People wanted to work at Skunk Works not because it was plush or prestigious, but because they loved the work." The mission called for the design of the first US jet fighter in

180 days. The group managed to produce a prototype of the P-80 Shooting Star 37 days ahead of the deadline.

Subsequently, the Skunk Works produced some of the most advanced military planes ever conceived, e.g., the F-104 Star-fighter—the first supersonic jet fighter—and the top secret U2—long-range reconnaissance plane. The *Skunk Works* has throughout the years undoubtedly contributed to Lockheed's advantage and leadership position in the jet fighter industry in the US and worldwide. No wonder now that Lockheed Martin, the much augmented and strengthened Lockheed after many a merger and acquisition, is still ahead of the game and has just been awarded the largest defense contract in the US history in the amount of $ 200 billion to build the Joint Striker Fighter. Call it luck. But the Lockheed people would like to believe that they absolutely deserve it.

The key challenge here for general managers is to foster the spirit of innovation within the firm and maintain an organizational environment and culture that encourage innovation: dare to experiment, dare to create, and dare to stun, and obviously, dare to fail and learn from the failure. Recent research on *intrapreneurship*, or internal corporate venturing, provides solid theoretical foundation for such skunk work and empirical evidence on how innovative firms proactively seek lucky breaks and inventions (e.g., Burgelman, 1993a,b).

GETTING LUCKY: EXTERNAL SOURCES AND INTERNAL MECHANISMS

For any strategist aspiring to create advantage and win, luck should expect to come only as bonus for good deeds but not as part of base salary. In ancient Chinese tales, there's such a story called "sitting by the tree and waiting for the rabbit." A farmer working in the field one day saw a running rabbit incidentally hit a tree and drop dead.

With this windfall gain, he thought this was better than hunting or toiling in the field. So he would sit by the tree thereafter and wait for more rabbits to run hitting the tree. Apparently, waiting for luck passively is a disservice.

How do we predict luck? We can't. But we can run down certain possible aspects, both within the firm and in the environment, where and when a firm is likely to get lucky and hopefully increase its odds in gaining competitive advantage from luck (Dierickx and Cool, 1989). Scanning the environment and predicting future trends help a firm be better prepared (Hambrick, 1982). Maintaining open, innovative, and stimulating organizational culture context will also expect to help. Table 5.1 highlights the various ways luck could strike from the external environment of the firm as well as the various intra-firm mechanisms for fostering useful weeds and skunk works. These external sources and internal mechanisms will be examined in detail in the next two sections respectively.

Table 5.1 Luck and Competitive Advantage: An Examination of Environmental Sources and Intra-Firm Mechanisms

Prepare to Improve Your Odds:
A Look at the External Sources of Luck
 Private of Asymmetric Information
 Unique Historical Events
 Changes in Social Cultural Trend
 Changes in Technology
 Shift in Customer Taste and Demand
 Government Regulation or Deregulation
 Faltering Competitor
 Dream Expediter
Take Advantage of Useful Weeds and Skunk Work:
Understanding Intra-Firm Mechanisms
 Seducing the Elites and Inducing Initiatives through:
 Spotting and Encouraging Bold Experimenters
 Fostering Faithful Champions of Grass-Roots Initiatives
 Creating Hotbed for Innovation

EXPLOITING LUCK FROM EXTERNAL SOURCES

This section discusses the various ways luck could strike from the external sources and how they impact a firm's competitive advantage. *Private or Asymmetric Information* allows the lucky firm to have advantageous positions in negotiation and bargaining, in competitive attacks or defense, or be first movers (Lieberman and Montgomery, 1988), gaining advantage over others in terms of customer relations, access to supply and distribution, and reaching a critical scale in operation and marketing before rivals flood in. *Unique Historical Events* afford some firms resource endowment or market positions that cannot be easily obtained by rivals at a later time. *Changes in Social Cultural Trend* may spell luck for some firms whose products happen to be in vogue while declaring other firms' products or service "out" and unfashionable. *Changes in Technology* often provide lucky breaks for small yet ambitious firms to challenge large established incumbents. *Shift in Customer Taste and Demand* could reverse the fortunes of rivaling firms overnight. *Government Regulation and Deregulation* could alter the rules of the game, dictating whether a firm is in favor or out of the game. A *Faltering Competitor* may give its rivals room for the necessary breath and escape from impending extinction. The presence of a *Dream Expediter*, e.g., a focal firm's complementor or substitutor of the focal firm's supplier, could bring new opportunity to the focal firm and enhance its bargaining position.

Private or Asymmetric Information

Information can make or break a firm. Asymmetry in information among rivaling parties could render a certain firm advantage over others by opening the window of opportunity for a particular party to act and create competitive advantage or avoid competitive disadvantage. Consider a military example. During the Three Kingdoms era in China, Shu and Wei, two of the three warring kingdoms, were crossing swords at one time. Wei attacked a Shu city where Shu's military headquarters resided. It happened that Shu's troops were all dispatched away while Wei attacked. With an empty city and little forces, the Chief of Shu decided to play tough based on information asymmetry. Instead of closing the city and hiding, the general decided to wide-open the main gate so as to confuse and intimidate the Wei attackers. He would send a couple of old and weak soldiers sweeping the streets, pretending nothing happened. He himself would drink and play music on top of the gate-fortress. Facing such a quiet city, the Chief of Wei would hesitate to break in for fear of hidden troops. The Wei chief, ever a cautious man himself, knew that the Shu Chief had never before engaged in irrational and hasty decisions involving high risk. And the empty city must be a sort of bate or stratagem to induce enemies. So the Wei troop retreated instead of attacking. Before they finally realized that the city was indeed empty and attacked again, the Shu chief was able to recall back his major troops and wait to engage the tired Wei attackers.

Know yourself and know your enemy, a hundred battles without peril.

Sun Tzu

Apparently, a firm can get lucky by manipulating competitive intelligence and hope to create information asymmetry, hence better chance of gaining advantage. Microsoft was lucky that Seattle Computer did not know about the IBM deal. Shu was lucky that the Wei chief knew not the strengths of his enemy. Similarly, Home Depot, the giant do-it-yourself home improvement chain store, in its early days, would usually not trash their empty boxes but would rather pile them up on the higher-level shelves in the store so as to create the illusion that they were always well-stocked (Marcus, Blank, and Andelman, 1999). The rival's ignorance and negligence spell lucky opportunity.

Unique Historical Events

Certain unique historical events can bring luck to a firm, especially international event, political, economic, and military, etc. For instance, the Oil Crisis in the 1970s jacked up gas price drastically in the U.S. This crisis suddenly made gas-efficient small-sized cars economically more attractive. Such an event spelled luck for the automakers from Japan, which were entering the lower end of the U.S. auto market with cars much smaller than those typical American made cars, and more gas-efficient. In the early 1990s, the Gulf War certainly helped CNN, the fledgling 24-hour news report channel on Cable TV, to establish itself and demonstrate the huge market potential for its then novel service.

Similarly, while Sony attempted to acquire CBS Record—an American icon—the label of John Sousa, Duke Ellington, Leonard Bernstein, Bob Dylan, and Michael Jackson, the parent company CBS twice said no due to board pressure against "Japanese invasion of American cultural industry" and the general sentiment reflected in the then Japan bashing (Reich and Mankin, 1986). Sony coveted the record company because it believed that by controlling a software concern, it could better promote its hardware, e.g., digital audio tape recorder. The stock market crash in 1987 presented a lucky opportunity to Sony, as then CBS boss Larry Tisch, believing in a permanent down turn, was in the selling mood. So Black Monday induced the deal on Sony's third try. Sony's record business had been a fair success, despite its later venture into the movie studio business which once caused them a $3 billion plus disaster.

To business firms, particularly those global in scope, they have to always ask questions like, what are the implications of a particular event to our particular business? Alertness in scanning the macro environment will likely helps better recognize the stochastic opportunities and capture windfall gains. Major global firms often maintain active contacts with various experts so as to better track and make sense of the these events, ranging from international politics, human rights issues, to global warming and El Nino effects. For instance, American Express periodically consults authoritative and knowledgeable figures like Henry Kissinger for prediction and interpretation of international events. By consulting with experts, it helps a firm not only predict and reduce potential threats but also gain advantage from lucky opportunities.

Changes in Social Cultural Trend

People are social animals. And social cultural trends change. A change in cultural trend or social vogue could deliver death blow to some firms in some businesses while boost a timely push to some firms in other businesses. The heath craze that swept the world in the past two decades or so made diet food and drink products fashionable and traditional high-cholesterol goodies miserable. Riding the diet trend and with the help from Coke and Pepsi, NutraSweet was able to establish a brand in an essentially commodity product and dominant position in artificial sweetener (Brandenburger and Nalebuff, 1996). Nike and Reebok were able to thrive with health craze, e.g., the vogue in aerobic exercises, gaining advantage over providers of other types of casual or even formal foot wears. In the same time, however, Kentucky Fried Chicken had to change its name to KFC, largely because of the pressure to hide the "unhealthy" image people typically associated with "fried" food.

To identify and predict future cultural trends helps a firm prepare for future luck. Some future-oriented consumer product firms are closely monitoring the consumption pattern of high school students who will soon grow up to be their core customers in the near future. As the saying goes, figure out where everyone is going and arrive before everyone does is perhaps the best bet at getting lucky. In this sense luck can be interpreted as vision meets opportunity and turns into reality. To the uninitiated, winner in the next round of game might seem lucky, to those with intimate knowledge of behind the scene story, it's never entirely a random process.

Changes in Technology

Technology often changes in discontinuous or revolutionary fashion, redefining relevance of a firm's knowledge and competence. The Encyclopedia Britanica's flop at the advent of Internet and the advancement of digital information technology illustrates this point (Evans and Wurster, 1997). And in this case, the lucky party was the ones who offered relatively inferior content yet quickly capitalized on new opportunities in on-line referencing and CD-ROM offering. Changes in technology bring more options for challenging companies to bypass the previously insurmountable barriers to entry and mobility, e.g., huge and sophisticated sales force of Britannica.

Just as the arrival of PC brought bad luck to typewriter manufacturers, Netscape's rise in 1995 with its Internet browser spelled potentially severe bad luck for Microsoft's empire in PC, derailing Gates' "The Road Ahead." Sun Microsystem's CEO Scott McNully even envisioned that "the network is the computer." If that's the scenario of the future, it would be a big problem for Gates' operation system based PC. Luckily for Microsoft, its huge installed base provided needed access to customers that enabled it to quickly match Netscape's move with a competing browser within six months and leverage its bundle-offering ever since.

To avoid unlucky incidents from major shifts in technology, and better yet, increase its odds of getting lucky, the deep-pocketed Microsoft is investing in various start-up companies and hedges the future. To improve its chance of dominance in software products for

Internet access through home TV, Microsoft has invested in Web TV, cable companies, and low-altitude satellite technology. Casting the net wide is expected to enhance opportunity. A tall tree in a low forest is bound to be lucky in getting more sunlight and air and hence grows further. It just might also be the first one to be wiped out by a strong thunderstorm, say a drastic technological discontinuity. Luck travels both ways.

Shift in Customer Taste and Demand

Customer taste changes. So it changes a firm's luck. General Motors was an empire assembled through mergers and acquisitions in the early turn of last century. With diverse lines of product offering and differing quality standard across its multiple divisions, it was not able to compete with the more integrated, efficient, and dominant Ford, the industry's pioneer. However, when more people were becoming car buyers and some wealthier second-time buyers came to the market, they began to demand more varieties in designs and colors across different price ranges. This demand Ford would not and could not satisfy, as it focused on producing only one model and color efficiently: "They can have any color they want—so long as it is black." The changes in customer tastes and sophistication spelled opportunity for GM and suited GM's existing strengths, helping GM secure its leadership position in the auto industry in the US which Ford was never to catch up throughout the 20th century.

The King's favor is no inheritance.

On the other hand, customer taste also sticks, affecting firms' luck. The New Coke incident at Coca-Cola in the 1980s saw Coca-Cola's attempted change to its century-old formula. Customers apparently were not as ready as Coca-Cola was in such a change. Shortly after the change, Coca-Cola had to put the old formula back to the market as the Classical. They were lucky that the customers had a sticky taste;

otherwise, the reintroduced Coca-Cola Classical would take a major dip, jeopardizing Coca-Cola's leadership in the soft drink industry. Retrospectively, this might be a lucky incident that provided Coca-Cola with lessons, publicity, and the New Coke. Commenting on the accusation that Coca-Cola intentionally staged the publicity stunt, one Coca-Cola executive replied: "We are not that smart. And we're not stupid either." Customer is the king.

A proactive firm often probes further into customer interests for lucky opportunities. For instance, Reebok's surge in the early 1980s in the US was largely fueled by the popularity of its aerobic exercise shoes. These shoes featured flashy colors and trendy designs that better suit the female customers' tastes and preference than do their performance-oriented Nike counterparts. In China, Haier, the leading white goods company, found that in some rural markets peasants were using its washers to wash vegetables instead of washing clothes! Sensing a great opportunity here, they quickly introduced a line called Little Sweet Potato to serve that newly-found product market in potato-growing regions, which proved to be hugely successful. Emphasis on understanding customers, so obvious and simple an idea, could never be over-repeated to one hoping to get struck by luck.

Governmental Regulation or Deregulation

Government regulation often causes luck to arise for certain firms. A case of luck can be found in the story of Central Security and Fire Equipment Co. (CSFEC). In 1994 at Zhengzhou, a city with a population of 6 million in central China, a huge fire set out in a major department store building in the city's busiest central business district. Due to heavy traffic jam in the district, poor access to the building, and lack of fire equipment in the building, the relentless fire soon destroyed the whole building, causing possibly the largest fire-related loss in the history of the city. One month after the incident, the Provincial and Municipal Governments promulgated strict regulations enforcing fire safety in all commercial buildings and premises.

The entrepreneurial boss of CSFEC, then a humble venture selling security and fire protection products, was always on the alert searching for business opportunities. Right after hearing about the fire from news report, envisioning the huge market potential, he quickly acted to borrow funds from any and all sources he could lay his hands on and brought in truckloads of fire fighting and prevention equipment, further enhancing its scale *vis-à-vis* its average competitors. Under the new governmental regulation, purchasing such equipment would soon be mandatory instead of by choice. With such a blessing, CSFEC had guaranteed sales to major businesses with great buying powers.

Similar to regulation, deregulation also often affects firms in a business asymmetrically. It spells luck for some while disasters for others. Take for example the commercial banking industry in the pre-deregulation era. Some banks, even many of the large local or regional banks, were used to and satisfied with their operation within their local banking community that was relatively stable. While banks with more expansion-minded CEOs, due to relatively more liberal and lenient regulatory practice in their home state, constantly sought opportunities to grow, often through merger and acquisitions. With the federal act on deregulation effecting in the early 1980s, the latter types of banks were much better prepared to expand on a national basis than the former type of banks. To the expansion-oriented banks, deregulation was their lucky break.

> *A great wind is blowing, and that gives you either imagination or a headache.*
>
> Catherine II (*The Great*)

A case in point is the bank now known as Bank of America, created from the merger between Bank of America and Nations Bank, formerly NCNB, a regional bank based in North Carolina. Presided by the expansion-minded Hugh McColl, Nations Bank consolidated its positions and jumped into the national scene. It became one of the top ten banks in the country in a decade's time in the 1980s, through frequent and large-scale mergers and acquisitions (*Fortune*, 1995a). Without deregulation, many of their high-profiled acquisitions would, however, not have the slightest chance of going through the barriers of FTC. But the same opportunities applied to all others in that time period, only NCNB alike took the initiative and seized the lucky opportunity afforded by the deregulation, shooting up to the number two position in the American banking industry, next only to Citigroup. In this recently ever-consolidating industry, either eat lunch or be lunch. You certainly need lucky breaks from deregulation, but you first have to have a sense of urgency and aggression (Hamel and Prahalad, 1989). Failing firms fail often not because they are unlucky, they fail because they are clueless in the time of change.

Faltering Competitor

Luck can also be found in involuntary act or faltering of competitors. Early in this century, music directors of major symphony orchestras of the US were all luminary European conductors who jealously guarded their fiefdoms from rivals and even their apprentices. On November 14, 1943, luck struck Leonard Bernstein, then a 25-year old assistant conductor of New York Philharmonic. The reigning maestro Bruno Walter was flu-stricken and had to miss the Saturday-afternoon concert, which was to be broadcast nationally. At one day's notice, without rehearsal, the junior Bernstein stepped in and launched his sensational debut, bursting into the premier classical music scene and getting coverage at the front page of *New York Times*. He would later go on to become the first American-born conductor to ever head a major U.S. orchestra and become the most celebrated American classical musician.

In war, luck often tips off the balance of power and even decides the outcome. Frederick the Great was once completely encircled by two hundred thousand enemy troops and waiting for annihilating when the Czar of Russia suddenly died, immediately breaking the coalition forged against Frederick the Great, who wound up emerging as the winner (Rogers, 1987). Similarly in business, death of the founder of an archrival—especially when internal power struggle ensures—often provides good opportunity to attack or to receive defected talents. A faltering competitor could render a firm advantage without ever engaging in a fight. For instance, the bankruptcy of a major home electronics retailer in a region may be a lucky opportunity to a long-waiting rival from other regions which has been coveting entry and filling the void. The Montgomery Ward bankruptcy in the 1990s provided lucky opportunity for Sears to easily lure its executives.

Dream Expediter

A firm can often gain advantage from luck through unexpected presence of badly needed help in supply, complementary products, or partners for collective action. For instance, when Coke's contract with Monsanto on NutraSweet was to be soon expired, Coke faced possible greater bargaining power by Monsanto as the latter had successfully established NutraSweet as a brand itself—a brand within a brand—and NutraSweet and Diet Coke were almost inseparable. Lucky for Coke, Holland Sweetener, an European competitor decided to jump in the game and submitted competing bid for Coke's business. Such a move into the arena by an unexpected player severely weakened the otherwise increased bargaining power of Monsanto. Coke was able to renew its contract with Monsanto and continue using the proven brand NutraSweet for a much better price (Brandenburger and Nalebuff, 1996).

When a bird and a clam fight, the fisher gains.
Chinese Proverb

In business arenas, many times, one firm's problems may be other's solutions. Solutions look for problems; problems wait for opportunities; opportunities propel solutions. For instance, when Matsushita tried to spin off its money-losing MCA studio, it just happened that the Seagram chief was, always fascinated by the luring glamour, ready to buy a ticket to Hollywood. To be sure, a lucky opportunity may not always churn out competitive advantage. What is important is to seize the opportunity to improve a business' potential in creating customer value through better positions, resources, and access.

Sony's surge into international economic arena was due in no small part to the managerial talent of Norio Ohga, whose long association with the company began with his letter as "a tough customer," criticizing Sony's new reel-to-reel recorder. A lucky incident for Sony. The co-founder Akio Morita was so impressed with the young Ohga and would offer him a job with Sony. As a classically trained baritone, Ohga's interest then was in voice and opera. After several rounds of persuasion and urge by Morita, Ohga finally joined Sony full-time, but not before completing a three-year study of voice in Europe. His passion for technology from a customer's perspective and managerial talent provided much needed addition to the prided Sony, which was then largely dominated by engineers. Similarly, Honda Motor's success also benefited from a blessed team—Sachiro Honda was lucky to have met Mr. Fujisawa whose financial and managerial acumen complemented Honda's technical genius. As Honda's passion lied in building the best engines and winning races, it took Fujisawa's managerial expertise to channel the firm's technical strengths to commercial viability (Pascale, 1984).

GAINING COMPETITIVE ADVANTAGE THROUGH USEFUL WEED AND SKUNK WORK

Advantage often emerges from spontaneous discovery and windfall gain within the firm, from self-championed initiatives, underground activities, and informal ventures. These activities may add extra momentum to the firm in addition to the more formal, explicit, and wide-reaching managerial initiatives. Whether or not a particular firm could actually gain advantage from skunk work or "useful weed," however, depends on multiple levels of factors: (1) availability of spontaneous initiatives at the grass-roots level; (2) ability of middle level managers to spot and champion the initiatives and conceptualize them into more general terms meaningful to wider organizational audiences and agendas; and (3) the vision and ability of top management to allow viable initiatives to shape and change the firm's corporate and/or competitive strategies. This section discusses the roles of the different players in this game and the mechanisms through which a firm could better husband its internal resources to enhance its odds of luck.

Seducing the Elites and Inducing the Initiatives

To benefit from skunk work and useful weed types of activities, the innovators and venturers within the firm need to better understand how to gain formal support and needed resources from the management (Bower, 1986) while the general managers need to know how to better design and shape a firm's structure, system, process, and culture, so as to more effectively foster the emerging of innovative initiatives (Burgelman, 1993a,b). Simply put, firm strategy is usually an interactive process of both top-down formulation and bottom-up formation. Innovators involved in skunk work need to seduce the organizational elites who set the firm agenda and allocate resources.

The elites are those actors within the organization who are qualified by "the rules of the game" and their positions of power to oversee the activities of the organizations (Kelly, 1976). The elites usually are those with top management positions or in certain cases people who belong to the firm's power coalition without holding formal or senior positions. Skunk work needs to frame itself as possessing potential for future advantage for the firm so as to gain endorsement at the top, although it may not be compatible with the firm's current strategy. It also needs to be packaged in such a way that, should the skunk work be successful, it reflects positively on and brings credit to those elites who championed it.

> *3M innovate for the same reason cows eat grass—because it is part of our DNA to do so.*
>
> Dr. M. George Allen
> Former VP of R&D at 3M

General managers who are responsible for firm strategy and competitive advantage ought to shape and manipulate the formal and/or informal organizational structure or context and create a climate that induces useful weeds and skunk work and helps them gain impetus. That is, any self-sponsored initiatives must move through the organizational ladder that is dictated by the organizational structure. An organization's current structure is usually designed to implement its current strategy and it therefore filters initiatives using the criteria of reinforcing the current strategy. Innovative initiatives by skunk works, however, often call for new directions of strategic adaptation. As such, an organizational structure that allows for and effectively promotes new self-sponsoring initiatives will help bring to light the benefits of skunk work and useful weeds type of activities. Moreover, general managers also should proactively search for worthy and viable initiatives to champion and endorse as special projects, so as to accomplish innovation that are otherwise impractical or inconceivable within existing organizational context.

Bold Experimenter

Bold experimenters are first movers within an organization who take certain initiatives that will later prove to have firm-wide implication yet are currently independent of, incompatible, or inconsistent with the firm's dominant strategy or standard practice. In the last two decades, China's economic reform has lifted people's living standard multifold. Most observers would credit the economic success to the open-door and reform policy of the late leader Deng Xiaoping. However, Deng was but the endorser of the reform who carried it out nation-wide. It was the bold experimenters that initiated the reform autonomously starting in the countryside. The pragmatic minded Deng's sympathetic attitude toward the grass-roots reform certainly helped.

> *White cat or black cat, so long as it catches mouse, it's a good cat.*
>
> *Deng Xiaoping*
> *Chinese Politician*

In Si Chuan and Canton, provincial governments first contracted out public-owned land to farmers to privatize the formerly collective farming activities. Such a skunk work practice dug a hole in the "iron rice bowl" of the old system and provided incentives for farmers to take better care of their land with longer-term concern and strive for productivity, because now they could keep the extra profit for themselves after meeting certain quota of supply to the government. The daring innovative practice of these pioneer provinces was tacitly permitted by a then more open-minded central government. After the success in these provinces, the household farming system was rectified by the central government and pursued as a formal national strategy. The skunk work brought the pioneer provinces competitive advantages over other provinces and helped the entire country regain economic momentum.

Consider also the example of Mr. Wang Xuan and The Founder Group, a technology venture incubated at Peking University. In the 1980s, when the laser printing technology was in its early stages of commercial development, Founder decided to bypass the then industry standard technology and work on the 4th generation laser printing technology for printing in the Chinese language. Such an innovative effort was criticized and doubted by many academic and industry experts. Overcoming all kinds of difficulties—technological, financial, and bureaucratic—and criticism from detractors, Mr. Wang Xuan and his Founder believed in their vision and worked hard toward making their Chinese laser printing system the industry standard. By the late 1990s, the Founder system had been used in more than 90% of the Chinese news press and thousands of publishing businesses, boasting strong presence also in Japan and Taiwan region. Consequently, the success of the bold experimenters at Founder brings Peking University not only financial resources but also the reputation as a pioneer in commercializing innovations done in elite Chinese universities.

Faithful Champions

To be successful, skunk work needs champions to promote its cause, make available funding, and provide protection from threat within and outside the firm. As skunk works is often secretive, isolated, and independent from the formal structure of its host organization, it may also cause unnecessary attention, jealousy, or even outrage or resentment from other parts of the organization or outside parties, a champion is called for to also insure its legitimacy. Warren Bennis and Biederman (1997) made the following insightful observation:

> *Every great group is an island—but an island with a bridge to the mainland. The Skunk Works operated as an independent community within Lockheed, its secret activities conducted behind unmarked doors. People who are trying to change the world need to be isolated from its distractions, but still able to tap its resources.*

And that bridge is precisely the role of the champion. Dealing with the outside stakeholders, e.g., CIA and Pentagon, the boss of Skunk Works, the late Kelly Johnson, would cultivate close ties with

Washington and personally seek and co-opt advocates for Skunk Works. Within Lockheed, the larger setting which hosted the Skunk Works, he did everything he could to protect his secret group from the meddling of corporate "suits," the bean counters, company men who would only abide by the rules and who could easily undermine the creative project by bringing it under corporate control.

While champions of skunk work try to justify its existence and value to top echelons and outside stakeholders, they often leave alone the creative or innovative part of the skunk work. The idea is to provide all the necessary resources and let the creative people do their own things. Johnson's successor Ben Rich would comment on the style as such: "We encouraged our people to work imaginatively, to improvise and try unconventional approaches to problem solving, and then got out of their way."

Hotbed of Innovation

A firm gains competitive advantage if its structure and culture encourage autonomous innovation activities better than do those of the rivals'. Matsushita used to firmly enforce its "one product, one division" structure. Such a structure facilitated internal competition and innovation. Because any one who developed a new product with commercial viability was able to create their own division, it provided incentives for people to innovate (Ghoshal and Bartlett, 1988). Because once a new product was spun off from its originating division, the old division had to find new sources of revenue to sustain. This forces people to innovate. Such a structure served as a hotbed for innovation and provided impetus for possible skunk work or useful weed type of efforts. For instance, after the tape recorder business was spun off from the radio division, skunk work in the division ended up creating the Karaoke machine, which was wildly successful in the Asian market.

Similarly, when Ministry of International Trade and Industry (MITI) shut out Sharp from its route to the computer industry on the ground that too many Japanese firms were competing in that industry, Sharp was forced to seek new business that would carry the firm. It pulled a skunk work over MITI and focused on one part of the computer accessories business. Their efforts paid off through their dominance in LCD technology, which provided much needed new source of revenue and competitive advantage in markets like laptop screens and other products using LCD, as well as first mover advantage in its View Cam, a line of camcorder with a built in screen that serves as a view finder and allows for instant replay.

Some organizations intentionally create skunk work type of projects to encourage innovation outside the dominant organizational structure. Examples include GM's Saturn Project, Ford's team that designed the new Mustang—which was also named Skunk Works, and the classical one—Xerox's PARC (Palo Alto Research Center) which designed the first computer for non-expert users. These innovative projects, however, create competitive advantage only if their technical innovation could be effectively capitalized on, creating commercial viability. Building skunk work and useful weed type of innovation into the overall firm's mainstream strategy and translating it into products that consumers would come to value. That, is the bottom line for gaining competitive advantage.

CONCLUDING REMARKS

Elusive yet debatable as a theoretical concept, luck has always been a frequently observed phenomenon that attracts much fascination by many, from practicing mangers to industry observers. This chapter provides a typology of various scenarios where luck strikes and confers a firm with competitive advantage. It treats luck as some sort of happening stemming from both chance event and human endeavor, ranging from pure serendipity in its ideal form to the case of prepared luck where random forces validate foresight and purposeful action. Taking a rather proactive approach, it aims to help guide general managers gain competitive advantage by pointing to the various external sources of luck as well as intra-firm mechanisms for better preparation.

In summary, while pure luck acts out of the control of human behavior, it helps for firms to be aware of the contextual conditions under which one's odds of getting lucky could be enhanced. Many lucky incidents may seem to be merely lucky incidents to the uninformed observers; they might just be the outcome of certain systematic and visionary efforts duly rewarded. In order to better improve a firm's odds, general managers have to be constantly on the alert to scan the environment, spot new trend, and act on transient opportunities. They also need to fight their own arrogance, ignorance, and negligence. Moreover, it helps that they remain open-minded and tolerant about useful weed and skunk work type of internal corporate venturing activities. To put the proactive perspective into extreme, luck is created.

Chapter 6   Managerial Initiative, Strategic Maneuver, and Strategic Co-option

This chapter examines more deliberate forces, managerial initiative, strategic maneuvering, and strategic co-option, as causes for competitive advantage. It coalesces the disparate array of literature on competitive advantage in International Management and Strategic Management. The integrative framework hinges on four general categories of factors, known as creation and innovation, competition, cooperation, and co-option, and discusses how they give rise to the three generic types of competitive advantages discussed in chapter one: ownership-based, access-based, and proficiency-based. Some specific determinants of competitive advantage are juxtaposed and presented within the proposed framework. Such a framework is advanced in the particular context of global competition.

Many an industry has witnessed accelerated and enhanced globalization, in both pace and magnitude, in the latter half of the 20th century (Levitt, 1983; Yip, 1995; Ohmae, 2000). At the dawn of the new millennium, such a trend of globalization in the international economic scene has been marching on unabatedly and has stirred up fierce competition even in industries previously regarded as being free from the onslaught of foreign rivalry. Consequently, such globalization unmercifully forces many firms, multinational corporations and local players, to reassess their competitive strategy and consciously create, renew, and hopefully sustain their competitive advantages in the global market place (Kogut, 1985; Porter, 1986, 1991; Ghoshal, 1987; Yip, 1989, 1995; Powell, 2001).

What are the determinants of competitive advantage in global competition? What strategic maneuverings could the firm engage in to gain global competitive advantage? These questions beg for serious attention from both International Management and Strategy researchers. To date, however, our understanding of the nature and causes of global competitive advantage remains fragmented and incomplete. Lacking a framework that helps piece together the disparate arrays of literature, researchers and practitioners alike are unfortunately constrained in their ability to systematically analyze how global competitive advantages arise and what factors may have caused them and determine their sustainability.

In the International Management (IM) literature, debates exist regarding the origins of global competitive advantage. While some researchers tout the merits of globalization and globally-coordinated marketing or competitive moves (Levitt, 1993; Yip, 1995; Ohmae, 2000), others choose to focus on country-specific origins for competitive advantage in the global market (e.g., Porter, 1990), and still others argue for a more balanced pursuit of global integration and local adaptiveness in the search for global competitive advantage (Bartlett and Ghoshal, 1989; Gupta and Govindarajan, 2001; Prahalad and Lieberthal, 2003).

In the Strategy literature, there exists a rich body of knowledge on the nature and causes of competitive advantage (Porter, 1985; Barney, 1991, Peteraf, 1993; Powell, 2001), ranging from the industry positioning approach (Porter, 1980, 1985), the commitment explanation (Ghemawat, 1991; Caves and Ghemawat, 1992), to the resource-based view (Wernerfelt, 1984; Barney, 1991; Peteraf, 1993) and the dynamic capability approach (Teece, Pisano, and Shuen, 1997). Moreover, extant work in Strategy on the dynamics of competition (Smith, Grimm, and Gannon, 1992; Chen, 1996), Schumpeterian innovation (D'Aveni, 1994; Jacobson, 1992), and cooperative strategy (Brandenburger and Nalebuff, 1996; Gulati, 1998; HBS, 2002) also help shed light on competitive advantage.

Though also fragmented and lacking integration, the various accounts of competitive advantage in the strategy literature, if extended into the IM research, will help enrich our understanding of the nature and causes of competitive advantage in the global arena. Surprisingly, little theoretical effort exists that integrates the various insights about competitive advantage in the IM and the Strategy literatures (cf. Gupta and Govindarajan, 2001). It is the purpose of this paper to bridge the two areas of research and attempt an integrative framework on the determinants of global competitive advantage. Such an integration is expected to help researchers paint a more complete picture in their theorizing on global competitive advantage and to provide management practitioners with a more comprehensive tool kit in their search for global competitive advantage.

Based on an extensive review of literature in both IM and Strategy, I choose to organize my integration around 4 major groups of determinants of competitive advantage, denoted as the 4Cs: Creation and innovation (Schumpeter, 1934, 1950; Hamel and Prahalad, 1989; Senge, 1990); Competition (Porter, 1980; Smith et al., 1992; D'Aveni, 1994; Chen, 1996); Cooperation (Hamel, Doz, and Prahalad, 1989; Contractor and Lorange, 1988; Dyer and Singh, 1998; HBS, 2002), and Co-option (Brandenburger and Nalebuff, 1996; Bailey, 1997; Doh, 2000). I coalesce the various accounts of competitive advantage in both IM and Strategy into these 4Cs and elucidate their respective theoretical underpinnings as well as practical illustrations.

As an initial effort, the choice of 4C is neither meant to be exhaustive or exclusive, nor entirely random or arbitrary. The major criteria of their inclusion are threefold: First, each has a long established research tradition with solid theoretical foundations. Second, there is empirical evidence attesting to their relevance to competitive advantage. Third, they have to be relevant and meaningful to global competition. Finally, this chapter, as a companion piece to Chapter 5 exploring the deliberate causes for competitive advantages, is also part of a larger framework (see Figure 5.1) that is well grounded in strategy research both theoretically and empirically. More detailed explanations of the rationale of the 4C treatment are offered in the literature review.

The chapter is organized as follows. It first reviews the relevant literature on competitive advantage. Then it advances the 4Cs framework and juxtaposes the determinants of competitive advantage in the global arena, followed by concluding remarks.

RATIONALE FOR THE 4C TREATMENT

Various forces and factors—environmental, organizational, or personal, could potentially determine the competitive advantages of a business firm. These factors and forces, using the firm as the unit of analysis, can be internal, working primarily within the firm's boundary, or external, effecting primarily outside the firm's boundary. Also, these forces and factors could be either serendipitous, arising and disappearing without the conscious control of the firm, e.g., luck (Barney, 1996a); or deliberate, subject to purposeful strategic maneuvers in competition, cooperation, or creative and innovative managerial actions in managing a firm's organizational structure (Chandler, 1962; Bartlett and Ghoshal, 1989), process (Senge, 1990; Gupta and Govindarajan, 1991, 2001), culture (Deal and Kennedy, 1982; Barney, 1986b), technology (Chandler, 2001), and people (Pfeffer, 1994; Stewart, 1997).

As the spontaneous or serendipitous causes of competitive advantage are basically out of the control of general managers in global competition (e.g., Ma, 2002), this paper chooses to focus on the deliberate factors that determine the rise and fall of competitive advantage: managerial actions and strategic maneuvers. Managerial actions refer to actions that focus on the internal working of the firm itself. They help enhance the firm's own level of playing and in themselves alone contribute directly to the firm's competitive advantages (Hansen and Wernerfelt, 1989). For the purpose of this paper, I term such managerial actions as Creation and Innovation (Schumpeter, 1934, 1950; Hamel and Prahalad, 1989), due to the fact that these actions are primarily endogenous and do not necessarily require interactions with competitors or other players in the product markets.

Strategic maneuvers, based on a search of literature, could be found in primarily three general categories: competition (Porter, 1980; Smith et al., 1992; D'Aveni, 1994; Chen, 1996), cooperation (Contractor and Lorange, 1988; Hamel, Doz, and Prahalad, 1989; Dyer and Singh, 1998), and co-option (Baron, 1995; Bailey, 1997; Doh, 2000). First, strategy literature is filled with war-like metaphors when it comes to the treatment of competition and its relationship with competitive advantages. This can be observed in such influential works from Porter's (1980) jockeying for positions to D'Aveni's (1994) hyper-competition, from the varying competitive dynamics (Chen, 1996) to the winner-take-all strategy (Hill, 1997), and from domestic rivalry to global dominance (Gupta and Govindarajan, 2001). As such, it is theoretically meaningful and practically relevant to systematically examine how competition affects a firm's global competitive advantage.

Second, in both the Strategy and IM literature, cooperative strategy has always been a focal concern (e.g., Contractor and Lorange, 1988; Hamel, Doz, and Prahalad, 1989; Brandenburger and Nalebuff, 1996; Gulati, 1998; HBS, 2002). In fact, inter-firm collaborative arrangements abound in international business (Porter, 1986; Yip, 1995). Not surprisingly, many of the writings on cooperative strategy to date have strong international flavors, ranging from the pioneering comprehensive account by Contractor and Lorange (1988), to the current treatment by Gomes-Casseres (1994) and Dyer and Singh (1998). Moreover, there exists a sizable body of literature on how international joint ventures and strategic alliances could help create competitive advantage in global competition (e.g., Kogut, 1988; Hamel, Doz, and Prahalad, 1989; Gomes-Casseres, 1994; Yan, 1998). Therefore, it is particularly germane and informative to examine our stock in the cooperative strategy literature and systematically assess the effects of cooperation on global competitive advantage.

Third, besides competition and cooperation, firms often engage in strategic maneuvers known as co-option, that help enlist the support of governmental agencies (Baron, 1995; Bailey, 1997), the third party players, e.g., neutral or independent players in a game (Brandenburger and Nalebuff, 1996; Hill, 1997), or influential local stakeholders (Doh, 2000). The underlying rationale for differentiating co-option from cooperation is threefold: (1) The object of a firm's strategic maneuvering in co-option is often a stakeholder that is not in direct competition or cooperation with the focal firm, as in the case of independent players who co-evolve with a focal firm's product spontaneously (Moore, 1996); (2) The object is often a non-economic or non-market entity (Baron, 1995), which can have powerful influence over how the focal firm could act in the global competitive arena, e.g., the government (Bailey, 1997). Interaction with such entities is therefore different from competition or cooperation with players in a firm's competitive environment (Porter, 1980); (3) The actual tactics and mechanisms used in the maneuver are often implicit or informal due to a host of political, cultural, or legal reasons, e.g., anti-trust, among others (Kogut and Singh, 1988; Bailey, 1997). As such, such co-option differs from explicit collaborative arrangements often seen in inter-firm cooperation.

In the next section, I shall present the various components of the 4C framework and elaborate on how they affect a firm's global competitive advantages. See Figure 6.1.

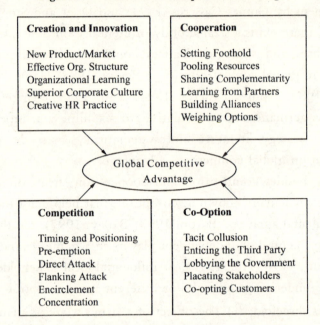

Figure 6.1 The 4Cs of Competitive Advantage

CREATION, INNOVATION, AND COMPETITIVE ADVANTAGE

Innovation lies in the heart of both strategy and entrepreneurship, two fields deeply concerned with how competitive advantage arises out of entrepreneurial creation and innovation (Schumpeter, 1934, 1950; Hitt, Ireland, Camp, and Sexton, 2001). "The fundamental impulse that sets and keeps the capitalist engine in motion comes from the new consumers' goods, the new methods of production or transportation, the new markets, the new forms of industrial organization that capitalist enterprise creates" (Schumpeter, 1950: 82—83). As the world economic system has been increasing globalizing and the free market gains wild popularity in emerging and transitional economies (Tan, 2001), innovation in creating new products/markets and new organizational practices become more and more important for firms in global competition.

A firm can gain competitive advantage through managerial initiatives that facilitate innovation (Hamel and Prahalad, 1989), efficiency (Williamson, 1991), and learning (Senge, 1990); initiatives that bring out the best in people to perform in winning oriented-culture (Pfeffer, 1994); initiatives that generate a host of multi-purpose knowledge and competence that are not dependent on any narrowly-defined product or business (Prahalad and Hamel, 1990), as well as dynamic capabilities that help the firm creatively apply these knowledge and competence to specific market opportunities (Teece et al., 1997); as well as initiatives that creatively align a firm's organizational structure and system to its global strategy (Egelhoff, 1988; Bartlett and Ghoshal, 1989; Gupta and Govindarajan, 1991).

It should be noted that the competitive advantage gained through Creation and Innovation, while it could fall within any of the three generic types, is often primarily proficiency-based, as it in general deals with learning, knowledge creation, competence and capability building, both organizational and technical.

Creating New Products/Markets

As taught by Sun Tzu thousands years ago, to win without fighting should be the supreme among all strategies. A firm can, under certain situations, win without the fight by carefully positioning itself to critical positions, which afford it later competitive advantages that are largely uncontestable. A firm can gain advantage by innovation in market positioning. It is not merely innovation in the technical arena, it is innovation in strategic sense. Instead of playing catch-up games following the leader's rule, a firm could change the rule of game and/or change the game itself (Hamel and Prahalad, 1989; Brandenburger and Nalebuff, 1996).

That is, a firm should avoid fighting an uphill battle but should engage in creative development of new resources, capabilities, products, and markets that allow the firms to be fundamentally different from yet superior to rivals (Hamel and Prahalad, 1989; Lieberman and Montgomery, 1988). Such creation and innovation aim at avoiding confrontation with strong competitors. It focuses more on the firm's own moves, and does not particularly concern over competition or cooperation. For instance, CNN positioned itself as the premium provider of news around the globe around the clock. Such exclusive focus on news reporting and often instantaneous coverage of important events any time when they happen earned CNN the trust and loyalty of its viewers. Redefining the rule of news reporting, CNN does not, in a narrow sense, compete against other news media, it competes against itself, creating new markets through innovative products/services.

Innovative Organizational Structure

Organizational structure is the basic set-up of an organization that dictates the workflow and the pattern of how people communicate and interact. Aligning organizational structure with strategy, i.e., maintaining fit between strategy and structure, provides a firm with competitive advantage (Chandler, 1962; Egelhoff, 1988). From an information processing perspective, Egelhoff (1988) posits that the structure of MNCs should be designed to allow them to achieve maximum performance in coordination and integration. Bartlett and Ghoshal (1989) conceptually argue for the important role of transnational structure in balancing the need of global integration and local adaptiveness and present ample corroborating case evidence.

Organizational Learning

Organizational structure merely lays out the channel and pattern of communication and interaction among various units of the global firm. Organizational processes, programs, and standard operating procedures, e.g., management information systems, direct the firm's activities, from strategic planning to routine functioning. Superior organizational process can provide the firm with competitive advantage through its contribution to organizational effectiveness and learning (cf. Winter, 1987; Nonaka, 1991; Senge, 1990). Organizational learning is a shared, collective process that involves people from grass roots to top management that focuses on generating, accumulating, and applying knowledge to enhance a firm's effectiveness, efficiency, and creativity. Gupta and Govindarajan (1991) argue that the control process of the MNC should enhance knowledge flow among its various units and subsidiaries. Prahalad and Lieberthal (1998) demonstrate that MNCs, which purposefully encourage headquarters or home bases to learn from their innovative foreign subsidiaries, possess competitive advantage over those MNCs that merely practice "corporate imperialism."

Superior Corporate Culture

Corporate culture can be defined as a shared belief and value system embedded with the norm and code that guide and regulate people's behavior within the organization (Deal and Kennedy, 1982). It often runs deep down in the heart of every living soul in the organization. A superior corporate culture in an "institutionalized organization" can help mobilize people toward the common goal of the firm and enhance efficiency, productivity, and creativity of the firm as a whole (Selznick, 1957). It does so through fine-ingrained concern, respect, and appreciation for people as human beings; celebration of the joy and fun of work; and infusion of value and meaning in what employees do to take care of customers. Corporate culture is often idiosyncratic and difficult to imitate. As such, a superior culture often provides a firm with sustainable competitive advantage (Barney, 1986b). For instance, Wal-Mart's culture of great service and superior customer value has helped them win respect in various foreign locations. 3M's culture of innovation plays a non-trivial role in its creation and development of a host of globally successful products (Bartlett and Ghoshal, 1997).

Creative Human Resource Practices

What has often been ignored in the discussion of competitive advantage is people. Skilled and experienced labor forces that are loyal and dedicated often provide sustainable competitive advantages in terms of accumulated intellectual capital and enhanced productivity (Pfeffer, 1994; Reichheld, 1996; Stewart, 1997). In the 1980s, both GM and Ford were trying to learn from their global rivals, Japanese automakers, the secret of superior quality and productivity. While GM focused primarily on upgrading its technological investment, e.g., the Just in Time system, Ford had instead chosen to focus on people and employee involvement. The success story of Ford's Team Taurus has demonstrated that people—the commitment of employees—are a source of competitive advantage that can be counted on even during life-threatening crisis of the firm.

Similarly, a MNC that is better at nurturing a loyal and stable managerial staff and workforce at its foreign subsidiaries is expected to possess competitive advantage over MNCs who fails to tap the potential of its overseas workforce. For instance, through its on-location Motorola University, Motorola was able to systematically train its workforce in China and other foreign countries, enhancing the competence of its overseas employees as well as its reputation as a responsible corporate citizen globally.

COMPETITION AND COMPETITIVE ADVANTAGE

Competition can be defined as action and response (Chen and Miller, 1994; Smith et al., 1992)—or preemption, attack, and retaliation—in competitive engagement against rivals. Competition often aims primarily at jockeying for positions, preempting rival action, and gaining valuable resources or access (Porter, 1980; Ghemawat, 1991; Chen and MacMillan, 1992). The competitive advantage gained through competitive maneuvers is often ownership-based, e.g., a strong market position, or access-based, e.g., winning over rivals by securing a dominant distribution channel in a jointly contested foreign market.

Timing and Positioning: First Mover Advantage

A firm can gain first mover advantage by being the first in occupying a market position or niche that allows for the gaining of resources, capabilities, and access that late movers cannot easily match (Lieberman and Montgomery, 1988). The first mover can enjoy advantages in technological leadership, experience-based economy, preemption of assets and positions, buyer switching cost, and customer awareness and loyalty (Porter, 1985; Lieberman and Montgomery, 1988). It also helps provide cash resources to plow back and invest in further enhancing a firm's first mover advantages. First mover's technological leadership, for instance, could be secured by setting industry standard, as exemplified in the case of the world VCR industry (Yoffie, 1990; Hill, 1997). First mover can also secure input factors on more favorable terms and preempt, or even eliminate, rivals' access (cf. Wind, 1997). In the IM literature, ample evidence also exists that supports the claim that early movers into foreign market enjoy competitive advantage over later movers (Luo, 1998; Luo and Peng, 1998; Pan and Chi, 1999; Pan and Tse, 1999).

Pre-emption

It is also worth noting that relating to the first mover advantage is often the pre-emptive effect the first mover's action could exert on other players in subsequent competition. A first mover can pick the attractive positions and force the rivals to take unattractive ones (Porter, 1985), e.g. Nike's choice of the upper end of the market. It can also preempt later rivals' ability to challenge and expand. P&G's introduction of the Pampers Phase was accomplished in 90 countries within a year. Sony, anticipating the potential of the 3.5" inch floppy disk, announced a 5-fold increase in its production capacity before IBM was even sure about its commitment to the 3.5" disk. Such a move quickly sealed Sony's lead in this market (Wind, 1997). The preemption effort provides the focal firm with competitive advantage by eliminating or constraining rivals' option space and by limiting, reducing, or neutralizing rivals' ability to create customer value in comparison to that of the focal firm.

Direct Attack

As rivalry intensifies with increasing globalization of business activities, which brings about a host of diverse competitors, high-speed market changes, and widening scope of competition, direct confrontation with rivals is often inevitable in certain businesses or markets. Smart ploy in positioning is impossible and changing the game unlikely. Nowhere to hide. Nowhere to run. Facing such a no-escape situation, the only sensible option for the firm is then to draw the sword and fight (D'Aveni, 1994). Direct attack aims at face-to-face rivalry against competitors. It conforms to the military principle of engaging in quick and decisive moves.

The Gillette Sensor launch 1990 in 23 countries almost simultaneously (within one year) represents a good example of direct attack where a major firm declares war against all rivals in an all out fashion (Wind, 1997). Such attack signals strong commitment of Gillette to excel and lead in this target market (cf. Caves, 1984; Porter, 1985; Ghemawat, 1991). The reason why Gillette could gain positional advantage from this launch is not only that the magnitude and speed of its assault are difficult to match but also its revolutionary product quality thanks to its R&D strengths accumulated through Creation and Innovation.

Flanking Attack

Different from direct attacks where firms engage in head-on rivalry, flanking attack attacks a rival from the side where the rival is least likely to retaliate due to ignorance or lack of interest, insignificance of the attacked market segment, or ineffectiveness in possible retaliation (D'Aveni, 1994). For instance, in the global market for microprocessors, Cyrix Corporation used flanking attack against Intel. Instead of competing against Intel in the mainstream microprocessor business, Cyrix once developed a math co-processor for Intel's 386 chips that would run 20 times faster than Intel's microprocessor. Such attack does not challenge Intel's overall market dominance, yet provided Cyrix with comparative advantage in a viable niche (Wheelen and Hunger, 1997).

Encirclement

This type of maneuver extends the flanking maneuver into extremes. Instead of attacking a rival in its stronghold directly, a firm would build up strengths in neighbor industries or geographic areas surrounding the rival's stronghold (Ghemawat, 1991). Wal-Mart used such strategy when it moved from rural areas to more urban areas. Wal-Mart did not hastily go into the cities where Kmart had stronghold. Instead, Wal-Mart built stores around the city in a ring fashion. The idea was to wait for the city to grow to Wal-Mart (Walton, 1992). Media News, an upstart newspaper group, owns 140 newspapers in the U.S., mostly small ones. Their strategy is to cluster several of their small dailies and/or weeklies owned in an area, typically suburban areas around major cities, combining business and some editorial operation and skimming off advertising avenues that would have gone to big papers in the major cities they surrounded (*Forbes*, 1997b).

Concentration

In fighting for competitive advantage, a major principle is concentration: to create advantage by concentrating a firm's resource at any point of encounter and create local superiority, even against a strong player whose overall strength is more superior. This principle, strongly advocated by the famed military strategist Liddell Hart, applies to multiple tactics discussed above, e.g., direct and flanking attacks, and could also find its theoretical affinity with the focus strategy popularized by Porter (1980).

An example of concentration can be found in Formule 1, a major motel chain in France. Avoiding the strong points of full service hotels, it chooses to focus on the functions, which the mass of budget travelers value the most: bed quality, hygiene, and room quietness. It drastically downplays or minimizes other amenities unimportant to these value-conscious customers, e. g., eating facilities, architectural aesthetics, lounges, room size, availability of receptionist, etc. Through such concentration, they can avoid being a lousy hotel that offers basically everything an up-scale hotel does but only at an inferior level. Instead it becomes a superior motel chain that offers unique and better value to its customers. And its parents wasted no time in rolling out the winning formula in other parts of the world (Kim and Mauborgne, 1997).

COOPERATION AND COMPETITIVE ADVANTAGE

Cooperation can be defined as the initiation and participation in collaborative arrangements with other players in a firm's environment. Cooperation usually aims at "relational rent" (Dyer and Singh, 1998): gaining access to customers, to complementary resources and capabilities from partners; learning and accumulating technical and organizational knowledge; and benefiting from scale and scope economies (cf. Contractor and Lorange, 1988; Hamel, et al., 1989). Moreover, a firm can gain competitive advantage through participation in the following collaborative arrangements: pooling resources with partners to enhance strengths; forming alliance with others to fight a third party; and joining multiple alliances to gain latitude (Contractor and Lorange, 1988).

It should be noted that, although a firm could also achieve ownership-based or proficiency-based competitive advantages (Hamel, et al., 1989), the immediate and direct outcome of a firm's cooperative maneuvering is often access-based competitive advantage (Dyer and Singh, 1998; Gulati, 1998).

Setting Foothold

A MNC, through cooperation with local partners, could set foothold in a target market, way before its full-fledged commitment to that market. Such foothold setting could prove to be an effective way of building contact, testing the water, and eventually gaining first mover advantage when a formal entry is desired (Lieberman and Montgomery, 1988).

Recently, Doh (2000) provides a comprehensive conceptual framework, which posits that local partner collaboration accentuates MNC's first mover advantage when entering a foreign market characterized by privatization. Empirically, many far-sighted MNCs adopt the measure of collaborative foothold and build reservoir of good will in countries where they will eventually attempt large-scale entry. For instance, HP-China stands as a classic example of how such a foothold could translate into competitive advantage over later comers who have to start the Guanxi game from scratch (Farh, Tsui, Xin, and Cheng, 1988).

Pooling Resources and Sharing Risks

Pooling resources together allows for collective strengths that are needed to tackle problems or challenges insurmountable to individual firms. Such cooperation also helps spread risk. Firms participating in such resource-pooling collaborative arrangements will gain advantage over those rivals, which have to venture alone and shoulder all the burden and risk (Hill, 1997). Such resource pooling kind of cooperation is often done through aggregation of strengths by players with similar resource profiles and product market activities. For instance, in the global oil drilling industry, many firms tend to join forces to pursue a particular project so as to enjoy greater scale economy (Contractor and Lorange, 1988).

Sharing Complementary Resources and Skills

Cooperation could also be undertaken by firms with complementary resources which jointly tackle a major project of interest to the concerned parties, e.g., R&D consortium where participating firms contribute varying expertise (Contractor and Lorange, 1988; Gulati, 1998). The NUMMI project between GM and Toyota stands as a fitting example as GM tried to access Toyota's expertise in small car manufacturing while Toyota wanted GM's know-how in selling to the U.S. market. Major firms with great marketing savvy in the consumer goods market also often join force to test new products in a new market. For instance, Coca-Cola and Nestle recently formed a joint venture to make and distribute canned coffee in Korea and Hong Kong SAR, exploiting their respective knowledge and skills in selling canned goods and coffee making.

Learning from Partners

Essentially all collaborative arrangements can be characterized as a learning race (Hamel, et all, 1989). To learn the underlying processes and capabilities that are most critical in creating customer values lies at the heart of cooperative strategy. Sony and Matsushita all benefited from their cooperation with Philips in learning how to make radios and tape recorders. Both have also benefited from their cooperation with American firms in early stages of the VCR development (Yoffie, 1990). Learning from partners made them strong competitors.

In high-tech industries, learning from partners becomes extremely important. In the fast changing computer industry, for instance, no firm can dominate the market through their own products alone. It's a business community where multiple firms collaborate and multiple alliances co-evolve. In such an environment, collaboration is a necessity and slow learners won't survive. It is a known fact that firms in Silicon Valley often sue each other for stealing technologies. Yet that does not change the fact that they are still cooperating at the same time when they are suing. The firm that can learn from its rival-partners more quickly will likely gain competitive advantage.

Building Alliances

A firm can also gain advantage if it could ally with certain players to jointly fight a common enemy (Gulati, 1998). Such alliance is often of transient nature due to the changing interests of the various players involved in a business. For instance, Caterpillar, in attacking the Japanese earth moving equipment market, enlisted the help of Mitsubishi to put pressure on their common rival Kumatsu. Kumatsu was reported to draw 80% of its global cash flow from Japan, its home market. The idea of the Caterpillar maneuver is to make noise at the rival's home front with a local helper so as to offset the rival's aggressiveness in the global market (Contractor and Lorange, 1988).

Weighing Options in Multiple Alliances

Firms often collaborate with multiple partners or straddle multiple strategic alliances to insure a foothold in the future of its industry or business (Gulati and Nohria, 1997; Gulati, 1998). For instance, The Limited and Liz Claiborne both maintain jobbers alliances in over several dozens of countries. Such alliances provide both firms with competitive advantage over rivals who rely on a single source of suppliers. In high-tech industries where technology changes frequently and quickly, firms participate in rival alliances so as to weigh their options and maintain future technical viability (Gulati and Nohria, 1997). Should any one firm's or alliance's product become industry standard, the straddling firm will always have a foothold based on which to build its market, e.g., Microsoft's investment in both cable and satellite technology for potential home Internet access through TV (*Fortune*, 1996c).

CO-OPTION AND COMPETITIVE ADVANTAGE

Strategic co-option attempts to align other parties' interest with that of the focal firm, providing possible competitive advantages by opening windows of opportunities, removing external obstacles, or neutralizing threats. It is often done through a third party to influence the firm's fight with rivals. It also could happen between rivals who tacitly collude to jointly deal with customers or a third rival (Porter, 1980). The major difference between strategic co-option and cooperative maneuver is that the former is much more subtle, informal, implicit, sometimes illegal, but most times without clearly specified binding measures. A firm could also directly co-opt customers.

It should be noted that, in general, competitive advantages gained through co-opting outside parties are primarily access-based, e.g., the right to access certain markets closed to other foreign competitors, or sometimes ownership-based, e.g., owning a special license obtained through lobbying.

Tacit Collusion

In an ongoing competition in the international market, firms often engage in tacit practices that are aimed to stabilize their overall competitive relationship and secure joint competitive advantages over other players (Ma, 1999). For instance, MNCs could practice mutual forbearance and soften their rivalry while collectively punishing other rivals who do not play by their rules. They could also compete vigorously on one dimension of the game while tacitly collude on other dimensions so as to maintain a reasonable competitive infrastructure and a healthy profit margin. For instance, Nike and Reebok, as archrivals, fight primarily on brand image in the global athletic footwear and apparel industry (Katz, 1994). The tacit understanding between the rivals is that price competition reduces the glamour of the business and leads to undesirable path for both, destroying the basic infrastructure of their rivalry. As such, each other's competitive practice, especially that of Nike's, usually tries to co-opt the rival to sustain non-price competition.

Enticing the Third Party

When two major rivals fight for the right of industry standard, the support of third party players, e.g., providers of critical components or complementary products, often play an important role in deciding which firm wins. Co-opting these third party players to serve a firm's interest could therefore provide competitive advantage. In the battle of VCR format in the 1970s, Sony's betamax and JVC's VHS were two competing formats. While Sony's arrogant attitude alienated potential partners, JVC aggressively persuaded other electronics manufacturers to adopt the VHS format. With more VHS format VCR flooding the market, major Hollywood studios would prefer releasing their titles on the VHS format. With the enlisted support of providers of the software, i.e., movies, JVC was able to dominate the VCR market (Yoffie, 1990; Hill, 1997).

Lobbying the Government

A firm could co-opt the government to gain advantage, e.g., inducing more favorable trade policy or tax credit, obtaining permission for entry into previously prohibited industries, using the home government to pressure foreign rivals or government so as to gain better access to foreign market or inputs, or appealing directly to foreign governments for support (D'Aveni, 1994; Bailey, 1997). For instance, when it comes to gaining competitive advantage through exports and foreign direct investment, many Japanese firms are equally competent at strategic co-opting foreign governments as they are at quality manufacturing. That is, they know how to cajole other people's uncles (Vogel, 1985).

Placating Influential Stakeholders

Besides the government, many other formal or informal institutions in foreign countries, social, cultural, religious, or other types, could have non-trivial impact on the success of a MNC and its competitive advantage in global competition (Baron, 1985). For instance, a MNC that is better at dealing with special interest groups, e.g., environmental groups, will possess advantage over a less adequate or environmentally-sensitive when attempting entry into country or regional markets where environmental groups wield tremendous power in affecting governmental policy making. Building Guanxi, friendly networks, with these influential stakeholders in the non-market arena often prove to be pivotal for MNC success (Farh, Tsui, Xin, and Sheng, 1998).

Sony Chairman Akio Morita penned a book *The Japan that Can Say No* for his countrymen in the 1980s, calling Japan to play tough against America, which apparently was not intended for American audience. The book, however, was quickly picked up by Pentagon and translated into English, the message of which largely irritated the Americans. To co-opt public opinions and business leaders alike in the U.S., Morita was to write later an article in *Harvard Business Review* touting the importance of Japan-U.S. cooperation.

Co-Opting Customers

A firm could also gain competitive advantage by co-opting the customers and the public through non-traditional marketing and appealing to them in non-economic ways (Baron, 1995). For instance, Body Shop uses environmental cause to promote business' social responsibility and win public sympathy and customer support over the world (Roddick, 1991). Sometimes firms also use economic incentives to co-opt customers into long-term relationship. GM introduced its GM Card program that allows customers to earn rebate on the credit card toward their next purchase of GM vehicles, a program that Ford quickly followed (Brandenburger and Nalebuff, 1996). Such co-optive practice toward the customers also sends a strong and clear signal to rivals. It suggests to rivals that they should move away from intense price competition and focus instead on better service as well as product quality and selection. In the end, the firms, which can successfully co-opt the customers into long-term relationship, gain competitive advantage.

CONCLUDING REMARKS

This paper sets out to advance an integrative framework that coalesces the rather fragmented literature on global competitive advantage. The framework hinges on 4Cs as suggested by a critical review of the literature: Creation, Competition, Cooperation, and Co-option. The major contribution of this chapter lies in that it helps make our understanding of the determinants of competitive advantage more complete and systematic, putting the various pieces into the greater perspective of global competition.

This chapter focuses on the various factors that the general management of a firm should attend to in gaining competitive advantages in global competition. It should be noted, however, that these factors represent a whole range of causes for competitive advantage and are context-specific, with some of them possibly being very dominant in certain context and others more relevant at certain times. For instance, in a highly regulated context of international competition, co-option would be more important than in cases where it favors fair play in market competition. In large scale and often-risky multinational projects, skills in collaborating with rivals will prove to be a better cause for competitive advantage than perhaps cutthroat competitive moves.

Furthermore, the relevance of the different causes not only varies with environmental context but also varies with different types of players. For instance, a dominant firm may be at potential disadvantage when it comes to the use of co-option strategy, as government and the public often appear to be more sympathetic toward smaller and less advantaged firms. Smaller firms may have to reply more on their own initiatives in creation and innovation due to their lack of opportunities in participating in more productive or lucrative strategic alliances or consortiums in their industries.

In summary, in international competition, general managers should not only be aware of the whole range of causes for competitive advantage, but also understand the intricacies of their intertwined relationships and the balances needed when pursuing these causes, e.g., the balance between cooperative and competitive moves between a MNC and a local firm, the balance between fair competition and co-optive measures, the balance between creative initiatives and preemptive maneuvers, etc.

Chapter 7 The Sustainability Challenge

Sustainable advantage refers to a competitive advantage that is long lasting in time and that is not easily destroyed or matched by rivals. As such, the challenge to sustainability of competitive advantage is to fend off triggers and forces that destroy or dissipate competitive advantage. This chapter attempts to systematically identify such triggers and forces. Deliberate or spontaneous actions that are triggered either internally or externally erode the sustainability of competitive advantage. Ignorance, negligence, arrogance, self-aggrandizement and overconfidence are identified as internal triggers. Environmental shift, competitive substitution, imitation, sabotage and bad luck are identified as external triggers. Examining the effect of such triggers and their interactions provides better understanding and practical guidance toward the sustainability challenge.

From *In Search of Excellence* (Peters and Waterman, 1982) of the 1980s, *Built to Last* (Collins and Porras, 1994) of the 1990s, to *Good to Great* (Collins, 2001) of the 21st Century, bestsellers in business helped articulate and popularize the varying paths toward the holy grail of sustainable competitive advantage and profiled the success for many a leading firm that defines the standard of excellence at the time. Yet, merely a decade or so later, quite a number of those once "excellent" firms had to struggle; and competitive advantages for those strong-built did not exactly last. Is it purely the tough turbulent environment to blame for a sort of bad luck? Is it possible that leading firms' own actions contribute to the fall from their glorious past? Simply put, what destroys leaders' competitive advantage or how do they actually lose them? To this question, bestsellers often remain silent.

In the academic literature, the process of creating competitive advantage has been addressed from a variety of perspectives. The conceptual development on destruction of competitive advantage, however, remains scant and fragmented. This conceptual gap motivates the research reported in this chapter. Given the scant attention on this important strategic issue, this research effort is of both theoretical value and practical relevance.

Multiple triggers are often at work that causes the destruction of a leading firm's competitive advantage. These triggers, internal or external to the firm, spontaneous or purposeful, interact and jointly affect the firm. However, for analytical purpose and ease of presentation, we examine these triggers in depth individually. Then we try to make sense of the whole phenomenon of competitive advantage destruction in a more integrative account, exploring the potential linkages and patterns among the various triggers. See Table 7.1.

Table 7.1 Challenges to Sustainability: Triggers and Forces that Erode Competitive Advantage

Internal Triggers and Forces
Managerial Ignorance: Don't Know
Managerial Negligence: Don't See
Managerial Arrogance and Self-Aggrandizement: Don't Care
Managerial Miscalculation: Don't Appreciate and Don't Want
External Triggers and Forces
Competitive Imitation
Competitive Substitution
Rivals' Sabotage
Paradigm Shift

INTERNAL CHALLENGES TO SUSTAINABILITY

Managerial Ignorance

Ignorance is an important construct that is attracting the attention of management scholars (Harvey et al., 2001). Leading firms lose their advantage due to their own lack of knowledge of the drivers of success. Firms may not be aware of the existence or importance of their core competencies. Certain resources are unique and valuable because they are socially complex and causally ambiguous (Barney, 1991). As such, the owner of unique resources that provide sustainable competitive advantage may not know the cause of competitive advantage. The firm's management may ignore the unique resources. For instance, inappropriate hiring of new personnel who do not fit in with the existing culture or group set-up could jeopardize a superior organizational culture or mode of teamwork. A company that thrives on its dedicated and loyal employees may lose its edge if it tries to substitute people with machines in order to save short-term overhead costs.

Managerial decisions with regard to acquisitions are spontaneous and without much thought to the potential problems in integrating organization cultures. AT&T's acquisition of NCR in the early 1990s yielded negative results owing to the disparate nature of the corporate cultures in the organizations. NCR's strong conservative (hierarchical) culture was at odds with the open work environment at AT&T (Carey and Ogden, 1998). Managerial ignorance results in blinding the firm from seeing external threats that will often emerge spontaneously. Actions of the firm arising out of ignorance lead to shocking unintended consequences such as eliciting strong retaliation from competitors, attracting environmental lobbyists or legal actions.

As proclaimed by Sun Tzu centuries ago, know yourself and know your enemy, a hundred battles without peril. Take a good look at your own firm. Do an internal audit from time to time and assess your strengths and weakness. Know your competitive advantage and the underlying sources, for what you don't know may cost you.

Managerial Negligence

Negligence and the lack of rewards, support, and non-acknowledgement of skunk works in a firm where innovation lies at the heart of its competition could also cause the firm to lose its advantage *vis-à-vis* rivals. For instance, the negligence of the top brass at Baring's Bank of UK went so far as to let a self-illusioned trader's bogus trading practice go unnoticed for so long that the accumulating loss almost rocked the bottom of this one of the most prestigious financial institutions in the history of UK.

A firm's top management might vaguely know its competitive advantage and its underlying basis; however, they might not be alert enough to match advantageous resource positions with emerging opportunity lines and commercial viability. Furthermore, failure in detecting accruing errors and, worse yet, failure in taking corrective measures, often give away a firm's once enviable position, destroying its competitive advantage.

Managerial Arrogance and Self-Aggrandizement

Arrogance is a not an uncommon trait of successful leaders. Arrogance leads to complacency and as a result, firms develop blind spots to threats in the competitive environment. Blind spots make the firm highly vulnerable to spontaneous attack from competitors.

Success doesn't beget success. Success begets failure because the more that you know a thing works, the less likely you are to think that it won't work When you've had a long string of victories, it's harder to foresee your own vulnerabilities.

Leslie Wexner
CEO, The Limited, Inc.

Successful firms have their own paradigms that make them blind and shifts in paradigms are required to bring about change (Kuhn, 1962). Mainframe computers are the basis of IBM's dominance and its reluctance to accept the advent of personal computers led to the erosion of competitive advantage. The same core competencies that help firms gain competitive advantage become core rigidities due to inflexibility and shortsightedness. Think about the engineering and organizational apparatus Henry Ford set up for the making of the once perfect "Model T."

The arrogance of the strong incumbents often blindfolds their top management teams and creates illusions that they are invincible. What worked before will always work. As such, they unjustly belittle their rivals, mock their presence, and allow their smaller rivals essentially unchallenged space to grow and experiment, until the rivals become too big to contain and too powerful to defeat. Think about Honda's famous entry into the US motorcycle market, when Harley Davidsons alike thought the Hondas were toys.

On the other hand, chief executives of firms experiencing huge and rapid success are prone to actions that have more to do with ego fulfillment than in the interest of the firm. The recently beleaguered Disney boss Michael Eisner had long been hailed as one of the most successful and celebrated CEOs corporate America ever witnessed, in a rank that is no less than that of Jack Welch. His achievement was secured through aggressive revamping of the Disney theme park business and decisive injection of strong doses of much needed creative power in its animation pictures. In the last 10 years, however, Eisner's suffocating micro management style, flat refusal to name a clear second in command and heir apparent, and super-sized compensation package even when Disney's stocks plummeted and failed to excite Wall Street all help contributed to his loss of confidence (*Business Week*, 2004). The once unassailable Disney reputation and its host of competitive advantages in customer goodwill, creative prowess, and service quality, etc. quickly fizzled into past memories.

Mickey Mouse was perhaps a star larger than life. Eisner turned out to be even a bigger star than Mickey. In turbulent waters, a visionary and a decisive leader may save a firm from downward spiral and financial distress. The irony is, however, that the same decisiveness or maybe tyrannical power (Ma, et al., 2004) that once worked wonders may not be tolerated anymore when the firm's performance is, again, in perennial distress. When a celebrated CEO's ego has to be massaged at the cost of the firm's long-term success and its wealth creation, both the CEO and the firm lose.

Managerial Miscalculation

A firm's competitive advantage could be destroyed through its own purposeful (in) action, carefully calculated strategic moves. At least two types of action are observed that destroy or terminate competitive advantage: firms either don't appreciate the current competitive advantage or don't want the advantage, often an inter-play of the two concerns.

A firm may not appreciate a particular competitive advantage and easily gives it away. For instance, a major personal care firm in Shanghai owned a well-known brand in Maxim. Yet with its merger with a foreign firm, it sold its brand name to a lesser competitor and used instead the foreign brand of its merging partners. Years later, it found that the sold brand was indeed a very popular one still attracting many loyal customers. The firm had to buy back this brand. However, the huge cost incurred in buying back the brand name taxed the firm heavily.

Similarly, under-appreciation of a firm's brand image may also reflect in a firm's choice to over diversify and lose its distinctiveness. For instance, Liz Claiborne, by diversifying in essentially every segment of the clothing business, washed down its distinguished image among professional women, their original target customers. Its competitive advantage against other designers in the "career" segment for professional women largely diminished, although it gained advantage in overall scale (Hill and Jones, 1996).

Decisions to make trade-offs to pursue or enhance other advantages result in termination of existing competitive advantage. Think about Intel's exit from the memory chip business and entry in to the microprocessor business. Think about Ted Tuner's move from the highly profitable billboard business he inherited to the television business. A firm has to know when to forgo an advantage (often a diminishing or potentially obsolete one) to gain a more important one for the future.

It pays in certain cases to make the right trade-off decisions, as I will explain in more detail in Chapter 9 when I discuss the management of a firm's constellation of competitive advantage as a whole. It may also cause a firm dearly in sustaining its competitive advantage when trade-off decisions (e.g., don't want a particular asset in a corporate portfolio) that are hastily made and lack convincing rationale and justifications. For instance, IDG, an early mover into the Chinese market, had achieved great success in its publishing business and information services, as well as its venture capital investment of various kinds. However, its gross miscalculation in prematurely dumping its shares in SOHU (one of the top three portals and a popular Internet site in China) at its rock-bottom price cost IDG a fortune, putting a major dent on its constellation of advantages.

EXTERNAL TRIGGERS OF DESTRUCTION

Competitive Imitation

Imitation by competitors drives down pioneering firm's competitive advantage (D'Aveni, 1994). Imitation often reduces the differential between the pioneering firm and the imitators in technological know-how, product distinctiveness, and manufacturing costs, hence destroying pioneering firm's competitive advantage. For instance, although Intel pioneered the PC memory device business, the Japanese firms that quickly imitated Intel's products and technology eventually drove Intel to make a deliberate decision to exit the business.

Apple's Macintosh derived its superiority and uniqueness from its graphical user interface (GUI), originally invented at Xerox's Palo Alto Research Center. Graph icons and the use of mouse to click on icons represented a big difference in the ease and convenience offered by rival PCs running on Microsoft's DOS operating systems. Microsoft's ingenuity lies in its ready willingness to develop application programs ability to learn about the GUI through its efforts to develop application programs for the Macintosh. The stealthy imitation by Microsoft resulted in the eventual dominance of the Windows operating system, nullifying the advantage held by Apple.

Imitation could be competitive suicide, as the imitator is trying to play incumbent leaders in the leaders' home courts where they claim superiority in market and/or resource positions (Hamel and Prahalad, 1989). Imitation, however, with innovative twist, may well turn the table against the leaders. Consider the rise of Japanese and Korean firms again Intel in the memory device business. Or consider Samsung, a latecomer, against Sony, a widely acknowledged pioneer (Ungson, Steers, and Park, 1997). Don't write off a humble imitator easily. Imitation is the sincerest form of flattering. Imitation is also the most deadly sugarcoated bullet that kills.

Competitive Substitution

Competitor's substitution can happen at both the product level and the technology level. First, a rival could neutralize a firm's product advantage by offering a substitute product that matches or surpasses the quality and/or function of the firm's product, or one that simply downplays the uniqueness of the firm's product. For instance, Compaq's IBM clone effectively neutralized IBM PC's competitive advantage by offering substitute products that were cheaper yet with the same function and technology. Second, a firm can use substitute technology to bypass the barrier of incumbent firm's technological advantage.

Amazon's entry into the book retailing industry was successful in eroding the advantage held by the leaders, Borders Group and Barnes & Noble. By leveraging the capabilities built to conduct commerce on the Internet Amazon substituted the conventional mode of book distribution, compelling the incumbents to incur large investments to ensure their survival. While Barnes & Noble survived the onslaught of a number of retailers online, Borders Group conceded victory and decided to partner with Amazon.

Substitution is often less easier to detect than direct imitation, which operates directly in the immediate domain of the leaders. A substitute firm often sails from a neighbor industry or areas outside the leaders' radar. Incumbent leaders may not clearly identify the substitutors as serious threats due to the rivals' seemingly non-threatening manner in its initial foray into the blind spot of leaders' competitive maps. Direct imitation reduces incumbent leaders' action space and chips away their advantageous positions. Substitutors move the mountain and sea. They make the leaders' games irrelevant and their corresponding core competence obsolete.

Sabotage

Sabotage refers to the acts of sabotage competitors undertake to undermine the advantage of leaders and pioneers in the industry. Ensuing legal battles are waged at a great cost resulting in the victory of the mightier and loss of the pioneer. Microsoft forced its way to become the dominant player in the Internet browser market by bundling their product with their operating system and by insisting that PC manufacturers load the browser on the desktop. Knowledge intensive industries such as pharmaceuticals and software are constantly under the threat of deliberate patent infringements. While it is possible for pioneers to protect their intellectual property rights, there are immense possibilities for acts of sabotage by rivals.

For instance, Cipla Ltd. a pharmaceutical manufacturer in India introduced generic AIDS drugs and offered to sell at $ 350 per patient annually compared to $ 15,000 for patented drugs from the pioneers of AIDS drugs such as Bristol-Myers Squibb and GlaxoSmithKline. AIDS being a serious problem in poor developing countries, the move made by CIPLA is an act of sabotage detrimental to the massive investments of leaders in the industry. Any move made to protect the patent rights, however legal is not viewed sympathetically with an acute need for affordable AIDS treatment.

(Anti) Competitive acts of sabotage are best dealt with proactive measures. Anticipation of rivals' actions and containment strategies are the best hope against sabotage. Containment strategies not involve defensive posturing, such as litigation but also offensive actions that will prevent acts of sabotage by competitors. Cooperation and co-option of potential competitors help create disincentives for any damage inflicting activity. Multinational pharmaceutical firms now set up shop in India by entering into cooperative agreements and establishing wholly owned subsidiaries.

Paradigm Shift

Paradigm shifts in the environment can invalidate competitive advantages of certain firms. Specifically, changes in social cultural trends, technological developments, and government regulations are among the major causes that could destroy certain firms' competitive advantage.

First, cultural trends change consumers' perception of different firms in an asymmetrical fashion, creating competitive advantage for some firms while destroying competitive advantage of others. For instance, the health craze in America in the past two decades severely tarnished the brand-image advantage of KFC while helping make possible the promotional advantages of firms like Nike (Miller, 1993).

Second, changes in government regulation also affect a firm's competitive advantage. For instance, the competitive advantages of the major tobacco makers were diminished by increasing governmental regulation (Miles, 1982). Similarly, the deregulation of the commercial banking industry brought a huge wave of consolidation, making the prior competitive advantage of many regional banks disappear because they now have to compete against larger-scale national banks.

Third, technological advancement, e.g., information technology, can also affect firms in asymmetrical fashion, therefore, redefining the relative position of firms on certain strategic dimensions. For instance, the advent of the Internet and the advancement of digital technology allowed smaller players in the encyclopedia business to challenge the dominance of Encyclopedia Britannica, whose sales force was unmatched. On-line offering of encyclopedia type of products largely changed the intense personal selling nature of the business, making Encyclopedia's advantage in huge sales force largely obsolete (Evans and Wurster, 1997).

Environmental shifts often redefine the relevance of participating firms' resources and capabilities in a new round of competition. They may threaten the leaders' positions from places where the leaders expect the least. General or macro environmental factors, e.g., political upheaval, social culture trend, technological advancement, etc. may rock the foundation of leading firms. Yet, these factors are not exactly initiated by imitators or substitutors, which make them even less easy to monitor and pay due attention to. The challenge to incumbent leaders is therefore even more daunting in this scenario.

Off course, relating to environmental changes, there's also the case of bad luck and crisis. Avian flu in Asia poses a great threat to KFC's advantage built on their motto "We do chicken right". Similarly, the public's fear for mouth and feet disease had severely hurt the entire beef producing and marketing industry in North America and beyond.

Crisis management is the key to prevent the loss of competitive advantage due to unforeseen events. Johnson & Johnson narrowly escaped their precarious situation following the deaths caused by Cyanide laced Tylenol tablets in 1982. Quick response and creative remedy under tragic or bad luck situation should be even more of a virtuous deed. This should be true especially for single product line firms, for they have nowhere else to escape to and nothing else to lean on.

THE MULTITUDE OF CHALLENGES TO SUSTAINABILITY

Examples abound of leading firms who lost their way in the sustainability game across a wide range of industries. Some of the erstwhile leaders closed shop and some are struggling to keep afloat in the turbulent waters.

Fading Glories of Yesteryear Leaders

For more than a century, Eastman Kodak was a successful pioneer in the photography industry. Eastman Kodak was to the photography industry as Ford was to the automobile industry and yet it lost the advantage it enjoyed in the industry. Is it because of the new entrants armed with new technology or is it because of Kodak's refusal to embrace the changing trends in consumer preferences?

Sears, Roebuck and Co. is the quintessential American retail giant that experienced near death experiences despite its glorious past. By 1999, Wal-Mart and Home Depot crept into the list of the thirty Dow Jones Industrial Average companies unseating Sears, which was part of the list since 1924. Is Sears not aware of its image that compelled it to reach Lands' End or is it really a well thought out move to bolster its flailing reputation?

Brilliant and innovative business ideas propelled Enron from a distributor of natural gas and owner of a large network of gas pipelines to a gigantic "market maker". It is now common knowledge that Enron collapsed. Is it the case of a few rotten bad apples or is the firm doomed to be a natural victim of its own meteoric rise?

So many challenges are to sustainability. So scant is due managerial attention. So fragile is the control and monitoring system, internal and external. Moreover, challenges to sustainability, forces and triggers both internal and external, often work together and jointly erode a firm's competitive advantage. This makes the general managers' job especially tough.

Multiple Triggers at Work: The Interaction Effects

In March 2004, Kodak was kicked out of the Dow Jones Industrial Average. An American icon and pioneer and once giant in the photography industry, Kodak proves to be an excellent example of how a company lost its competitive advantage and how a company attempts to survive the sustainability game.

Initially, Kodak *ignored* the potential threat from advances in digital photography. Later Kodak was compelled to pay attention to the promise of digital technology in imaging. Despite its initial attempt at investments in R&D, Kodak *neglected* the comprehensive nature of digital photography markets. The major *environment shift* caused by advances in technology enacted out Moore's law in the digital camera markets. In 2001, digital cameras became extremely popular and the trends suggested that digital photography is bound to overtake the market for traditional photography.

Kodak decided to focus on the application of digital technology in wholesale and retail photofinishing and by expanding their presence in emerging film markets. Kodak was *arrogant* enough to wager on the potential of markets for film photography in India, China and other Asian countries with the assumption that the consumers in such developing countries cannot afford the high prices of digital cameras. Currently, the trends suggest that digital photography is slowly becoming the norm in the rapidly growing economies of India and China (*Financial Times*, 2004)

Rapid growth in digital technology had an impact on Kodak's current financial situation and position within the camera and film industry. Specifically, digital technology threatened Kodak's mainstay film-based segment. Dynamics within the market have Kodak on the defensive and reacting aggressively by engaging in fierce price-cutting tactics with the risk of losing profitability from its film segment and the further risk of losing its status as the leading film manufacturer.

Thus, Kodak's future health faces a double threat. On one side, competitors such as Fuji are chipping away at Kodak's profitable consumer film business. On the other, the technology revolution (the explosion of the Internet and advancements in digital technology) is undermining Kodak's conventional camera and film interests.

Kodak's initial ignorance, followed by its negligence and its arrogant posture combined with the major shift in the technological environment caused by the convergence of several industries attracted a host of new and formidable competitors. Kodak found itself in unfamiliar territories included desktop printing and digital storage. Taking advantage of Kodak's reluctance to enter the digital market rivals like Sony made aggressive entry into the market and developed the market by taking a lead in setting standards. Kodak is now alleging that Sony's infringement of Kodak's patents is an act of *sabotage*.

CONCLUDING REMARKS

In this chapter, I presented an array of examples from various industries illustrating the numerous ways in which leaders could not sustain their respective competitive advantages. The framework summarizing the triggers and forces that challenge sustainability of competitive advantage has important and practical managerial implications.

In the world of business, firms win or lose and leaders come and go. Unlike sports where one can toil in minor leagues for life, business has no minor league—you lose, you are out, there's rarely any lasting place for the mediocre (Wernerfelt, 1984). Unlike Hollywood where an actress could win an Oscar way in her 80s, CEOs enjoy no luxury of multiple failing roles. They worry about achieving competitive advantages when they don't have possession of them. They worry about losing them once they possess them, thirsting for even more.

While Andy Grove claims that "only the paranoid survives" or Ted Turner believes that "perhaps the only way to be secure is to never to feel secure," Ralph Waldo Emerson long ago remarked that: "Every hero becomes a bore." Well, some sooner. Some not. It is perhaps against human nature to ask the leaders to be always on the alert. Complacency and arrogance seem so natural when a leader is showered in success. Yet, awareness of the various potential pitfalls, I hope, will help the heroes last longer.

Chapter 8 Competitive Advantage and Firm Performance

Competitive advantage is perhaps the most widely used term in strategy that remains, however, poorly defined and operationalized. This chapter makes three observations regarding competitive advantage and conceptually explores the various patterns of relationship between competitive advantage and firm performance. First, competitive advantage does not equate superior performance. Second, competitive advantage is a relational term. Third, competitive is context-specific. It examines three patterns of relationship between competitive advantage and firm performance: (1) competitive advantage leads to superior performance; (2) competitive advantage without superior performance, and (3) superior performance without competitive advantage. The ultimate purpose of this chapter is to help generate a healthy debate among strategy scholars and practitioners on the usefulness of the competitive advantage construct.

As I conclude the first part of the book, it provides an opportune time to reflect on and improve over our working definition of competitive advantage offered in Chapter 1 and systematically explore the effect of competitive advantage on firm performance, the ultimate score card of general managers. The notion of competitive advantage has been a cornerstone of our field. As such, research on competitive advantage occupies a central position in strategy literature (e.g., Porter,

1980, 1985; Rumelt, 1984, 1987; Barney, 1986a, 1991; Ghemawat, 1986, 1991; Peteraf, 1993; Teece, Pisano, and Shuen, 1997). However, the notion of competitive advantage itself has rarely been systematically addressed and, to date, remains poorly defined and operationalized. Is competitive advantage what it takes to compete, a characterization observed during competition, or an outcome of competition? Is competitive advantage contingent on the competitive situation or is it a more general trait of the firm? Put differently, how is competitive advantage different from competence, strengths, and, ultimately, performance?

This chapter, addressing the above questions, makes three observations regarding competitive advantage. First, competitive advantage does not equate (superior) performance. Second, competitive advantage is a relational construct. Third, competitive advantage is context-specific. In presenting these three observations, this chapter proposes suggestions to refine and operationalize "competitive advantage." It then conceptually explores the relationship between competitive advantage and performance, which is argued to be much more complex than it is currently being treated in the literature. Concluding remarks follow.

COMPETITIVE ADVANTAGE IS NOT PERFORMANCE

The structural approach (Porter, 1980, 1981, 1985) and the resource-based view (RBV) (Wernerfelt, 1984; Rumelt, 1984; Barney, 1986a, 1991) are two dominant perspectives in strategy which purport to explain competitive advantage, sustainable advantage in particular. It seems, however, that neither perspective readily differentiates competitive advantage from superior performance. Instead, they are treated more as interchangeable constructs.

Competitive Advantage: The Structural Approach

The structural approach rooted in IO economics posits that strong defensible market position (read power) in an attractive industry renders sustained competitive advantage (Porter, 1980, 1985). Here, industry positioning plays an important role in determining the firm's competitive advantage. Using the structural approach, Porter (1980) advances the industry analysis framework (five-forces) whose "ultimate function is to explain the *sustainability* of profits against bargaining and against direct and indirect competition." (Porter, 1991: 100, *emphasis original*). To achieve sustainable profit, a firm needs sustainable advantage, in either cost or differentiation (Porter, 1980, 1985).

In this sense, Porter defines competitive advantage in rather specific and concrete ways that seem to implicitly equate competitive advantage to profitability (performance), and sustainable advantage to sustainable profitability. That is, competitive advantage is treated as an outcome (of positioning) and should be pursued as an end in itself. An important question arises: Is either cost advantage or differentiation advantage sufficient and necessary for superior performance? If the answer is no, then we should perhaps conclude that competitive advantage, within Porter's perspective (1980, 1985) at least, does not equate performance.

A government-sponsored near-monopoly firm in certain industries, for instance, could enjoy high profit without either cost advantage or differentiation advantage over rivals. Also, it is highly conceivable that the firm with the lowest cost in a market may not enjoy better performance than a rival that happens to have (for whatever reason) overwhelming advantage in access to distribution. Although competitive advantage in cost or differentiation may increase the likelihood of better performance, competitive advantage *per se* is not the same as performance. At least, cost advantage and differentiation advantage, two generic types identified by Porter (1980), are not necessarily the ultimate determinants of performance. Superior performance could also come from other types of competitive advantage, e.g., speed (Stalk, 1990; Eisenhardt and Brown, 1998) or flexibility (Sanchez, 1993, 1995), or perhaps more practically, combinations of multiple competitive advantages.

As such, maybe we should not use the general term competitive advantage as a surrogate for superior performance, nor should we assume that competitive advantage, whatever type, automatically leads to superior performance. Competitive advantage and performance are two different constructs and their relationship seems to be complex.

Competitive Advantage: The Resource-Based View

The RBV (Rumelt, 1984, 1987; Barney, 1986a, 1991; Dierickx and Cool, 1989; Grant, 1991) provides another perspective on competitive advantage, which is hailed as a possible paradigm capable of elucidating and integrating research in all areas of strategy (Peteraf, 1993). The basic tenet of the resource-based view is that unique resources are the sources of sustained competitive advantage (Barney, 1991). To generate such advantage, a resource must be rare, valuable, inimitable, non-tradable, and non-substitutable, as well as firm specific (cf. Barney, 1986a, 1991; Dierickx and Cool, 1989; Grant, 1991).

A notable work is the integrative account by Peteraf (1993) that summarizes the cornerstones of competitive advantage from the RBV. Heterogeneity in resource endowments provides competitive advantage (indicated by monopoly or Ricardian rents). Ex post limitation to competition sustains the rents. Imperfect mobility of the resources sustains the rents within the firm. Ex ante limits to competition guarantees that cost of securing resources not offset the economic rents.

In RBV, a firm's unique resource is treated as being inherently related to performance. The unique, inimitable, and immobile resource is valuable precisely in the sense that it generates economic rent (Barney, 1991). Here the linkage between competitive advantage (unique resources) and performance (economic rent) is more direct than that in Porter (1980): it does not even have to specify cost advantage, differentiation advantage, or any other types of competitive advantage. If a firm has valuable, rare, and inimitable resources, then superior performance ensues. That is, the definition of such resources (as the essence of sustained competitive advantage) already has inherent performance implications.

Several questions arise. Does the RBV assume that there is only one particular type of unique resource (hence one type of sustained advantage) in a particular industry? Does the prescription by the RBV preclude the situation where more than one firm can have such resource(s)? If firm A has resource X that fits the RBV prescription and firm B has resource Y that also meets the RBV criteria, then what determines which firm has competitive advantage over the other? Or does it matter? If we can identify the resources that bear the dictation by the RBV and use them to directly predict performance, do we still need constructs like competitive advantage or sustained competitive advantage?

Based on the above review of the two dominant perspectives on competitive advantage in our field, I come to the following tentative conclusions, which will be further elaborated on in later sections. First, competitive advantage and performance are two different constructs. Second, if competitive advantage, either defined by position or resource, is used casually as a surrogate of superior performance, it is not only redundant but also tautological. Third, competitive advantage, whatever type, does not guarantee superior performance. Finally, for competitive advantage to be a theoretically useful construct, it has to be better defined and operationalized.

COMPETITIVE ADVANTAGE IS A RELATIONAL TERM

In this section, I seek to understand competitive advantage at its most basic level of analysis and in the most basic form. I argue that competitive advantage is a relational term. It is essentially a comparison drawn between a focal firm and its rival(s) on certain dimension(s) of concern in competition. Specifically, I examine competitive advantage in the context of its reference point (Fiegenbaum, Hart, and Schendel, 1996) and according to its magnitude and composition, and comment on its operationalization.

Reference Point

Competitive advantage, as a relational term, depends on the reference point. That is, we must answer the question such as "against whom?" and "on what?" Does competitive advantage mean that one firm must be superior than all rivals? Or does competitive advantage mean only to be a pair-wise comparison between two rivals of concern? Porter's (1980) description of the cost leader advantage seems to suggest that the cost leader has absolutely the lowest cost position among all firms in an industry, hence perhaps his justification for equating such (cost) competitive advantage to superior performance.

In reality, however, competitive advantage could be, and often is, assessed between any pair of rivals on certain dimension(s) that has competitive ramifications. For instance, among three chain stores A, B, and C that compete in an industry where, say, number of locations is a major area of competition, A has the largest number, B the middle, and C the smallest. Then we could infer that, assuming the number of locations is of linear importance in competition, firm A has competitive advantage over B, which in turn has competitive advantage over

C. In this case, we can compare a particular firm with the other two; we can also choose any two focal firms of interest to conduct pair-wise comparison. Such pair-wise comparison on a specific and discrete dimension of competition features competitive advantage in its most basic form and at its most basic level of analysis.

Notice that such conception of competitive advantage separates competitive advantage from firm performance, treating them as distinct constructs. Firm A may have more locations than Firm B, but Firm B may have more sales volume per location due to competitive advantages in other areas, e.g., merchandise selection and service quality. In this sense, Firm B may actually have better performance (profitability) than Firm A. However, just because Firm B performs better than Firm A does not mean that Firm A doesn't have competitive advantage over Firm B in terms of number of locations. It simply means that there are often multiple dimensions of competition that jointly determine firm performance. A firm may have to have multiple competitive advantages to enjoy superior performance.

In this sense competitive advantage is not an undifferentiated, overall determinant of performance. It is a firm's relational score on a particular competitive dimension *vis-à-vis* that of rivals that may contribute to superior performance. However, we shall not deny the possibility where one dimension of competition single-handedly determines performance and hence competitive advantage on that dimension is the determinant of superior performance. This is only a special case within the general conception of competitive advantage discussed above.

In summary, I propose the following definition of competitive advantage: the differential between two competitors on any conceivable dimension that allows one to better create customer value than the other. This definition builds on Porter (1985) in emphasizing the importance of creating customer value. It moves down from the generic types of competitive advantage, i.e., cost and differentiation, to a more basic level and form of competitive advantage. In addition, this definition also facilitates the operationalization of the construct: first identify the dimension of competition and then compare a pair of firms against this dimension. It provides a baseline understanding of competitive advantage and readily accommodates the description of competitive advantage by both the structural approach and the RBV, two dominant perspectives in our field. This said, however, competitive advantage is still an elusive construct, like transaction cost (Williamson, 1991) in the choice of market and hierarchies, mutual forbearance in multipoint competition (Gimeno and Woo, 1996), and employee participation in organizational behavior (Ledford and Lawler, 1994), we could infer its presence and function but could not easily capture or measure it directly.

Magnitude

Given the above definition, two types of competitive advantage can be conceived: heterogeneous (binary) vs. homogenous (differential). The resource-based view hinges on the concept of resource heterogeneity (Rumelt, 1984, 1987; Barney, 1986a, 1991). Moreover, Barney (1991) treats sustained competitive advantage as an equilibrium term: all attempts to imitate a valuable, rare, and difficult-to-imitate resource cease to exist. In this sense, resource heterogeneity sustains, hence competitive advantage sustains. Here heterogeneity seems to suggests that one firm possesses a unique resource and other firms could not imitate or match it. The differential among them, theoretically, approaches infinity.

Presented in its strongest form: you either have it or you don't. Those who have it have competitive advantage; those who don't don't. Similar to Porter's conception of cost advantage (1980), here the RBV also focuses on the situation of "best of all" instead of merely pair-wise comparisons among competitors. The examples of such valuable, unique, and difficult-to-imitate resources certainly abound, e.g., De Beers monopoly of supply of raw diamond and Coca-Cola's brand name (in a league of its own). However, there also exists vast competitive space where imitation is prevalent and competitive advantage, if any, is only relative and temporal (D'Aveni, 1994): no where to run, no where to hide, the only option is to fight in hypercompetition.

If firms by and large could imitate rivals' resources and products, then these firms are by definition competing on some common dimensions. In such cases, on these common dimensions at least, competitive advantage is the differential between rivals, regardless of whether some of them also have heterogeneous competitive advantage based on other unique dimensions of resources or products. Such differential in (homogenous) firm resources is perhaps the most commonly observed form of competitive advantage, e.g., productivity and other efficiency-related factors.

Composition

Another important concern is the composition of competitive advantage. A competitive advantage could be a discrete one based on a firm's differential with a rival on one specific dimension of competition, e.g., presence at the retail shelf space. A competitive advantage could also be a compound of multiple individual advantages that work together as an integrative whole. In this sense, a compound advantage can be regarded as a higher-order advantage to a discrete advantage. For instance, Wal-Mart's competitive advantage in low cost is a compound of multiple discrete competitive advantages that include location, information technology, warehouse and transportation systems, and corporate culture, among others (Ghemawat, 1991).

Although many discrete competitive advantages could contribute to a firm's performance directly, e.g., dominance of retail shelf space, they also contribute to form compound competitive advantages, which in turn contribute to firm performance. Typical compound competitive advantages include efficiency of organization and production process (cost advantage) and quality and innovation in products (differentiation advantage) (Porter, 1980), and speed and flexibility of market response (Stalk, 1990; Sanchez, 1995). The more compound a competitive advantage, the closer it is to have direct performance implication in the causal chain of performance analysis.

Operationalization

Regarding operationalization of competitive advantage, some cautions have to be taken. Although I define competitive advantage as differential between a pair of rivals, the direction of the differential is of importance. This may cause problems especially when the "pairwise" assumption is violated, e.g., statistical analysis done on a large sample of subjects, where firms' relative competitive advantage is determined by their score on certain dimensions. Take again the store chains as an example. The number of locations may not have a linear effect on competition and value creation. After a certain critical number has been reached, increases in number of locations will likely cannibalize a chain's own stores, reaching into less densely populated areas, and diminishing headquarters managerial attention to individual stores.

As such, uncritical use of the raw scores of a group of firms on a certain dimension that has implication for competitive advantage does not always capture the essence of competitive advantage. This is especially true when the underlying dimension of competitive advantage has an curvilinear effect, e.g., extent of diversification (Rumelt, 1974). As such, the same amount of differential may not mean the same degree of competitive advantage, and a positive differential on the very same dimension may mean competitive advantage in one situation, i.e., between a pair of firms below the optimal point, but competitive disadvantage in another, i.e., between a pair of firms beyond the optimal point.

Moreover, the measurement of compound competitive advantage

may pose even more problems. It is so because of the multiple dimensions involved and a compound competitive advantage may not be a simple summation of individual competitive advantages. As such, the traditional measures of adding scores from multiple dimensions as well as the bilateral linkage between a variable and performance featured in typical statistical analyses may not always capture the essence of such compound competitive advantage. So far as analysis is concerned, simultaneous modeling, e.g., Data Envelopment Analysis (DEA) (Chance, Cooper, Lewin, and Seiford, 1994), and other more sophisticated methodologies which capture a firm's position against a rival on multiple frontiers at the same time seem to be more appropriate analytical tools.

COMPETITIVE ADVANTAGE IS CONTEXT-SPECIFIC

Competitive advantage is a relational term between a focal firm and rival(s) within a specific context of competition. Competitive advantage is not a universal, general, and overall characterization of a firm or certain aspects of a firm. Similar terms to competitive advantage could be found in competence and strengths, which seem to be generally regarded as firm-specific traits, but are also argued to be meaningful primarily within a certain context. I first discuss the situational nature of these terms and then explore the context-specific nature of competitive advantage.

Prahalad and Hamel (1990) treat core competence as a unique set of resources and capabilities, both technical and organizational, which allows a firm to be competitive in a wide range of end product markets. However, core competence can also turn into core rigidity (Leonard-Barton, 1992). For instance, the highly skilled and sophisticated sales force of Encyclopedia Britannica used to be its core competence over lesser competitors. Yet with the advent of the digital era, that intense personal selling business has been transformed largely into one that values convenience and low cost, allowing lesser competitors to compete more effectively and diminishing the core competence of Britannica (Evans and Wurster, 1997).

Similarly, firm strengths is another term that is often used to refer to or imply competitive advantage (Leaned, Christensen, Andrews, and Guth, 1965; Andrews, 1971). But such a term is also argued to be highly situational in nature. Grant (1998: 13) observes:

> *Is Michael Eisner a strength or a weakness for Walt Disney Company? To the extent that he has masterminded Disney's revival over the past 14 years he is an outstanding strength. Yet his quadruple heart-bypass surgery and inability to implement a management succession plan suggest that he is also a weakness.*

To be sure, the terms strengths and weakness, in its original context of SWOT analysis (Learned et al., 1965), are used in conjunction with opportunities and threats that characterize a firm's external environment. The moral is that a firm's strategy should explore the fit between the firm and its environment. As such, strengths (and the underlying resources and traits they represented) are by definition dependent on the environmental context. It is not necessarily that the core competence and strengths *per se* that render competitive advantage. It is the fit between such firm attributes—strengths, resources, core competencies, capabilities, whichever is in vogue in the literature—with the requirement in specific competitive context that really matters.

Somehow this message seems to get lost in the past two decades or so in strategy research. The structural approach made the analysis of competitive environment more systematic and rigorous (Porter, 1980, 1985). The RBV, largely as a reaction to the structural approach (Wernerfelt, 1984), made the analysis of the firm more systematic and rigorous (Rumelt, 1984; Barney, 1991). Consequently, competitive advantage seems to be defined either as a market position (Porter, 1980) or resource position (Wernerfelt, 1984). Maybe it is high time that we revisit the message of fit embedded in the original SWOT framework and conceptualize competitive advantage accordingly, for neither market position nor firm resources and capabilities in themselves could illuminate the "ultimate" source of competitive advantage (Collis, 1994).

Recent research has already been pushing toward the direction of marrying the two dominant perspectives in out field. Mahoney and Pandian (1992) encourage the dialogue between the structural approach and the RBV and explore their similarities. Amit and Schoemaker (1993) propose mid-range concepts like strategic industry factors (industry requirement) and strategic assets (firm attributes) and argue that the overlap between the two creates competitive advantage. Teece, Pisano, and Shuen (1997), advocating the dynamic capability approach, calling attention to the importance of "identifying new market opportunities and organize effectively and efficiently to embrace them." That is, matching a firm's resources and capabilities along changing market opportunities (Collis, 1994) is a fundamental task in creating competitive advantage given its context-specific nature.

Consider the following example derived from an ancient Chinese anecdote. Two teams decide to engage in horse racing. Each of them has three horses, one in each of the three speed categories—slow, medium, and fast—with their respective speed distribution as follows—represented in rather stylized numbers to illustrate the point—in Figure 8.1. The race includes three rounds and winning is on a best 2 out of 3 basis. Given the relative resource strengths of each team, different lineups as presented in Figure 8.1 will definitely have different implications on the two teams' competitive advantage in each round of the race and the overall game. Clearly, whether a particular horse (resource) of the team creates competitive advantage or disadvantage depends on the competitive context.

Figure 8.1 Competitive Context and Competitive Advantage

	Line-up I		Line-up II	
Teams	A	B	A	B
Fast Horses	10 →	9	10 ↘	9
Medium Horses	8 →	7	8	7
Slow Horses	6 →	5	6 ↗	5

Team B is at competitive disadvantage in the first line-up, for every horse it has is weaker than that of Team A in each of the three categories. Using this line-up, Team B has no chance of winning at all. Yet, rule permitting, Team B could attempt the second line-up to concentrate its resources and create some local competitive advantages so as to win the total game. Instead of spreading its resources too thin, Team B could choose to focus on where it can create competitive advantage: running its faster horses against Team A's respective slower horses. Such maneuver creates a relative differential in strengths in certain points of contact with the rival. And the local competitive advantage gained in two rounds of the competition will translate into an overall competitive advantage and winning.

Fictitious example notwithstanding, it does help illustrate that competitive advantage is not only relational but also context-specific. In the strategy literature, in addition to the conceptual treatment reviewed earlier (Amit and Schoemaker, 1993; Collis, 1994; Teece et al., 1997), there also exists empirical evidence suggesting that a firm's competitive advantage, its effect at least, varies according to industry context. In an empirical study of firm performance, Wernerfelt and Montgomery (1986) raise the question "What is an attractive industry?" What their results demonstrate is that the answer to that question varies by firm, the cost structure of the firm to be specific. Industries with high growth rate are likely to shield inefficient firms while industries that are more stable make the inefficient firms particularly vulnerable. As such, a firm with a low cost position will have greater competitive advantage over a high cost rival in low-growth industries than if they are to compete in high-growth industries (Wernerfelt and Montgomery, 1986).

In summary, I have made the following observations so far: Competitive advantage does not equate to performance, although it could contribute to superior performance. Competitive advantage is a relational term characterizing a focal firm's comparison with rival(s) along any comparable dimension of competition. Whether or not a firm's particular attributes render competitive advantage depends on the competitive context. Finally, the relationship between competitive advantage and firm performance seems to be more complex than it is currently being treated in the literature, by either the structural perspective or the RBV.

COMPETITIVE ADVANTAGE AND PERFORMANCE

Competitive advantage and performance could have different patterns of relationship. I examine their relationship using the following three categories: (1) competitive advantage leads to superior performance; (2) competitive advantage without superior performance; and (3) superior performance without competitive advantage.

Competitive Advantage Leads to Superior Performance

Most research in strategy, with the structural perspective and the RBV as the epitome, focuses on this scenario. We can argue that competitive advantage helps a firm better create value for the customers hence contribute to firm performance. Discrete competitive advantages, e.g., the location of Wal-Mart stores' in the 1970s and 1980s (Ghemawat, 1991), on the one hand, contribute to firm performance directly. They also, on the other hand, contribute to the composition of compound competitive advantage, e.g., Wal-Mart's cost advantage, which in turn contributes to firm performance.

Such compound competitive advantages include, as discussed earlier, cost advantage and differentiation advantage (Porter, 1980), which are especially important in industries where the structural characteristics are likely to have long term ramifications for competition. Adding to these two basic types of competitive advantage are flexibility (Sanchez, 1983, 1985), speed (Stalk, 1990; Eisenhardt and Brown, 1998), and innovation (Hamel and Prahalad, 1989; Kim and Mauborgne, 1997, 1999), competitive advantages that are particularly important in high technology industries and other emerging industries.

In a bilateral fashion, competitive advantage, be it discrete or compound, resource-based (Barney, 1991) or market position based (Porter, 1980), is expected to be positively related to firm performance. However, given a pair of firms that compete in a particular market, to predict which firm has more superior performance requires more than bilateral analysis on any particular type of competitive advantage. In most cases, superior performance requires multiple competitive advantages over rivals (Stalk, et al., 1992; Teece et al., 1997). That is, it is often the combination of multiple competitive advantages that determines whether a firm has superior performance over rivals. This makes it possible the scenario that a firm may have many competitive advantages yet does not have superior performance, a scenario to which more space for discussion will be allotted, since the current scenario is already well documented in the literature.

Competitive Advantage without Superior Performance

There are at least four types of situations under which we could observe that a firm has competitive advantages yet does not enjoy superior performance: (1) a firm may have a discrete advantage that fail to develop into a compound advantage; (2) a firm may have a great competitive advantage over all rivals yet fail to fully tap its potential; (3) a firm may have multiple competitive advantages over a rival but does not have the right combination or lacks competitive advantage in one critical area, which could turn the table; and (4) management intentionally sacrifices a competitive advantage.

First, a discrete competitive advantage is more remote than compound competitive advantage within the causal chain in explaining firm performance. The more remote it is from performance in the causal chain, the more noise factors will overwhelm or diminish its effects. For instance, an organization may have the latest and the most sophisticated hardware, a discrete advantage in enhancing the efficiency of its operation. Yet, without the right people who are skilled, dedicated, and willing and able to learn (Pfeffer, 1994), this competitive advantage may not materialize into any compound advantage, e.g., speed, low cost, or flexibility, that can greatly contribute to performance. As such, this firm may not have superior performance over a rival firm that is at competitive disadvantage in the area of hardware but has a great routine built on the human expertise (Nelson and Winter, 1982; Winter, 1987).

Similarly, a chain store may have the greatest locations, but poor management could wash out that particular advantage and fail to establish any compound advantage, e.g., differentiation, cost, and flexibility, and create superior performance. It often takes competitive advantages in complementary areas to develop a particular discrete competitive advantage into a compound competitive advantage and contribute to firm performance more directly and greatly.

Second, a competitive advantage that potentially will have the greatest impact on the firm's competition and performance may not be clearly recognized and exploited by the firm. Although the RBV has articulated the conditions under which a resource could create sustained economic rents, it remains inconclusive on whether a firm could a priori systematically identify such resources (Barney, 1989; Dierickx and Cool, 1989). It is highly possible that, due to causal ambiguity and social complexity (Barney, 1991), a firm itself may not recognize its unique resources and exploit the potential competitive advantage it will render. Moreover, such resources underlying the potential competitive advantage may even be treated by management as waste or distractions if not being applied to a fitting competitive situation, a case attesting to the observation that competitive advantage is indeed context-specific.

The case in point is the Graphic User Interface (GUI) for PC developed at Xerox's Palo Alto Research Center (PARC) in the early stages of the PC business. Their technology in GUI design may prove the best weapon for creating a differentiation advantage in the PC business. Yet the leadership at Xerox decided to shelf this technology and go with other plans. Such a lack of understanding of its real competitive advantage at hand failed Xerox in its entry into the booming PC business, to say nothing of creating superior performance in that business (Hamel and Prahalad, 1994).

Apple Computer, learning from and improving on Xerox's GUI, went on to create the Macintosh line computers. Its competitive advantage in innovation and differentiation brought it superior performance. However, advantage in innovative products and differentiation can only go so far. Not being able to establish the industry standard among corporate users and failing to achieve cost advantage, partly due to lack of scale (installed base), both Apple's market standing and its performance suffered facing strong competition from Microsoft, which brings us to the next point.

Third, a firm may have competitive advantage in many or all but the most critical areas over rival(s) or it may lack the right combination of competitive advantages. Depending on competitive contexts, firm performance may be determined by just one critical dimension of competition or by a combination of multiple factors. For instance, in the winner-take-all industries (Hill, 1997), e.g., the VCR industry, success in controlling the industry standard could perhaps vindicate all competitive disadvantages in other areas. Sony, as a first mover, initially had many competitive advantages over JVC, e.g., innovation and differentiation. Yet losing in the industry standard war to JVC's VHS format due to lack of network building diminished Sony's many competitive advantages in the VCR business (Yoffie, 1990). Sony had to play the game according to the standard set by JVC and reduce its own β system into a niche product, hurting its performance in the business.

Often times, it also takes the right combination of competitive advantages to create superior performance. For instance, EMI, the first mover in the CT scanner business, used to possess advantages through its technological innovation and differentiation (Lieberman and Montgomery, 1988). Yet due to its relative small size, it did not have the resources to manufacture its products efficiently at a large scale and market them world-wide, hence lacking competitive advantages in cost and speed of market entry, advantages that are critical to quickly and firmly establish a global presence. GE, a later mover, armed with competitive advantage in cost, differentiation, and speed, quickly established a dominant presence globally, and nullified the first mover advantage of EMI in technology. GE's combination of advantages in multiple areas helped contribute to its superior performance in the business.

Finally, a firm's competitive advantage in certain area could be diminishing due to intentional sacrifice or trade-off made by the management. As such, the contribution of such competitive advantage to performance is losing momentum and the firm may not enjoy superior performance in that area of business. Consider Microsoft's Microsoft Network (MSN). It had a huge advantage over rivals, e.g., AOL, in reaching customers, because it was the only on-line service offered in bundle with Windows 95, hence automatically shipped with 90% of all new PCs sold in the world (Yoffie and Cusumano, 1999). However, in order to push its Internet Explorer (IE) and rival Netscape in the web browser business, Bill Gates decided to grant AOL similar status on Windows 95 in exchange of AOL's preferred treatment of IE on AOL.

Such a move certainly reduced the competitive advantage of MSN and hurt its performance. But for Microsoft the firm, it may be a wise move, for it boosted IE's market share, a critical market for the future. The competitive advantage Microsoft demonstrated in its speed of response and flexibility in maneuvering, in addition to its cost advantage (scale economy) and differentiation advantage (near monopoly) in its PC operating system business, may well contribute to the overall performance of the firm, saving the not so superior performance of MSN.

Superior Performance without Competitive Advantage

Can a firm have superior performance without competitive advantage? It depends on how we define competitive advantage and on the time span of analysis. Factors like governmental regulation (Baron, 1994; Bailey, 1997), luck (Barney, 1996a), and environmental shock (Meyer, 1982) could all alter the normal relationship between competitive advantage and firm performance. First, governmental regulations could artificially raise a firm's performance, e.g., profitability, by restricting competition and granting the focal firm monopoly or near monopoly power. Is such artificial monopoly competitive advantage or non-competitive advantage? If we treat governmental regulation as merely an external factor that shapes the context of competition, then the artificial advantage enjoyed by a firm should not be considered competitive advantage, especially when that firm has no real advantage whatsoever over potential competitors which are denied entry into its markets or reduced to peripheral players toiling in unattractive niches. Then this is clearly a case of a firm enjoy superior performance without competitive advantage. If we define competitive advantage broadly as including both market (economic) and non-market (political) advantages (e.g., Baron, 1994), then we can also argue that firms that are treated favorably by the government have competitive advantage in political skills, e.g., lobbying (D'Aveni, 1994).

Consider also the case where the government decides to offer subsidy to firms in certain business so as to make them cost competitive and encourage export. If the government only offer subsidy to firms whose cost is higher than certain level, then, at least in the short run, it is possible for the firm which is immediately above the threshold level to have better performance than the one immediately below the threshold level which does not receive governmental subsidy, although the latter has cost advantage over the former. In the long run, however, due to the help of the governmental subsidy, the former firm may indeed develop a competitive advantage over the latter. Second, the same logic could also be applied to the effect of luck (Barney, 1986a) and environmental shock (Meyer, 1982). A firm could enjoy better performance instantaneously over a rival which has competitive advantage, simply because the focal firm receives a one-time serendipitous boost to its profit due to pure luck. In the long run, such lucky incident may also have impact on the firm's resource base, creating sustainable competitive advantage. Such non-repeatable historical experience or path dependence explanation of resource-based advantage is well documented in the RBV literature (Rumelt, 1984; Barney, 1986a, 1991).

Similarly, a environmental shock or jolt (Meyer, 1982) could also alter firms' relative competitive advantages over each other. For instance, hospital A may have competitive advantage and superior performance over hospital B in the same geographic area. But a strike in hospital A may interrupt its operation and hurt the hospital tremendously. In the short run, hospital B may enjoy better performance than hospital A, although Hospital A still holds competitive advantage over hospital B. In the long run, if hospital A is not resilient enough organizationally, it may suffer demoralization, defecting of key personnel, and declining in service, reputation, and customer base, losing its competitive advantage.

Finally, time lag can also make possible the situation that even a firm's competitive advantage has diminished, but the residual customer good-will could still provide a one-time boost to the firm, showering it with superior performance for that specific period of time, even over rivals who do enjoy competitive advantage. This case also suggests that proper caution has to be exercised to take into consideration the time lag phenomenon when analyzing the relationship between competitive advantage and firm performance. That is, it may not make sense in certain cases to measure competitive advantage and performance at the same time point when studying competitive advantage-performance relationship. For instance, the current year R&D intensity does not necessarily captures a firm's competitive advantage in creativity or technical innovation in that particular year. As such, a higher intensity ratio does not suggest competitive advantage. Better understanding of the relationship between flow variable and stock variable on the competitive dimension of concern could help mitigate this problem (Dierickx and Cool, 1989).

CONCLUDING REMARKS

In this chapter, I have presented three observations on the construct of competitive advantage and conceptually explored competitive advantage as a relational and context-specific construct. I also attempted an examination of the complex relationship between competitive advantage and firm performance. Obviously, this chapter raises more questions than it answers.

One of the most important tasks facing us is that we have to decide on the ultimate research question, or the ultimate dependent variable, of our field. If competitive advantage and performance are essentially the same, then it doesn't matter which construct we use, we simply use the two terms interchangeably. This chapter has suggested, however, that competitive advantage and performance are indeed two different constructs. If our ultimate dependent variable is performance and the ultimate question "Why do firms differ in performance?" (Barney, 1994), then we have to justify why we need competitive advantage as an intermediate variable between its underlying dimensions and firm performance. If our ultimate dependent variable is simply competitive advantage, and whatever follows follows (i.e., superior performance as a natural benefit of competitive advantage), then we have to answer the question "How do you know an advantage when you see one?", i.e., the criteria we use to identify competitive advantage.

Overall, one conclusion seems to have emerged from the tour of literature that we have taken in this chapter. That is, for competitive advantage to be a theoretically meaningful construct for Strategy Management research, its definition must be more clearly and rigorously stated and its operationalizations better specified. Before we can do that, competitive advantage will only remain a heavily loaded term, used largely for convenience but not theoretical preciseness.

PART TWO
Constellation of Competitive Advantages

Chapter 9 ARTS: An Integrative Framework

To achieve persistent superior performance, a firm needs competitive advantages, a constellation of them. Superior firms typically do not do just one thing well; they often excel in multiple aspects. Nurturing an evolving constellation of multiple advantages and undertaking timely renewals help carry the firm through competition over time. To maintain healthy dynamics of a firm's constellation of advantage, the following tasks should be carefully attended to: establishment of dominant advantage which defines the firm's core purpose and identity; accumulation of supporting advantages to complete the constellation; amplification of complementary advantages for maximum performance; trade-off among competing advantages for long-term viability; and renewal of both dominant and supporting advantages, in adaptation to changes in the firm, competition, and the general environment. Knowledge of the relationship between and interaction of multiple advantages is essential for managing a firm's advantage constellation, a critical challenge facing general managers.

Winning firms often win because they know best how to create and renew a constellation of advantages: how to excel in doing multiple things well and how to change and adapt to new competitive situations. As such, viewing the firm as an evolving constellation of advantages is to say that a firm is a vehicle for winning.

A firm is a vehicle for winning.

Author

To help firms systematically analyze how to harness competitive advantages and win, an analytical framework can be advanced for understanding the dynamics of the firm's advantages as a constellation. Advantages come in various shapes and sizes and they evolve through time. Analyzing the constellation of a firm's advantages longitudinally allows us to observe competitive advantages in action, i.e., how individual advantages emerge, interact, and vanish; how the constellation changes and renews itself; and how its changing composition affects the firm's performance.

"Constellation of advantage" is defined as a host or system of competitive advantages that are of various causes and sustainability. Constellation of advantage is an evolving system. Its composition changes over time as existing advantages are eroded and new advantages arise. Every firm's constellation of advantage has its unique structure and dynamics. Understanding the key components of a typical constellation and the interaction among different advantages through time, however, helps general managers better attend to their advantage constellation.

CONSTELLATION OF ADVANTAGE: COMPONENTS AND DYNAMICS

A typical constellation comprises dominant advantage(s) and supporting advantages. See Figure 9.1. Dominant advantage(s) is the centerpiece of the constellation while the supporting ones make it more complete and effective. Some advantages are complementary that can amplify each other. Some advantages are competing ones that sometimes require trade-off. In addition to sustaining existing advantages, creating new advantages is needed to assure the long-term viability of the constellation. The major role of the general managers then is to strive for a healthy balance between various advantages in the firm's constellation and carry out timely renewal, in adaptation to changes in its environment, competitors, customers, and the firm itself.

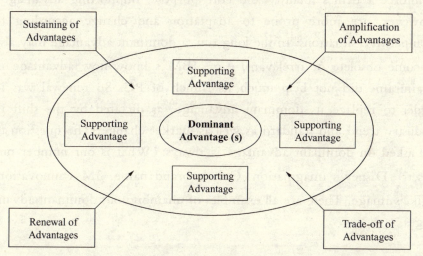

Figure 9.1 The ARTS in Managing Constellation of Competitive Advantage

We first explain the relative roles of dominant and supporting competitive advantages as the major components in a constellation and then use the ARTS framework (Amplification, Renewal, Trade-off, and Sustaining) to describe the dynamics of a constellation.

DOMINANT AND SUPPORTING ADVANTAGES

Dominant advantage helps define a firm's core purpose and identity. "At KFC, we do chicken right." And right is the slogan that captures a firm's distinctive competence and unique image. With the centerpiece in place, supporting advantages could be established to better serve the firm's mission. For instance, superior locations, prompt service, and clean room would all be possible areas for KFC to create supporting advantages. Similarly, while Canon's dominant advantage is its superior capability in image processing, its supporting advantages lie in its marketing savvy and manufacturing prowess.

Dominant advantages should be more sustainable so as to help reinforce a firm's identity and core purpose. Supporting advantages, however, are more prone to adaptation and change according to competitive situations. In the long run, a dominant advantage may also become obsolete or irrelevant, e.g., IBM's know-how advantage in mainframe did not help much its launch of PC. So renewal was in order to replace its dominant advantage, as dictated by the shift in industry trend and standard as well as market change. The question to be asked on dominant advantage is always:"What is our number one asset?" Disney's imagination. Coke's brand name. 3M's innovation. Nike's image. These are all examples of unambiguous dominant advantages.

THE ARTS FRAMEWORK

Amplification of Advantages

A dominant advantage could be amplified through a complementing advantage, even a borrowed one. Consider the DirecTV example. The dominant advantage of Hughes Electronics is in its satellite technology, not its competence in commercial viability. To launch its new venture in the commercial market, Hughes desperately needed to establish a cost advantage that few defense contractors could boast. So it took on RCA and Sony, more market savvy consumer electronics firms, as partners to supply its signal decoders for the customers and digital tape recorders and tapes for programming (*Business Week*,

1996a). In so doing, it was able to amplify its satellite technology by applying it to the commercial market, supported by access to partners' cost advantages.

As has become well known by now, partly due to the government's antitrust law suit, Microsoft has been constantly amplifying the effects of its advantage in the operating system business by bundling it with other products, e.g., Internet browsers. Similarly, in the original negotiation with IBM on the licensing agreement of the PC operating system, Microsoft insisted on being allowed to license the system to other makers of IBM compatible PCs. This move, aiming at attaining the largest installed base possible, helped enhance the status of the MSDOS Operating system as the *de facto* industry standard, amplifying its advantage to the scope of essentially the entire PC industry (*Fortune*, 1995c).

Renewal of Advantages

A firm's advantages need to be renewed to insure its continuous viability and persistent superior performance. Without ability to renew their dominant advantages facing the threat of computer-based word processors, major players in the typewriter business had to reduce their business to market niches, struggling for survival. During the PC revolution, IBM, on the other hand, was able to adapt to renew its advantage—at least for a while in the 1980s—in the computer industry through the introduction of its IBM PC, although its open architecture nature later gave away the advantage to Microsoft and Intel, which co-defined the Wintel format.

Facing hostile environmental changes, some of the major cigarette firms, however, fared much better in renewing their advantages due to their deep-pocket financial resources. For instance, the dominant advantage of Philip Morris used to be the brand name of its cigarette and skills relating to the making and selling of cigarettes. With the decline in the cigarette market due to increasing health concern and government regulation, Philip Morris was forced to seek new opportunities to sustain its growth and profit (Miles, 1982). As Philip Morris stands now at the top echelon of the *Fortune* 500 list, its dominant advantage has been its superior capability to market a host of food and drink products and other packaged goods essential to people's daily lives. Similarly, 3M has reinvented itself many times, from mining to manufacturing and from sandpaper to scotch tapes and post-it notes and to thousands of hi-tech products, always on the cutting edge of technology (Ghoshal and Bartlett, 1997).

Trade-off of Competing Advantages

A constellation sometimes hosts competing advantages. For instance, Reebok International and its acquired subsidiary, Avia, all possessed strong brand image, an advantage over most rivals in the business except for Nike. Should the firm let the two brands keep their independent images or should they assume a uniform identity? A trade-off had to be made. At one time in the late 1980s, backed by corporate policies that encouraged internal competition, the Avia division would run TV commercials that directly attacked the flagship Reebok brand (Miller, 1993). Apparently, such an attack did not help the firm's overall advantage in brand image.

In an evolving constellation, competing advantages also often vie for the position of the dominant advantage. Consider the example of *Encyclopaedia Britannica* (EB) mentioned earlier. Its dominant advantage used to be its authoritative content and credibility. In an intense personal selling business such as theirs, however, they had subsequently assembled a well-oiled machine in marketing and sales. And the content compiling itself would at certain points constitute only 5 percent of the total cost, and selling would consume the rest of the cost. Should the dominant advantage be anchored on the content providing or should it be on the salesforce? It appeared that sales prevailed. While CD-ROM and online reference burgeoned, readily available cheaper substitutes, inferior in content quality though, garnered enough customer attention. The sales of the printed version of multi-volume *Encyclopaedia Britannica* would plummet by 50 percent or so in the early 1990s (Evans and Wurster, 1997). Facing such a severe threat, EB has to work extra diligently to consolidate its position in the digital world. Should they choose to focus on authoritative content and reputation as their dominant advantage, would they have fared better facing new competition? Or, in anticipation of the advent of Internet and other digital-based forms of competition, could EB have been bold enough to cannibalize its own advantages in salesforces?

Sustaining of Advantages

There are at least two basic approaches toward sustaining of competitive advantage. The first one relies on unique resources (Barney, 2002) or defensible position (Porter, 1980) and tries to discourage imitation. This approach, more or less, assumes a once-and-for-all mentality. For instance, Xerox's technological leadership in document duplication and its enviable leasing and maintenance force used to serve as tremendous entry barriers against newcomers and provided the firm with a dominant position in the copier business. To further deter imitation, it protected its technology through 500 plus patents. Xerox's competitive advantage sustained for decades until Canon's worldwide attack against Xerox, armed with its own innovation and improved technology, design, and target marketing (Hamel and Prahalad, 1989).

The second approach relies on constant innovation to create a series of temporal advantages so as to sustain the firm's overall advantage through time, especially in the context of hypercompetition where firms constantly engage in intense rivalry (D'Aveni, 1994). For instance, Intel has been able to gain a series of competitive advantages through competitive maneuvering in its microprocessors business. Before competitors fully imitate any generation of its chips, it will come up with a newer generation to keep rivals at bay, even at the expense of cannibalizing its own products before they reach maturity. Such consecutive introduction of new products requires that the firm be persistently competitive and innovative. This is indeed a proactive approach toward the sustaining of competitive advantage in an industry where "only the paranoid survive" (Grove, 1996).

CONSTELLATION OF ADVANTAGE IN ACTION: THE WAL-MART CASE REVISITED

Location as Dominant Advantage

The single most important factor that launched Wal-Mart as a formidable player in the discount retailing industry was no doubt its initial choice of store locations. Targeting small rural towns underserved or not served at all by any large-scale discount retailers would prove to be a brilliant starting point, laying the foundation of Wal-Mart's low price strategy and its explosive and astronomical growth in the years that followed. This choice, highly imitable in its early years, was not much noticed and not matched by rivals. Once the locations were established, the strategy was, however, no longer easily imitable (Ghemawat, 1991). By then, Wal-Mart had already achieved monopoly and hence local scale economy in these locations that would deter entry. It had also gained expertise from its accumulated experience in site choice and store development that surpassed any rivals. Moreover, Wal-Mart was drying up the potential pool of ideal location candidates, moving from its stronghold in the South to eventually every continental state in the country.

The implementation of the location strategy was to saturate a market area by spreading out and filling in: to build stores following a pattern that its warehouses and distribution centers could reach them within one day's drive, and the district managers could control and take care of them. That set the outer boundary. And they then went on to fill the territory and saturate the region. This method also helped in enhancing and sustaining the location advantage. The saturation strategy left no room or loose bricks for rivals to break into Wal-Mart's strong sphere of influence. And the cluster of stores in a region demonstrated its commitment to serve and lead in the region, which helped deter new entry hence sustain its advantage. Kmart once tried to enter with three stores into the market of Springfield, Missouri where Wal-Mart had 40 stores within a 100 miles. Kmart found it miserably tough to play against Wal-Mart's concentrated strengths (Walton, 1992).

Capability-Based Dominant Advantage

As time went by, the initial location advantage that served Wal-Mart so well would, realistically speaking, become less powerful with its source for replenishment vanishing; and become more or less irrelevant for stores in more urban areas. Price competition would be intense as opposed to the rural areas where it had basically established a local monopolistic position. But remember, as a superbly managed firm, Wal-Mart is an advantage constellation. Should Wal-Mart have relied solely on its initial location advantage, it would be nowhere near where it is today in the American business landscape. It has throughout the years amassed multiple advantages at its service. All these individual advantages directly and indirectly translate themselves into Wal-Mart's ultimate dominant advantage: the ability to achieve low cost in merchandising. The low cost advantage, centerpiece of its everyday low price strategy, is based on knowledge and efficient business processes that help them do many things well and on ownership and access to superior resources and capabilities.

The dominant advantage of Wal-Mart has changed from its initial advantage in location to more capability-based efficiency advantage as they learned to serve the locations better. Wal-Mart's current dominant advantage lies in its knowledge and capability in moving the greatest quantities of goods in the most efficient way on earth: faster and cheaper. Consequently, the shape, size, components, and the configuration of the constellation have also changed with the change in dominant advantage. The constellation is now much more diverse and complete than it was before. Many of the advantages associated with or derived from the location advantage have more or less sustained, for 30 odd years, and lasted even till today.

Developing Supporting Advantages

During the early years, as Wal-Mart was busy enhancing and sustaining its location advantage, its then dominant advantage, other advantages would derive themselves from the location advantage. For instance, the market saturation strategy spread the Wal-Mart reputation by word of mouth in its rural market regions. This saved in no small amount in advertising costs. They could get by simply by using only one circular about every month—as opposed to rivals' frequent sale ads on paper and through other channels—a practice that they still use even today. They did not have to advertise and run special sales every now and then. The subsequently developed everyday low price policy would get the customers into the store and generate sales volume (Walton, 1992, p. 111).

Of supporting advantage, Wal-Mart could also boast its Store Opening Plan and its ability in tailoring store plans to suit different towns' needs: customized store building. Supporting advantages also arose from their distribution center and warehouse system, plus their own trucking fleets whose drivers doubled as liaisons between stores and distribution centers, which all contributed to support the market saturation strategy and the overall location advantage. These advantages combined, with the later addition of advanced information systems, enabled Wal-Mart to distribute merchandise from warehouses to stores within 48 hours and re-shelf a whole store about twice a week (Stalk et al., 1992).

Renewing Multiple Advantages

When it came to the 1980s and Wal-Mart began to push into the cities, they were already renewing its constellation with new advantages like, among others, established bargaining power over, and partnership with, vendors and suppliers; pioneering the comprehensive use of information technology; and developing advanced skills in inventory management. Wal-Mart's size or scale itself would provide bargaining power over vendors. With the use of information technology, they could easily track sales numbers and forecast trends and inventory needs for individual stores and company wide. Information technology also allowed Wal-Mart to share information with vendors that enabled them to better plan their production schedules to suit Wal-Mart's inventory need. Efficiency in communication and data exchange resulted in better management of vendor relationships. Wal-Mart would pay in shorter time than rivals. Vendors could offer better prices (Stalk et al., 1992). With the renewal of these new advantages, Wal-Mart left rivals even further behind. By the later 1980s, it was poised as a capability-based firm that grew out of their early reliance on a constellation dominated by location advantage.

Amplifying Extant Advantages

The advantage over rivals furnished by Wal-Mart's efficient transportation system, warehouse to store communication, and inventory management system had already put Wal-Mart ahead of the game in distribution over the rivals. With the adoption of information technology, it put Wal-Mart's lead even further. Its satellite system, allowing for instantaneous communication and information sharing within the corporation, helped make their advantage in distribution and inventory management much stronger.

Wal-Mart did not only grow through expansion of the Wal-Mart stores at the retailing sector, it also expanded into the wholesales club segment. Often built next to Wal-Mart, its Sam's Clubs provided newer opportunities to exercise their muscle in location choice, customized store configuration, transportation and distribution; and further increased their size and buying power. As such, applying its existing advantages to multiple market opportunities amplified these advantages and also enhanced its overall cost advantage. Recently, Wal-Mart has also amplified its competitive advantage in distribution, inventory management, and greater scale economy by venturing into the grocery business, opening super Wal-Mart stores that combine supermarkets and retailing, which proved to be an increasingly significant source of Wal-Mart's domestic growth (*Fortune*, 1998).

Undertaking Trade-off and Renewal to Build a Better Future

Different advantages may conflict with each other. Sometimes they can be integrated and sometimes not. When integration is not possible, a trade-off or compromise has to be made. This requires the ability to see the big picture as well as self-discipline. In the early years of Walton's venture, he had already controlled more than a couple Ben and Franklin franchises. His advantages in variety store business abounded, ranking his the best in sales and profit in the entire chain and among the best in the region. Discount retailing then, however, only showed its potential and Walton, by launching Wal-Mart in small towns, was going against the industry's convention.

So a choice had to be made. One advantage had to be terminated, voluntarily. What advantages to gain, what future to build? It was discounting that triumphed. Walton was not narrow-minded by his success in managing variety stores. What he dreamed of and did was to chase and shape the future. It was a choice of potential advantage over established advantage, a shot at long-lasting advantage over a proven short-term advantage. It was decisively shedding-off the variety store mentality and a total embrace of the discounting concept (Walton, 1992, p. 125).

To seize an opportunity and to know when to forego an advantage.

As Wal-Mart masterfully manages the evolution of its constellation of advantages, even greater challenges lie ahead. Its continuous market saturation strategy might already have over-flooded the whole country, as evidenced by its 3,000 odd stores. How will they further grow? Is there any new trend arising in the retailing industry? What's the future of the industry like? Does Wal-Mart's current constellation of advantage enable them to build and shape that future? If not, how should the constellation adapt?

Searching for new growth opportunities, Wal-Mart has in the 1990s ventured into the world market, building stores in Canada, China, Mexico, and some other countries in Latin America (*Fortune*, 1998). What advantages they already have are still advantages in the global market? Given the poor infrastructure and lower living standard in some of the countries they entered, can Wal-Mart still position itself as a low price leader? What should their dominant advantages be in these countries, now and in the future? Are their current advantages and potential advantages domestically compatible with those needed internationally? What trade-off or integration has to be made?

Winners are the ones that look into the future, ahead of the rivals that is. Any one particular advantage in Wal-Mart's constellation might erode or terminate, but the constellation of advantage won't easily. Looking into the future, knowledge and capability in moving the greatest amounts of goods with the highest speed and lowest cost possible will still be the key for winning in retailing, domestic or international. Advantages that are based on such knowledge and capabilities and those that help further create or gain such knowledge and capabilities should be in the firm's advantage constellation.

CONCLUDING REMARKS

To win in the game of business, a firm needs competitive advantages, a constellation of them. As the example of Nike, GE, and Wal-Mart demonstrate, multiple advantages are needed to create persistent superior performance. Nurturing an evolving constellation of advantage will help carry the firm through competition over time.

General managers should strive to maintain healthy dynamics of the constellation, making trade-offs among competing advantages, balancing the relationship between dominant and supplementing advantages, leveraging and amplifying existing advantages, as well as replenishing the constellation with new advantages. Knowledge of the dynamics of the constellation is expected to help general managers in performing their fundamental task—to deliver persistent superior performance.

Chapter 10 Advantage-Based View of the Firm

This chapter elaborates on advantage-based view of the firm, which integrates major extant theories on competitive advantage. Treating the firm as an evolving constellation of competitive advantage determined by the firm's action, resource and capability, as well as market positions, this chapter juxtaposes the different schools of thoughts and theoretical paradigms that help inform a firm's constellation of competitive advantage. Taking a holistic approach, it also outlines some of the major practical challenges in maintaining a healthy constellation and calls for due managerial attentions in successfully dealing with them.

Faithful and aspiring pilgrims on the journey to the Holy Grail of competitive advantage often find themselves bombarded by various theories and perspectives that claim to provide *the* authoritative road map, *the* secret path, or the *newest* edition of the official travel guide. These theories and perspectives, among others, range from industry analysis (Porter, 1980, 1985) to the resource-based view (Barney, 1986a; Rumelt, 1984; Wernerfelt, 1984); from core competence (Prahalad and Hamel, 1990) to dynamic capability (Stalk, Evans, and Shulman, 1992; Teece, Pisano, and Shuen, 1997); from time-based competition (Bower and Hout, 1988; Stalk and Hout, 1990; Stalk, 1990) to knowledge-based competition (Winter, 1987; Nonaka, 1991); from managing culture (Deal and Kennedy, 1982; Barney, 1986b) to managing people (Pfeffer,

1994; Ulrich, 1997); from commitment (Caves, 1984; Ghemawat, 1991) to innovation (Schumpeter, 1934; Rumelt, 1984; Jacobson, 1992); from strategic intent (Hamel and Prahalad, 1989) to corporate vision (Collins and Porras, 1994, 1996), and from hypercompetition (D'Aveni, 1994) to co-opetition (Brandenburger and Nalebuff, 1996).

How do we make sense of the plethora of these theories? Despite some overlap and similarity in theoretical roots, foci, or priorities, these extant theories on competitive advantage, especially recent ones, tend to emphasize the uniqueness and newness of their respective approaches or messages, touting theirs as *the* new tools for the new era of business reality. Most of these theories and perspectives, however, could be termed as *single-factor theory*. That is, they often choose to focus on and underscore the supposedly effect of one particular factor, be it industry structure, firm endowment, time, culture, or cooperation. The point is, however, that single-factor theories, useful as they may be for understanding certain particular competitive advantages, often cannot fully explain successful firms' persistent superior performance.

The purpose of this chapter is to attempt a theoretical integration that helps put extant theories on competitive advantage into perspective. In doing so, it is expected that the explaining power of the various theories of competitive advantage can be amplified and our knowledge of firm performance enhanced.

This chapter reviews and critiques major strategy theories on competitive advantage and advances an integrative framework that coalesces these extant theories. The organizing concept of the framework is still *constellation of competitive advantage*, as explained in Chapter 9. In this Chapter, I offer an alterative interpretation, which, using a more theoretically grounded perspective, complements the ARTS framework developed in Chapter 9.

I first discuss the limitations of single-factor theories, the need for integrative theorizing, as well as the basis for an advantage-based view of the firm. Then I review major extant theories on competitive advantage, and juxtapose them into the respective categories of action, resources, and positions, which ultimately shape and change a firm's constellation of competitive advantages. Finally, I identify major challenges in managing the firm's constellation of advantages.

LIMITATIONS OF SINGLE-FACTOR THEORIES: THE HONDA STORY REVISITED

The business world in reality is not necessarily organized along any elegant theoretical lines. As such, the same strategic phenomenon often has to be viewed from multiple perspectives for us to capture the richness and complexity of the phenomenon. This is exactly why a more holistic perspective is often needed to better explain a firm's superior performance. Take for example the various explanations for the "Honda Effect", dubbed by Henry Mintzberg as "the only known fact in the entire management literature" (Mintzberg, 1996). Given that the Honda case has perhaps been repeated to death in strategy research and teaching, I won't bother with any details here but choose instead to expound the possibility that the different explanations can be juxtaposed and coalesced.

The original BCG report focused on formal (strategic) analysis and came to the conclusion that cost efficiency derived from *experience curve* and scale economy underlay Honda's competitive advantages and its success in the world motorcycle industry. Adding to that was the "segment retreat" reaction from the more myopic American and British manufacturers. The BCG report demonstrated the power of systematic and formal analysis of the logic embedded in a strategic phenomenon. This rational account, however, would be disputed by the now famous "Honda Effect" story (Pascale, 1984). Richard Pascale's interview with Honda executives who were involved with its entry into the U.S. motorcycle market suggested an evolving process that involved failures, myopic market planning and targeting, trial-and-error learning, adaptation, and luck.

Based on Pascale's account of the Honda story, Mintzberg would see Honda's case as a perfect example supporting his articulation of the *emergent strategy* as a pattern accumulated from a series of decisions. While Mintzberg (1996) might see the interactive and incremental process as being strategic, Richard Rumelt (1996) argued instead that the strategic thinking was blown out of proportion and the story was plainly, from a resource-based view, that a *unique endowment* of talents in Honda, the person and the firm. As such, superior, idiosyncratic resources and capabilities in the technical area at the operational level, according to Rumelt, was largely responsible for Honda's success.

Similarly, Prahalad and Hamel (1990) would explain the Honda success as a story of building, utilizing, and amplifying a firm's *core competence* to serve its strategic intent, its obsession with winning (Hamel and Prahalad, 1989). Coupling their account of Honda's motorcycle business with Honda's entry into the American automobile industry, they would regard Honda's action and strategy as to build worldwide leadership in making engines for application to the widest possible range of products or businesses. George Stalks and associates at BCG (1992) would later add another twist to the core competence explanation. Core competence in engine building allowed Honda to participate in seemingly disparate and unrelated businesses, e.g., motorcycle, automobile, lawn mowers, generators, etc. But what differentiated Honda from competitors was its focus on *capabilities*, among which, dealer management and speedy product realization are of central position. Stalks and associates would also argue that core competence and capability represent two different yet complementary dimensions of strategy.

The Schumpeterian perspective (Schumpeter, 1934) would see the key to Honda's initial success as its *innovation* in building small engines and in creating a new game in the niche market of small bikes. This enlarged the overall scope of the motorcycle business and allowed Honda to secure stronghold in the niche and helped fuel its battle over rivals industry-wide. As such, Honda destroyed the old equilibrium in the motorcycle industry where it also established new market niches and set new standards in manufacturing quality and efficiency.

Its superior technical strengths in designing and manufacturing small engines and its dominance in the niche market would also help erect *entry and mobility barriers*, viewed from a industry structure perspective, and deter cross-market entry or retaliation from incumbent rivals (Porter, 1980; Caves and Ghemawat, 1992). Clearly, we cannot, and should never, underestimate the ambition to win by any Japanese companies. Honda might seem to be myopic and less prepared in their initial entry in the US market, but do not forget the following fact. As Ghemawat (1991) insightfully pointed out, Honda's entry in to the US was engineered by the visionary Mr. Honda, who had defied the conventional wisdom and the wishes of the Ministry of International Trade and Industry (MITI) and its trading companies that Honda should first occupy the Southeast Asia market. Honda was *committed* to conquering the U.S. market.

Reflecting on the Honda story, what was *the* single factor that propelled Honda to global success? Strategy or luck? Core competence or capability? Efficiency, unique endowment, or market power? Did they create something totally new or was it just better and cheaper? Realistically speaking, no one single factor would explain the whole story of Honda's success yet every one of them is more or less useful. The Honda story teaches us at least two lessons. First, successful firms often, either intentionally or spontaneously, do many things well and they build evolving, multiple advantages to gain and sustain their success. Second, adopting multiple theoretical lenses may potentially help us understand the various elements of the overall strategic phenomenon in more depth and completeness.

AN ADVANTAGE-BASED VIEW OF THE FIRM: A HOLISTIC PERSPECTIVE

A firm's *raison detre* lies in its competitive advantage over rivals in serving customers. At least for successful firms it is so. Winning firms often win because they know best how to create and renew their competitive advantages: how to excel in doing many things well and how to change and adapt to new competitive situations. From a winner's perspective, a firm is not merely a collection of product-market activities (Porter, 1980, 1985), a bundle of idiosyncratic resources (Penrose, 1959; Rumelt, 1984; Wernerfelt, 1984), a set of core competence or capabilities (Prahalad and Hamel, 1990; Stalk, et al., 1992). Instead, it should be treated as an evolving constellation of competitive advantage. Such a view of the firm can be termed as an advantage-based view of the firm. It views the firm as the vehicle for winning. Wining—achieving superior performance—is the bottom line. All single factors emphasized by extant theories are simply means, not the aim in themselves. The major thesis of the advantage-based view is that there are multiple ways to achieve competitive advantages and multiple advantages are often needed to achieve persistent superior performance.

What is the mission of the advantage-based view of the firm? How does the advantage-based view come to terms with extant theories of competitive advantage? Simply put, the advantage-based perspective builds on them instead of replacing them; it integrates them instead of supplementing them; it is an issue-driven, holistic perspective instead of a single-factor theory, or discipline-based special lens or treatment. While a single-factor theory often emphasizes a special case, e.g., time-based competition, the advantage-based view works at a more universal or general level. In a nutshell, it tries to skim prior strategy research and weave them together using a single, coherent and logical framework: constellation of competitive advantage. To develop such a framework, let me first review the building blocks.

EXTANT THEORIES ON COMPETITIVE ADVANTAGE

Table 10.1 presents a brief summary of the major extant theories on competitive advantage in the strategy field, organized around three dimensions: a theory's view and treatment of the firm, its core theoretical concepts, and its dictation on the task of strategy. These extant theories serve as major building blocks of the advantage-based view of the firm.

Table 10.1 A Summary of Major Extant Theories on Competitive Advantage

	View of the Firm	*Core Concepts*	*Task of Strategy*
Market Power View	A Collection of Product-Market Activities	Industry Structure Market Positions Bargaining Power Entry/Mobility Barriers Monopoly Rents	*Positioning* To put a firm in a strong, defensible position in an attractive industry
Resource-Based View	A Bundle of Idiosyncratic Resources or a Set of Capabilities	Unique Resources Core Competence Firm Capabilities Ricardian Rents	*Differentiating (on resource)* To exploit unique resources and capabilities and conceive and implement strategies that are non-duplicable
Commitment View	A Carrier of a Series of Irreversible Investment Decisions	Commitment Persistence of Strategy Entry Barriers Mobility Barriers	*Selecting Commitment* To create a sustainable position through a series of investment decisions that are irreversible

(Continued)

	View of the Firm	Core Concepts	Task of Strategy
Schumpeterian View	A Vehicle for Innovation and Creative Destruction	Innovation New Combination of Resources New Processes New Form of Organization Entrepreneurial Rents	*Innovating* To upset the current industry equilibrium and create new games where an innovating firm wins
Efficiency View	A Mechanism of Production and Transaction	Economy in Transaction Operating Efficiency Economizing Efficiency Rents or Quasi-Rents	*Economizing* To achieve first-order economy and be as efficient as possible
Ecological View	A Specie or organism in a Business Eco-System	Evolution Co-Evolution Environmental Selection Business Eco-Systems Keystone Specie	*Co-Evolving* To strive for leadership in as well as viability of a business eco-system
Hyper-competition View	A Vigilant and Paranoid Warrior	Hypercompetition 4 Competitive Arenas Competitive Escalation New 7 Ss Analysis Temporal Advantage	*Fighting* To constantly fight and win individual battles so as to win the whole game through time
Co-opetition View	A Unitary and Rational Player who Attempts to Optimize	Competition & Cooperation Substitutes vs. Complements PARTS of Game Win-Win	*Co-opeting* To balance competition and cooperation and choose the best option given rivals' action. Try to change the game and create win-win

Industrial Organization Economics

In the 1980s, Porter (1980, 1985) revolutionized the strategy field by formalizing industry analysis, working within the Structure-Conduct-Performance paradigm of Industrial Organization Economics (Porter, 1981). This approach treats the firm as a collection of product-market choices and activities, whose position in the industry and the industry's structure determine its conduct (read strategy) and performance (Bain, 1956). According to the structural approach, a strong, defensible market position (read power) in an attractive industry renders sustained competitive advantage possible. And the attractiveness of an industry is dependent on the configuration of five competitive forces in the industry—an extended definition of industry—rivalry among incumbent firms, threat of new entry, threat of substitute, supplier bargaining power, and buyer bargaining power.

Porter regards the ultimate function of his industry analysis framework (five-forces) as to explain the *sustainability* of profits against bargaining and against direct and indirect competition. The primary task of strategy then, according to the structural approach, is industry positioning. Once arrived in a defensible position in a structurally attractive industry, the strategic task of the firm is to erect and manipulate the entry barriers and fend-off incumbent and potential rivals so as to defend the position and sustain its competitive advantage.

The Chicago School of Industrial Organization, different from the structural perspective which emphasizes market power, argues that firms become big and powerful because they are efficient (Demsetz, 1973; Stigler, 1968). Demsetz (1973) posited that it was efficiency rents that provided firms with superior performance, not monopolistic power *per se*, although the Chicago School did not dismiss the possibility of monopoly rents. In this sense, natural monopoly could ensue when one firm is bale to efficiently serve the whole market. And the supranormal performance of such a firm is considered the reward of their efficiency.

The Resource-Based View of the Firm

Penrose (1959) elucidated her theory of the growth of the firm, where she treated a firm as a bundle of resources, including managerial resources as its kingpin. In the strategy field, a research stream known as the resource-based view builds on the insights of Penrose and emphasizes firm resources and capabilities as the source for sustainable competitive advantage (Wernerfelt, 1984). That is, certain organizational resources are valuable, rare, and difficult-to-imitate; and they are often immobile and firm-specific, non-tradable, and non-substitutable. These unique resources will provide a firm with sustainable competitive advantage hence persistent superior performance (Barney, 1986b, 1991; Rumelt, 1984; Cool and Dierickx, 1989; Grant, 1991). Contrary to the structural approach that focuses on product market imperfections, the resource-based view emphasizes the imperfections in market for resources or strategic factors, which cause and sustain resource heterogeneity among firms (Barney, 1986a; Zajac, 1992).

The best strategy for a firm then, according to the resource-based view, must be based on certain unique resources that are immune from imitation and substitution. Parallel to the entry barrier concept of the structural approach, the resource-based view relies on the concept of resource position barrier—isolating mechanisms that prevent or discourage imitation—to explain sustainable advantage (Lippman and Rumelt, 1982; Wernerfelt, 1984; Rumelt, 1987; Grant, 1991). Recent research on core competence by Prahalad and Hamel (1990) and the stream of research on organizational capabilities (Stalk, et al., 1992; Teece, et al., 1997) could also be generally considered being within the intellectual paradigm of the broadly defined resource-based view of the firm. Teece and colleagues (1997) define dynamic capability as the capability to configure and coordinate multiple competencies and reconfigure these competencies along changing market opportunities.

The Commitment Approach

A research stream stemming from the Industrial Organization economics that also employs game theoretic analysis centers its attention on commitment. Caves (1984) made the pioneering contribution in this stream of research and Ghemawat (1991) formalized its major elements. As commented by Caves (1984), many compe- titive moves are strategic in the sense of involving substantial precommitments of resources that are irreversible. Defining commitment as the firm's tendency towards the persistence of its respective strategy over time, Ghemawat (1991) argues that commitment is both sufficient and necessary to explain sustainable advantage. Without commitment, there would be neither persistent difference in organizations' performance levels nor any need to anticipate the future.

The major argument is therefore that strategy is manifested in a few investment decisions that are irreversible. Careful choice of sequential decisions on commitment under uncertainty is the key determinant of creating and sustaining firm advantage. Research on commitment, in the Industrial Organization tradition, emphasizes the role of entry barriers and mobility barriers. For sustainable advantages to realize, commitment in terms of irreversible investments will have to translate into entry or mobility barriers that deter incumbent and future rivals (Caves and Ghemawat, 1992). Like other game theoretic models, here the environment is assumed to be relatively stable, albeit uncertain, so that commitments can have long-lived consequences in sustaining a competitive advantage (cf. Porter, 1991).

Schumpeterian Economics

Arguably the foremost economist in our century who understood best the nature of capitalist economy, Schumpeter (1934, 1950), would anchor his theory of economic development on innovation. He argued that the profit-seeking entrepreneur-capitalist would constantly attempt to destroy the old equilibrium through *innovation*, the engine of the self-propelling market economy. Schumpeterian competition, due to the creative destruction nature, is by definition not stable and certainly less predictable. Yet it is exactly the characteristics of uncertainty that invites strategy. In the uncertain, complex, revolutionary, and rapidly-changing world of Schumpeterian competition, it is the entrepreneurs' vision, judgment, and risk-taking in their strategizing facing uncertainty that drive the growth of the economy and put innovating firms on top of all contenders (Amit and Schoemaker, 1993).

Inspired by Schumpeterian thinking, Hamel and Prahalad, in advocating their perspective on strategic intent (Hamel and Prahalad, 1989), core competence (Prahalad and Hamel, 1990), and competing for the future (Hamel and Prahalad, 1994), hail the importance of entrepreneurial vision and ambition. Creating something totally anew and doing things in drastically different ways lie at the very heart of strategy. The best strategizing then is arguably to always have the ability to create new games and/or change the rule of games. And that is the spirit of creative destruction.

Transaction Cost Economics and the Efficiency Perspective

Transaction cost economics focuses on the economy of various governing mechanisms in transaction, the basic unit of analysis of business activities. Transaction cost economics treats the firm as a mechanism to facilitate efficiency in production, organization, and transaction (Coase, 1937; Williamson, 1975, 1991). According to Williamson (1975), the firm, characterized by managerial hierarchies, is an alternative to the market mechanism in organizing production and exchange activities. The reason that justifies a firm's existence and its boundary at any time is that the firm is more efficient than market in minimizing transaction cost—the cost arising from and associated with searching for, negotiating, and enforcing deals and transactions. Williamson comments on the implication of transaction cost economics to strategy and firm advantage as follows (Williamson, 1991: 75).

> [E]conomy is the best strategy. That is not to say that strategizing efforts to deter or defeat rivals with clever ploys and positioning are unimportant. In the long run, however, the best strategy is to organize and operate efficiently... economizing is much the more fundamental. That is because strategizing is relevant principally to firms that possess market power—which are a small fraction of the total (ephemeral market advantages ignored)... All the clever ploys and positioning, aye, all the king's horses and all the king's men, will rarely save a project that is seriously flawed in first-order economizing respects.

Williamson defines first-order economizing as effective adaptation and elimination of waste. Citing the explanations of Japanese firms' success in global competition, Williamson (1991:87) further observes that:

> The more favored explanations, at least in the popular press, are of strategizing kind. I submit, however, that the Japanese have long been aware that economy is the best strategy. The main explanation for their success is that first-order economizing has been assiduously pursued.

Clearly, the explanation for the aforementioned Honda success, from Williamson's perspective, would primarily be, more likely than not, efficiency-based.

Ecological Perspective

The ecological perspective treats the firm as a specie which tries to adapt to changes in, and exploit resources from, its business eco-systems and is subject to environmental selection (Hannan and Freeman, 1977). A major theoretical focus of the ecological view is the competition between different business eco-systems in addition to competition between species within the same business eco-system. That is, environmental selection happens at both the individual species level within a business eco-system and the multiple eco-system level (Moore, 1996). In this sense, a specie might be a keystone piece around which its immediate eco-system builds, but the whole eco-system in which it resides and dominates might be at the same time subject to total elimination. As such, any specie aspiring for leadership in its eco-system must evolve in the way that better position it in the immediate eco-system, as well as in the future battle between its eco-system and other similar systems, so as to insure the robustness and resilience of its eco-system.

Adopting the ecological perspective, Moore (1996) argues that competition, traditionally conceived as being conducted for dominance at the individual product or industry level, is dead. What is most needed is a new language that better describes the new competitive landscape. Instead of thinking in such terms as a firm competing in a discrete industry, managers should think in terms of species or organisms evolving and co-evolving in business ecosystems. Different insights could be gained on the sustainability of firm advantage from such a conception of competition. That is, to gain and sustain advantages, a firm needs to push its products or technology to be the keystone piece, i.e., industry or system standard, of its evolving eco-system; and it also needs to be alert about and to deter the challenges of competing eco-systems.

Hypercompetition

Recently, D'Aveni (1994) coined the term hypercompetition to describe a competitive situation where rival firms constantly jockey for positions through escalating efforts in four interrelated arenas: price and quality, timing and know-how, stronghold, and deep pocket. The defining characteristic of the hypercompetitive market is that sustainable competitive advantage is impossible. As such, this perspective views the firm as a hypercompetitor that attempts to out-maneuver rivals and create temporal advantages on a routine basis. Building on prior research of competitive action and response (Porter, 1984; Smith, Grimm, and Gannon, 1992; Chen and MacMillan, 1992; Chen and Miller, 1994), D'Aveni (1994) also presents various competitive weapons through the "New 7s" that help firms disrupt the status quo and win.

Hypercompetition at its core, however, is indeed a Schumpeterian competition in an extreme version, i.e., the wave of creative destruction is rather short in length and its happening frequent. As such, the battle in hypercompetition is to kill or be killed. D'Aveni (1994) further argues that cooperation is no way out of hypercompetition. Cooperation is contestable and often escalates conflict instead of placating it. So the only way to survive in a hypercompetitive world is to bravely embrace hypercompetition. Firms adept at fighting competitive battles are likely to gain advantages, albeit temporal ones, in hypercompetition.

Game Theory and Co-Opetition

Game theory treats the firm primarily as a unitary player with rationality (or super-rationality) which attempts to optimize its utility given available public information and other players possible range of actions. Game theory is a way of thinking. It helps us frame issues into interactive choice situations. It is a modeling technique and consists of some clearly stated principles and some prototypical games, e. g., prisoner's dilemma. It is also a language system that helps simplify more complex decision-making situations (Camerer, 1991; Saloner, 1991). Recently, Brandenburger and Nalebuff (1996), based primarily on game theoretic reasoning, have formalized a new analytical framework named co-opetition that features a mindset that combines competition and cooperation. It advises firms to change the game and win.

Co-operation, simultaneous engagement in competition and cooperation, emphasizes the important roles of both competitor and complementor in the game of business. What is often omitted or ignored in business decisions, Brandenburger and Nalebuff (1996) argue, is the consideration of complementors, who enhance the focal firm's value in the eyes of customers. And that omission is largely responsible for the traditional idea that treats business games as wars, as cutthroat competition. Adding the role of complementors back into the picture, opposing the usual element of competitive substitutes, helps firms think about cooperation and win-win scenarios. The major message of the co-opetition approach is that firms gain advantage if they could change the games they face, more specifically, change the PARTS of the game: players, added-value of different players, rules of the game, tactics in playing the game, and scope of the games.

THE NEED FOR THEORETICAL SYNTHESIS

Management theory is often a fashion business (Abrahamson, 1996). Whenever a "new theory" or "newest best practice" comes into the business world, advocates of them would tend to emphasize its "newness" and why it should be *the one* that is destined to displace all the "old thinking" or "traditional theories" which, as they argue, seem to be so out of touch with the "new reality" (cf. Eccles and Nohria, 1992). The fact is that all theories have drawbacks and are subject to refutation. This said, we could also enhance our knowledge by exploring the linkages among the various theories and how they could be coalesced. Combined, they may better explain competitive advantage and superior performance.

Single-factor theories as I reviewed above, however insightful they may be, can only go so far alone. Any factor will only provide a certain particular advantage. Relying on any single advantage to sustain a firm's superior performance seems rather shaky. In the end, what is strategic often changes. Market power, efficiency, innovation, commitment, unique resources, however valuable, are all means. The ultimate goal is winning. To this end, a firm needs multiple advantages and its constellation of competitive advantage has to change with the environment adaptively. To help firms achieve this end, any theory or perspective that informs competitive advantage should be dissected and juxtaposed in the context of those competing and complementary theories and frameworks.

A synthesized view amplifies their respective merits and facilitates general managers' informed choice. The advantage-based view is just such an integrative perspective. Theoretically, it builds on extant theories of competitive advantage. Practically, as an integration of extant single-factor theories, the advantage-based view of the firm is expected to more completely embrace contemporary business reality.

> *And as water shapes its flow in accordance with the ground, so an army manages its victory in accordance with the situation of the enemy. And as water has no constant form, there are in war no constant conditions.*
>
> Sun Tzu

Consider the example of Sony. Essentially all extant theories and perspectives reviewed here could be applied to describe it yet none alone can accomplish the task completely. Sony, as one of the largest electronics manufacturer in the world, certainly enjoys *market power* because of its strong market position globally, e.g., its dominant position in the Walkman segment of the personal electronics market (Cooper, 1997). Its *efficient* manufacturing capability and outsourcing expertise provide operating advantages. Sony is a firm that is known to be a pioneer, not a follower (Collins and Porras, 1996). *Innovation* lies at the heart of the whole corporation (D'Aveni, 1994: 103). It would constantly push out new products and models to overwhelm the me-too competitors.

And Sony is a company that is willing to make *commitments*, for good or ill, even when a technology's commercial viability is uncertain. Their commitment to their β format in the VCR industry cost them arms in that lucrative market because it failed to become the industry standard (Yoffie, 1990). From an ecological view, Sony failed to establish its leadership position in its business eco-system of fellow VCR producers. Same can be said about their stubbornness in going alone on Mini-Disc and Digital Audio Tape (DAT), not sharing its format through network or alliance (Hill, 1997). Nonetheless, one has to appreciate Sony's remarkable consistency and discipline in implementing its strategy: be a pioneer and the proprietary beneficiary of its new technology.

Sony's miniaturization skills have often been cited as a classical example of corporate *core competence*, which enables it to enjoy a commanding lead in portable and pocket size electronics (Prahalad and Hamel, 1990). Its unique *capability* in quickly preempting all niches and price-levels of their electronics products helps it keep rivals at distance. In this sense, Sony would definitely be a leading company in the so-called *time-based competition* (Stalk, 1990).

Although it favors proprietary technology, Sony is also no stranger to *cooperation* and learning-inspired collaborative arrangement. To tackle technical challenges and share risks in R&D, Sony would in the late 1970s and early 1980s jointly develop the CD format with Philips (McGahan, 1991). Once it learned enough from the partner and ironed out major technical obstacles, it would decide to make greater commitment in manufacturing facilities faster than did Philips and preempt the worldwide market of CD players. As Philips read the CD format as essentially a high-end consumer product, Sony treated it as the future industry standard and a potential blockbuster for the firm, which would succeed its color TV and Walkman as the next star product and help sustain its growth.

As a regular participant in strategic alliance as Sony is, it is perhaps also not any far from D'Aveni's (1994) description of a typical *hypercompetitor*. Instead of keeping its products absolutely unique and top scale, it chooses to flood every niche of the market; to build share by ruthlessly slashing prices; to enhance its dominance by continuous model succession in all price ranges. Kenichi Ohmae (1988) criticized such strategy as being myopic, driving the competition to a level where profit margin is unnecessarily thin. Criticism not withstanding, Sony certainly stroke it big in the CD player business (McGahan, 1991).

The Sony example is not merely an exception but reflects a general mentality and practice of Japanese style competition. That is, to target markets where products are R&D based and customers value products quality and reliability; change the nature of products from elite, up-scale novelty items to mainstream, middle class level goods and commodity; quickly build mass production capabilities with efficient business processes that deliver both low cost and high quality; aggressively market the products, build share, create dominance, and eventually conquer the market world-wide. To see this logic in practice, just look at some of the key industries where the Japanese excelled: cameras, quartz watches, home electronics, automobiles, and office equipment.

To be sure, with Sony as an example, the Japanese style competition is multi-perspective, all-round, and all-out. To them, the target is not any specific niche. It is winning in the whole market around the globe. They can be a humble learning collaborator (McGahan, 1991), a nasty hypercompetitor (D'Aveni, 1994), an efficient manufacturing machine, a powerhouse with unique resource, capability, or core competence (Prahalad and Hamel, 1990), a committed and disciplined player, a relentless innovator, and a winning inspired power grabber (Hamel and Prahalad, 1989). It is not that the competition is merely increasingly time-based (Stalk, 1990), capability-based (Stalk, et al., 1992), innovation-based (Hamel and Prahalad, 1990), or cooperation or group based (Gomez-Casseres, 1994). It is that the speed and intensity of competition are all accelerating and the scope and variety of competition ever widening, due to the Japanese style competition and the consequent awareness of firms worldwide about the actual and potential global implication of such competition in any industry and business.

Competing against such complex, multi-faceted, competitors, any single-factor theory will not likely be enough to serve as appropriate guidance. What is needed is an analytical framework that integrates multiple single-factor theories and covers a wider range of possible strategic options and activities. To this end, the advantage-based view of the firm stands squarely to help general managers analyze such competitors in the scene of global competition.

CONSTELLATION OF COMPETITIVE ADVANTAGE: AN INTEGRATIVE FRAMEWORK

As mentioned earlier, the advantage-based view treats the firm as a vehicle for winning. This winning perspective facilitates the definition of a firm's mission, the fundamental reason of its very existence in business; and its identity, its institutional image in society. A firm is in business precisely because it can deliver certain customer value better than others can. The firm's image and identity derive from its unique contribution to the society in economic and non-economic ways that makes it a winning team. As a management philosophy, the advantage-based view of the firm is useful in funneling a firm's strategic attention to its core value, distinctive competence, and unique capabilities. The advantage-based view prompts a firm to focus on what it does best. It mandates that a firm should engage in activities where it enjoys the most advantage over others, where it has a chance to win. For instance, GE's policy of insisting that every one of its businesses be in the top two spots of its respective industry perfectly illustrates such a point (Bower and Dial, 1994).

The defining characteristic of the advantage-based view of the firm is that it treats the firm as a multidimensional, evolving *constellation of competitive advantage*. Such a constellation consists of various types of advantages that are simultaneously at work, where different advantages may reinforce, augment, and even derive from each other; temporal advantages might be sustained; obsolete advantages get to be replaced by new ones. Moreover, it treats the firm not only as a constellation of competitive advantages, but also as a constellation that constantly and deliberately renews itself. The constellation is an evolving system. Its composition evolves as existing advantages are eroded and new advantages arise. At any moment then, the system may host simultaneously emerging or potential advantages, temporal advantages, as well as sustainable advantages.

A well-balanced constellation of competitive advantage is the fundamental determinant of a firm's persistent superior performance—consistent and sustained above-normal performance through time. As such, the central activity of strategic management is to create and maintain a healthy dynamics for its evolving constellation of competitive advantage, by constantly searching, realizing, sustaining, and amplifying individual advantages as well as renewing the constellation of competitive advantage with new advantages, in adaptation to changes in its environment, competitors, customers, and the firm itself.

A firm's competitive advantage constellation often consists of factors that are emphasized in extant single-factor theories. The fundamental difference between the advantage-based view of the firm and single-factor theories, however, lies in their respective explanations for persistent superior performance. While single-factor theories often emphasize the importance of a sole factor, the integrative advantage-based view credits the constellation of multiple advantages instead. See Figures 10.1 and 10.2 for a graphic comparison.

**Figure 10.1 Persistent Superior Performance:
Explanations by Some Extant Theories**

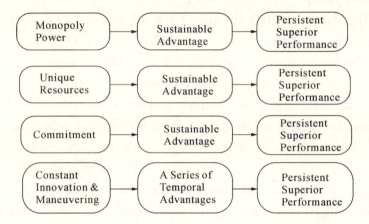

**Figure 10.2 Persistent Superior Performance: Explanation
by the Advantage-Based View of the Firm**

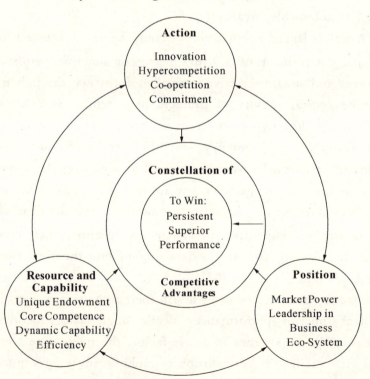

Clearly, the various single-factor theories' explanation would be true within the framework of the advantage-based view. That is, the linkage between firm attributes, advantage, and performance described by the single-factor theories is a subset of and also holds true in the integrative model of the advantage-based view. In this sense, the advantage-based view provides a more general and universal framework.

The integrative framework consists of three major components: firm resource and capability, position, and action. All three components draw on factors emphasized in extant theories on competitive advantage and contribute to a firm's constellation of competitive advantage in different ways.

Resource and Capability

This component draws on the resource-based view (Wernerfelt, 1994), broadly defined, and the efficiency perspective in transaction cost economics (Williamson, 1991) and the Chicago School in Industrial Organization economics (Demsetz, 1973). Firm unique endowment, e.g., Caterpillar's extensive worldwide sales and maintenance network (Bartlett, 1985), core competence, e.g., Canon's competencies in imaging (Prahalad and Hamel, 1990; Ghoshal, 1992), and dynamic capability (Teece, et al., 1997), e.g., Nike's ability to coordinate multiple competencies in designing, manufac- turing, and marketing (Miller, 1993), all provide the respective firms with competitive advantages. As far as efficiency is concerned, Wal-Mart's ability to quickly move great quantities of merchandises with low costs, for example, stands as a major source of its competitive advantage (Ghemawat, 1991; Stalk, et al., 1992).

Position

This component draws on the structural approach to industry

analysis (Porter, 1980) and the ecological perspective to strategy (Moore, 1996). A firm's market power provides competitive advantage, e.g., Home Depot's size and huge purchasing power allow it to bargain more effectively against suppliers. Similarly, a firm's leadership position in its business eco-systems also renders the firm competitive advantage. For instance, in the global cellular phone markets, two major business eco-systems vie for industry standard, the TDMA (Time Division Multiple Access) championed by Ericsson and allies vs. CDMA (Code Division Multiple Access) championed by Qualcom. Ericsson's leadership in the TDMA alliance and its dominance in the European markets as well as some Asian markets provides Ericsson with an competitive edge (*Forbes*, 1997a).

Action

This component draws on the Schumpeterian perspective (Schumpeter, 1934, 1950), hypercompetition (D'Aveni, 1994), co-opetition (Brandenburger and Nalebuff, 1996) and commitment (Caves, 1984; Ghemawat, 1991). Firm action in innovation, competition, cooperation, and making selective commitment contribute to its constellation of competitive advantage. First, innovation helps firms gain advantage. For instance, 3M's innovation in technology constantly provides new products to propel its growth (Bartlett and Mohammed, 1995). Second, competitive action contributes to gaining advantage. The intense competition between Nike and Reebok helps bring the best our of each rival and further differentiate the two super powers from the rest of competitors (*Fortune*, 1995b). Third, collaborating with competitors could also render competitive advantage. Sony's cooperation with Philips in CD technology, for instance, contributed to its mastering of some of the critical technical knowledge and processes, allowing Sony to quickly dominate that business (McGahan, 1991). Finally, commitment in laying out a persistent pattern of strategy through a series of investment decisions helps firms achieve competitive advantage. For example, Wal-Mart's commitment to serve the rural areas in retailing provided it with scale economy, monopoly power, and entry barriers to deter latecomers' challenge (Ghemawat, 1991).

Capability, Position, and Action: Relationships

While firm action can directly contribute to competitive advantage, it often helps in strengthening a firm's position and enhancing its capabilities. Through action, a firm exercises its capabilities to gain and consolidate its market positions. Through action, a firm sharpens its routine and enhances its capabilities. For instance, the aggressive action of NationsBank in pursuing merger and acquisition helped the former regional bank climb to the position of among the top 5 in the U.S. in a decade's time. In the process, NationsBank accumulated valuable experience and honed its skills and capabilities in identifying targets for acquisitions, making deals, and post-merger integration (D'Aveni, 1994; *Fortune*, 1995a).

A firm's market position also dictates the range of possible options for a firm's action and affects the firm's potential capabilities and their exercise in the firm's action. For instance, Microsoft's large installed-base of its windows operating systems allows it to leverage this dominance and bundle its other products, e.g., MS Explorer the web browser, with its windows system. Such market power makes it more advantageous for Microsoft in its competitive action against rivals in a whole range of software product markets. Microsoft's strong market position also helps attract fresh talents and enhance its technical expertise, knowledge base, and capabilities in product innovation (*Fortune*, 1997c).

A firm's capability also determines a firm's action and its market positions. For instance, the superior technical and marketing know-how of Nintendo enabled it to gain a worldwide dominant position in electronic games. Gillette's technical capability in product innovation and its dynamic capability in coordinating cross-country marketing and promotional efforts enabled it to launch in 1990 its Gillette Sensor line of razors simultaneously in two dozens or so countries, a competitive action difficult to match by any rivals. Gillette's superior capabilities and well coordinated action helped consolidate its market position in the cartridge razor business globally (Wind, 1997).

CONSTELLATION OF COMPETITIVE ADVANTAGE: THE INTEL EXAMPLE

To see a constellation of competitive advantage in action, consider the example of Intel, one of the top five firms with the highest market value in the U.S. The persistent superior performance of Intel in the past three decades comes from its relentless strategic actions and maneuvers, strong market positions and leadership in setting industry standard, as well as its superior capabilities in product innovation, manufacturing, and effective marketing campaigns (Grove, 1996).

Action: Innovation, Hypercompetition, Commitment, and Co-opetition

Intel is an action-oriented company. It resorts to various options of strategic actions in striving for leadership in its business eco-system: innovation, competition, commitment, and co-opetition.

Intel is an innovator. Its initial dominance in the computer memory device business derived from its technical innovation and path-breaking products in DRAM (Dynamic Random Access Memory) chips and EPROM, the erasable programmable memory device. The seed for Intel's dominance in microprocessor for PCs was sewed when Intel invented the 8080 microprocessor, and later 8086. Its 8088 microprocessor, an 8-bit version of the 8086, was chosen by IBM when it launched its PC in 1981. Intel's constant innovation in microprocessors helps push out a score of new products in its X86 series and the Pentium series. Innovation propels Intel's successive dominance in its core business (Grove, 1996).

Despite its dominance in the microprocessor business, Intel does not rest on its laurels and rely solely on its strong market position to fend off rivals. Instead, Intel is a fierce competitor, a paranoid warrior embodying the aggressive spirit of its CEO Andy Grove. Its constant introduction of new-generation chips, from 286, 386, 486 to Pentium, Pentium MMX, and Pentium Pro, insures that Intel always has a competitive edge over rivals which imitate Intel's designs. In the hypercompetitive environment of Intel's business, Intel's real advantage is being faster than its rivals. Intel challenges and competes against itself to expand the technological boundary.

To establish a dominant position in any business, a firm needs commitment. Intel's commitment was made on microprocessors. Intel's commitment to maintain leadership position in the microprocessor business was tested when its CISC (Complex Instruction Set Computing) architecture was challenged by the RISC (Reduced Instruction Set Computing) processors, a format championed by Motorola that had been widely used in workstations. Sticking to the logic that high switching costs prevent customers from easily shifting between different technological standards, Intel refocused its effort to support the momentum of 486-based computers and enhanced its commitment to the CISC format (Grove, 1996).

Such commitment was undertaken also because of the belief in co-opetition and in the role of complementors, or "fellow travelers" in the technical journey in Grove's term. It was the willingness of major computer manufacturers like Compaq to build the 486-based computers that largely influenced Intel's decision. Intel knew fully well the value of complementors whose products enhance the value of Intel products.

For instance, its co-opetive relationship with Microsoft helped define the Wintel PC standard. The complementarity of Intel's microprocessors and Microsoft's operating systems allowed the two firms to dominate the PC hardware and software businesses throughout the last two decades or so (*Fortune*, 1996c).

Although, Intel, Microsoft, and major computer makers fight to claim the value created in the PC business, these firms also cooperate to explore new ways to enhance the total value. For instance, Intel's *Intel Inside* campaign, not only effectively promoted its brand to the end customers, but also enhanced the credibility of computer manufacturers' products. Intel would provide rebate on its chips and lure manufacturers to collaborate on its *Intel Inside* campaign. Firms like Compaq and IBM were reluctant initially to participate due to the fear that the Intel brand would overwhelm their respective computer brands, but eventually jumped on board once they saw the sheer weight of Intel and its tenacity in promoting its microprocessor standard. It simply makes sense to communicate to the end customers that one's computers are based on an open (more exactly, dominant) standard in microprocessors.

Capabilities: Designing, Manufacturing, and Marketing

Intel's unique strengths lie in its technical capability to develop path-breaking products. Critical to its success are also its capabilities in manufacturing and marketing. With its superior design capabilities, Intel was able to develop innovative products that set the industry standard. Its 80386 chip won 200 design wins within one year of introduction. However, as Intel learned from its DRAM business against Japanese competitors, superior design capabilities must be matched by superior manufacturing capabilities to secure long-term success in the computer chips businesses (Grove, 1996).

Designing and manufacturing complement each other. To speed the design process, Intel designers would involve manufacturing early during the chip designing, insuring manufacturability. Intel possesses manufacturing facilities all over the world. In order to enhance its manufacturing quality and productivity, it has closed inefficient pants, enhanced clean-room discipline, and used more automation. Both its designing and manufacturing capabilities jointly define Intel's unique technical competence that makes it possible the speedy introduction of new generations of chips to the market (Nanda and Bartlett, 1994).

Intel's marketing capability allows it to go beyond its immediate customers—major computer makers who adopt Intel's microprocessors—and connect directly with its end customers. Its *Intel Inside* campaign has become one of the best staged advertising and promotion schemes in history, along side classical examples of NutraSweet and Dolby. Since its introduction in 1990, Intel has become a well-known consumer brand. As a result, customers, computer literate or not, would insist on having *Intel Inside* their computers, figuring that it must be something good and essential if so many major names in the computer business like IBM, Compaq, and Dell, relentlessly promote it (Aaker, 1996).

Positions: Market Power and Leadership in Business Eco-System

Intel is a company that strives for dominance. It is a winning-driven firm. Like GE, It competes where it has competitive advantage, or potential competitive advantage. This would mean refusing to linger in a business where it no longer has competitive advantage. Although it held dominant position in the DRAM business in the early years, the 1980s would witness the drastic decline of Intel's global market share to a non-factor in this business, due to the rising of Japanese firms which boasted greater manufacturing quality and efficiency. In 1986, Intel decisively chose to exit the memory device business, the very business it created. This bold act demonstrated Intel's determination to be a winner as well as its ability to adapt to environmental changes (Grove,

1996).

As it focused on microprocessors, it would always try to supply the entire needs of the industry. This means Intel has to first establish its position as bearer of the industry standard. That is exactly what Intel has been able to achieve since its initial dominance in microprocessors with its IBM license. Each generation of its chips has set the industry standard respectively, based on which imitators have to operate. Such dominant market position enables Intel to exploit scale economy in its manufacturing and marketing. Intel is not shy either in exercising its strong muscles. The *Intel Inside* campaign mentioned earlier is just such an example where Intel's sheer weight would influence other players to play Intel's game (Johnson, 1997).

Together with Microsoft, Intel has played the leadership role in the PC business eco-system. Its new generations of chips allow Microsoft to develop software products that take advantage of their higher speed. Microsoft's operating systems that run on Intel chips reinforce the industry-standard status of Intel's chips. Microsoft's development of more sophisticated software products, especially those involved with video applications, further challenges Intel to come up with more advanced microprocessors. So far, the Wintel standard had basically won over the Macintosh format in the PC business eco-system and holds court to the challenges of other business eco-systems, e.g., the microcomputers and the Internet, where Intel also actively searches for new growth opportunities (*Fortune*, 1996c).

In summary, shifting its commitment from the memory device business to the microprocessor business, Intel has throughout the years constantly built and renewed its multiple competitive advantages. As demonstrated above, the integrative framework of constellation of competitive advantage helps us more systematically examine the secret of Intel's persistent superior performance from multiple perspectives.

CHALLENGES IN MANAGING CONSTELLATION OF COMPETITIVE ADVANTAGE

Several key challenges face general managers when they try to build and maintain a firm's constellation of competitive advantage. These challenges call for due managerial attention in managing the system's dynamics.

Market Power Vs. Efficiency

In a virtuous cycle, firm efficiency leads to the building of market power; and market power helps facilitate efficiency. For instance, the great purchasing power of Wal-Mart gives rise to scale economy in its supply hence contributes to its merchandising efficiency. Such efficiency in turn helps consolidates its market position (Ghemawat, 1991). In a vicious cycle, market power brews inefficiency and inefficiency erodes market position. Market power is often a reward of past efficiency, unique endowment, or luck. In the short run, it could afford a firm a cushion or buffer that allows it to milk its established position and, from time to time, even be somewhat inefficient. In the long run, however, if market power is not enhanced and replenished with new sources of efficiency or innovation, it is nothing but an illusion of the firm's invincibility. It creates too much slack and slows down a firm's responsiveness to the market. The declining of Kmart in retailing points to its relative lack of efficiency, despite its previous dominant market position (Stalk et al., 1992; Moore, 1996).

Keeping in mind the dilemma of market power and efficiency helps general managers to assess their respective roles in the firm's constellation of competitive advantage. Market power itself is no inheritance; those which result in it—among them, efficiency in business process—are more fundamental an advantage source. Efficiency itself may contribute to firm advantage; yet strong market position further amplifies efficiency advantage. The debate between structural approach and the Chicago School highlights this seeming dilemma (Bain, 1956; Demsetz, 1973) and the difference between market power-based strategizing and economizing as argued by Williamson (1991) illuminates the need for a more balanced view on both efficiency and market power.

Endowment Vs. Capability

Endowments of unique resources alone could often provide competitive advantage (Barney, 1991). And firm capabilities typically arise and derive from their underlying resources. The dealer and service networks of Caterpillar, as an uniquely valuable and difficult-to-replicate resource, are largely responsible for its capability to respond to customer service request promptly (Bartlett, 1985). Firm capabilities, managerial ones in particular, also enable the firm to search for, utilize, deploy, and renew its resource endowment. Microsoft's recruiting capabilities help them to locate the best freshly minted engineers world wide and most experienced veteran managers in the industry, enhancing their endowment of technical and managerial resources.

On the other hand, firm capabilities often arise from knowledge-based activities which the firm has to nurture within itself carefully. While unique resource endowment often stems from luck, path-dependent events (Barney, 1996b, 1991), knowledge-based capabilities require clear vision and consistence in their development with the support of many activities (Winter, 1987; Teece, et al., 1997). As such, they may be even more difficult to imitate and yet more subjective to managerial intention and creation. Transforming resource endowment into capabilities and building knowledge-based capabilities remain high on the agenda of managing constellation of competitive advantage.

Commitment Vs. Flexibility

Commitment is necessary and often sufficient for an advantage's sustainability (Ghemawat, 1991). Flexibility, on the other hand, insures the firm's viability in case that changes in the firm and/or environment deem the original commitment and the need of which obsolete. Without commitment, it may not be possible to have sustainable competitive advantage; without flexibility, a firm might be unduly stuck with an obsolete advantage. To what extent should the trade-off between commitment and flexibility lie, not only for particular advantages but also the entire system, remains a lasting challenge.

Innovation Vs. Imitation

In the capitalist society, innovation may be the ultimate mean to proactively create advantage. 3M, the classic example of an innovative company, insists on that 30% of its annual sales must come from products introduced in the most recent 4 years (Bartlett and Mohammed, 1995). Such institutionalized innovation insures its competitive edge, although the advantage created through innovation is not always sustainable due to imitation.

A first mover may enjoy the advantages like experience economy, market leadership, industry-standard setter, favorable access to supply and distribution, as well as customer loyalty (Lieberman and Montgomery, 1988). Later mover, however, could also enjoy advantages, that are unavailable to first movers, e.g., free-rider effect, shift in consumer trends and/or technical standards which favors second movers that are in a better position to solve market or technological uncertainty. Sony always attempts to be a pioneer and lead while Matsushita is better known for its me-too strategy. Both strategies could work simultaneously in many business contexts, which makes possible the situation of equi-finality.

Should the firm be a leader or follower? Should the firm's constellation of competitive advantage be filled primarily with those that derive from innovation? Should it consist of more second-mover advantages? Schumpeterian perspective (1934) helps general managers in contemplating the timing of and trade-off between innovation-based and imitation-based competitive advantages.

Competition Vs. Cooperation

Competition creates advantage. So does cooperation. Competitive maneuvering creates superior positions; neutralizes rivals' advantages; preempts rivals' possible moves; and deters entry and access by rivals (Porter, 1980; Chen and MacMillian, 1992; D'Aveni, 1994; Wind, 1997). Cooperation builds gateways for access to partners' expertise and technology; access to materials, labors, capital, customers, and distribution. It enables risk-reduction, scale and scope economy in R&D. It also helps firms co-opt or block competition (Hamel, Doz, and Prahalad, 1989; Brandenburger and Nalebuff, 1996).

To cooperate is also to compete. Environmental situation changes and firm needs change, so should the firm's strategy and its target rivals or partners in competition or cooperation. Should a firm's advantage system draw its advantages primarily from competition or cooperation, or both? What criteria should a firm use to make such a choice? Research efforts on hypercompetition (1994), co-opetition (Brandenburger and Nalebuff, 1996), as well as the structural approach (Porter, 1980) are expected to be relevant in addressing this challenge.

Act Alone Vs. Act in Group

In stable and more certain environment where changes occur rather infrequently, it might still be possible or even advisable to build up product or market dominance through purely a firm's individual efforts. Yet in the emerging business landscape, firms often find themselves, for proactive or defensive reasons, tangled in webs of networks, groups, alliances, or other collaborative arrangements (Gomez-Casseres, 1994). Therefore, how to manage a firm's constellation of competitive advantage in the context of its business eco-system remains a major challenge (Moore, 1996).

Individual firms may have advantage over rivals based on their product quality or efficiency. Should these firms, however, reside in a collapsing business eco-system, they need to attend to the possibility that rival eco-systems may render theirs obsolete or irrelevant. Similarly, a technically stronger firm may also sail in a losing path simply because it was locked out from a winning standard due to its participation in a losing alliance (Ghemawat, 1991; Hill, 1997). So the decisions have to be made. To create and renew its advantages, should a firm go alone in its market or should it choose to take part in groups and alliances? To what extent should a firm draw advantage from its own attributes vs. its membership from a strategic alliance? The ecological perspective will be useful in helping general managers facing these issues (Moore, 1996).

Temporal Vs. Sustainable Advantage

A healthy and balanced constellation of competitive advantage hosts advantages of various types and time sensitivity. Both temporal and sustainable advantages contribute to the persistence of superior performance. The need for and possibility of sustainable advantage vary from firm to firm and business to business. Without sustainable advantage, a firm will not be secure in its long term survival. Relying solely on sustainable advantage, often built on market or resource position barriers, may hinder the firm's ability to adapt or fight in case of need. Strive to gain temporal advantage from competitive maneuvering helps sharpen a firm's routine and keeps it alert and fit (D'Aveni, 1994).

While the structural approach (Porter, 1980, 1985), the resource-based view (Barney, 1991; Wernerfelt, 1984), and commitment approach (Caves, 1984; Ghemawat, 1991) inform the nature and cause of sustainable advantage; Schumpeterian perspective (1934) and hypercompetition view (D'Aveni, 1994) emphasize the value of temporal advantages. Combined, they help general managers better assess the relative composition and the balance between temporal and sustainable advantages in a firm's constellation of competitive advantage.

Current Vs. Future Advantage

Competent firms often enjoy advantages over rivals and are aware of their current competitive challenges. Superior firms, in addition to their current advantages, think about and prepare their system of competitive advantage for the future. As such, these firms are willing to make sacrifice, to undertake trade-off between current and future advantages and between mature and emerging potential advantages. It is not too rare to see that leading firms, from time to time, cannibalize their own products or technologies. Firms like Intel, Canon, or Sony constantly introduce new generations of products to set the standard and push the game to a situation where they could possibly enjoy perpetual lead.

When should a firm disregard, abandon, or terminate its current advantage and strive for new ones? What guides the firm's choice in balancing current and future advantages? Again, extant research on Schumpeterian competition, hypercompetition, and commitment, among others, illuminates these challenges and helps general managers deal with them effectively.

CONCLUDING REMARKS

- A firm is a vehicle for winning. To win is to create the best customer value, to be better than the best. Winning justifies a firm's existence. At least for successful firms it is so.

- The essence of strategy is about winning. Persistent superior performance is the best score board or report card of a firm's strategy and its strategists.
- To achieve persistent superior performance, the best strategy is to build and manage a constellation of competitive advantage, a system comprising multiple advantages that also evolves.
- The advantage-based view makes full use of extant theories of strategy. It integrates existing wisdom and insights into the framework on constellation of competitive advantage.
- It is the general managers' fundamental task to create, shape, and renew the firm's advantage system. This requires good sense about the dynamics of the system and knowledge of the various challenges in managing the system.

Implications for Strategic Management Research

Using the lens of constellation of advantage is expected to enhance the explaining power of our theories. Instead of trying to locate *the* ultimate source of *the* sustainable advantage, based on whatever view of the firm—either as a collection of product-market activities or a bundle of resources—and focusing on whatever factor that is in vogue-market power, unique resources, core competence, dynamic capabilities, time, speed, innovation, and so on, we need to attend to the phenomenon of the firm's multi-level and multi-type *advantage constellation.* For this reason, this book offers the first cut of an advantage-based view of the firm.

Anatomy and constellation of competitive advantage, the two fundamental frameworks of the advantage-based view, help lay out a foundation for future work to build on: to further study how the anatomy of advantage affects firm performance, what advantages should be in a constellation, how changes in the constellation affect performance, and under what conditions constellation of advantage could turn into constellation of disadvantages. More sophisticated methodology, e. g., data envelopment analysis, should also be used in addition to more traditional methods, so as to map out simultaneously the frontiers of best practice on multiple dimensions of competitive advantages.

Implication for Strategic Management Practice

The managerial implication of the advantage-based view of the firm is that a firm needs to better understand its instrument for winning and better manage its entire system of advantage as an integrative whole. In the quest for persistent superior performance, no one thing really matters in the long run. Viewing the firm as a host of multiple evolving advantages, then we will see the power as well as the limitation of the various extant theories. The firm is no longer just a feudal monopolist, a lucky possessor of unique resources, a paranoid hyper-competitor, a trusting collaborator, an entrepreneurial innovator, or a shrewd strategizing opportunist. It's none of them. And it's all of them.

Instead of being obsessed with any specific tools to create and maintain an advantage, strategists need to be obsessed with winning, whatever it takes. This requires them to effectively choose from and utilize multiple tools to assists in their task of strategizing. Realistically speaking, banking on a single-factor advantage, however sustainable it may be, will likely turn out to be impractical, although it just might, on rare occasions, render the firm a chance for persistent superior performance. Building an evolving system of advantage, a system that hosts and creates multiple advantages, I believe, will certainly make a firm's chances greater and better. And, that, is the spirit of the advantage-based view of the firm.

Epilogue

You ask, what is our aim? I can answer that in one word: victory at all costs, victory in spite of all terror, victory however long and hard the road may be; for without victory there is no survival.

Sir Winston Churchill
Speech to House of Commons, 1940

For nothing can seem foul to those that win.

William Shakespeare

The two brilliant quotes from two brilliant English men eloquently remind us the necessity of winning. Now do the following exercise. Name ten firms from UK in the last half of the 20th century that have fundamentally changed the way people live and work around the globe. Does it take you for a long while? And then do the same exercise for Japan. You will definitely find it much easier to complete the latter assignment. Ironically, Sir Winston and the British won World War II against the Nazi with the Allied Force, but it was Japan that was winning the global economic war in the ensuing years since World War II.

Check out the top ten banks in the world thirty years ago and the list of top ten now. Thirty years ago, none of the Japanese banks was even on the map; some thirty years later, Japanese banks would dominate the global top ten consistently. In 1988, all the top 12 largest banks in the world ranked by deposits were Japanese. In 1994, all top ten banks in the world ranked by assets were from Japan. One thing is for sure: Japan didn't just get rich because they had world-class bankers. What they had actually produced were primarily winning firms, firms that came to dominate world-wide consumers' market and created superior customer value in so many business areas, automobile, home electronics and appliances, office equipment, etc.

Firms like Sony, Honda, Matsushita, and Canon are winners in their respective global markets. Diverse and different as their businesses are from each other, they share one common characteristic: Determination to win. Sony's mission in the 1950s was much larger and heroic in scope: to elevate the Japanese culture and national status. More specifically, to be a pioneer, not a follower, doing the impossible; to experience the joy of advancing and applying technology for the benefit of the public; to improve the image of Japanese made products. Honda aspired to be the next Ford, pioneer and innovator in the auto industry. The founder of Matsushita laid out a 250-year strategic plan to fulfill the mission of providing the best goods at the lowest cost to the greatest number of people possible. In 1991, the president of Canon described the vision for the company as such: to become a premier global company of the size of IBM combined with Matsushita.

> *The aim of any Japanese corporation is ensuring its perpetual survival. Unlike the venture businesses and U. S. corporations, our greatest objective is not to maximize short-term profits. Our vital objective is to continually earn profits on a stable basis for ensuring survival.*
>
> *Ryuzaburo Kaku*
> *Former President, Canon*

WINNING: SURVIVAL AND IMPACT

Such is the ambition to stay as a global winner on a permanent basis. To be sure, there are also plenty of American firms that are winning it big in the global market: from Coca-Cola to McDonald in food and drink; from Procter & Gamble to Johnson and Johnson in personal care and pharmaceuticals; from Microsoft to Motorola in computer, high-tech, and tele-communications. These firms shape and change the way people live and work worldwide. Just like the ambitious Japanese corporations, these firms vow to perpetuate their win by constantly renewing and enhancing their constellation of advantages.

And now Samsung, LG, and a host of Korean firms are increasingly making big splashes in the international economic scenes (Kang, 1989; Ungson, Steers, and Park, 1997), followed by some leading Chinese firms, e.g. Haier and TCL, which are also making giant strides in conquering the global market (Zeng and Williamson, 2003).

Veni, Vidi, Vici—I came, I saw, I conquered.
Julius Caesar

Successful people secure their names in history through posterity; successful firms secure their place through impact. The advantage-based view will so advise: focus on winning and strive for impact! Winners command more resources and demand greater customer and societal attention. This is not only true for private firms, but also true for national economies. Just consider how much earthly-resources the US consumes and the impact it has over the world. Consider how much global economic resources the Japanese have as its input to its huge industrial machine. Also, do not forget how the newly emerged economies in Asia are now increasingly conquering the world market and garnering respect. In this sense, to win is to achieve impact around the globe. And impact preludes superior performance. To win and achieve impact, a firm needs a viable constellation of advantage, so does a nation.

> *The most important thing in the Olympic Games is not winning but taking part... The essential thing in life is not conquering but fighting well.*
>
> *Baron Pierre de Coubertin*
> *Speech at Banquet to Officials of*
> *Olympic Games. London. July 24, 1908*

Coubertin's point may be well taken. But the modern day Olympic Games are also known as the ultimate race to challenge the best, to be faster, higher, and farther. Merely taking part in the games may be important or even honorable to any individual players. What people often remembered and admired, however, are winners, who excel, glorify, and inspire. Winners command more impact. The Olympic Games are indeed the games for winners in the league of winners. Without a winning record, there's not even a chance to take part. Without the will to conquer, how could one expect to fight well? If a fighter does not hope to win, why even fight at the first place? Business games share the same logic. Winning is the bottom line. To certain extent, competition in business may be even more intense and winning more necessary than in sports where worse performing teams will always have the next season.

> *A central difference between sports and business is that in business patterns of entry and exit ensure that a firm always will be up against the best in whatever market it chooses to compete. The second best competitors are forced out, leaving a situation where there is no second division in business.*
>
> *Birger Wernerfelt*
> *Professor, MIT*

This strong statement by Wernerfelt notwithstanding, business firms, in most situations if not all, have to fight the best to survive and thrive. This corresponds well to Intel CEO Andy Grove's notion "only the paranoid survive" in hypercompetitive environment. For there will be no business as usual. Instead, there will always be younger and hungrier firms that aspire to have the giants toppled. If you don't win, others will. If you lose, there might be no tomorrow. Hopelessly optimistic and confident people and teams make things happen; winning obsessed and inspired firms conquer and change the world.

CALL TO ACTION

A kernel idea of the advantage-based view is action. You won't tumble if you don't move. But you probably won't win either if you are not in motion. Winning calls for action to actually create and change the constellation of advantage.

In order to take action and win, a firm needs to institutionalize the winning philosophy and cultivate the winning attitude throughout the entire organization. It needs to mobilize people at all levels of the firm to act toward the ultimate goal of winning. To win, a firm also needs appropriate theoretical guidance, guidance that helps them better understand time-tested wisdom as well as contemporary business reality, so as to better manage its constellation of advantage.

In addition, firms also need supportive social environment and governmental policies that help them win. As a matter of fact, often times, firms have to also actively and effectively deal with unfavorable government policies and distrusting social environment, just as they enthusiastically build their constellation of advantage in the economic and competitive arena. For essentially all the text book examples of great firms that we use as models in business schools—those started from scratch by visionary entrepreneurs and came to power and sustained their advantages in their business—are always subject to and usually do go through lengthy and often demobilizing Antitrust investigations.

PUBLIC POLICY IMPLICATION

Winners necessarily dominate the market and, as a reward, are therefore often big in size. If we believe in the Chicago School that big firms become big because they are efficient and good at creating customer value, then we ought to salute the big winners instead of scorning them with jealousy and suspicion. If we believe in Schumpeter that the beauty and power of market economy is in creative destruction, then we shall have faith in the market system and be confident that there will always be innovating firms from generation to generation, like Microsoft, Wal-Mart, and Intel, that redefine their respective industry and competition.

Eliminate monopoly power and you throttle innovation.

Richard Rumelt
UCLA Professor

No inefficient firms could sustain in the long run, without government subsidy that is! If innovators could not capture the value they create, incentive for creation will be lessened. If a winner is not duly rewarded, the appeal of winning will be discounted. In the US, interestingly, largely because of the antiquated Antitrust law and American style egalitarianism, the government as well as the public would always have some inherent suspicion and distrust over the winners, the big players. Such a mentality and legal causes severely constrain American firms' ability and action to win in the increasingly more competitive global market. What winning firms would accomplish through their efficiency and superior capability is often being blamed as using unfair competitive practice or exercising unfair competitive advantage-based on their market power.

Thou shall no kill, but tradition approves all forms of competition.

Arthur Hugh Glough (1819-1861)
The Latest Dialog

Traditional American idealism must combine with a thoughtful assessment of contemporary realities to bring about a usable definition of American interests.

Henry Kissinger
Former US Secretary of State

Historically speaking, there is perhaps no such thing as fair competitive advantage. Advantage itself by definition suggests inequality, asymmetry, and differential. And competition was never fair. If it is fair, there will be no competition, just showing up; and winners will be determined automatically. In reality, firm endowments vary and opportunities are rarely if ever equal.

The Antitrust laws might be a valid institution in insuring fair play when American industries were in their infancy and social and competitive environments relatively placid. In the turbulent time of global competition, the old laws may not be relevant any longer. American firms, haunted by trust-busters at home and competing against players often backed by national government with coordinated industrial policy in the global market, necessarily become vulnerable. To effectively compete in the global market, a new mentality is badly needed. The American experience should be a lesson to the aspiring governments in emerging economies. A nation's competitiveness depends on the world dominant firms it produces.

> *Abide not by thy ancestors' law. Learn instead why and how thy ancestors institute the law.*
>
> Han Fei Zi, BC
> Chinese Philosopher

To be sure, government has and should have its legitimate concerns over social welfare and public good. It is a fact of life that inequality exists and competition is rarely fair. But it is only because of inequality that disadvantaged people or firm fight for equality. It is precisely the existence of unfair play that induces the cry for fair play. Whatever the case, the game will still be played. Government needs to do what it does. And so does the firm. This said, those firms that have better skills and capabilities to deal with such social and legal issues possess competitive advantage. That is, in its constellation of advantage, a firm needs social or institutional advantage. Without social legitimacy, a strong economic entity will not sustain its momentum and its very survival might also be in question.

In modern times, industrial society or information age, no single national economy, stronger ones that is, have been built on small firms that can't dominate in the world market. Alfred Chandler, Jr. eloquently argued, and meticulously demonstrated using examples spanning major Western industrialized economies, the paramount effect of scale and scope economy and the indispensable role of general managers as "visible hands" in the era of managerial capitalism.

It is no secret that many global companies are larger and more powerful than some sovereign governments. But realistically who's to regulate the global market? Way before European governments were arguing about or out-bargaining each other on the term and future for a unified currency in Europe, the Euro, firms like Visa and Mastercard have already quietly begun to make that, a unified currency, a reality.

In the increasingly global market, only the best company in providing superior customer value will survive and thrive. Countries that produce no such companies and those hinder or destroy such companies will be miserably left behind in the new global economy. Contemporary business history shows that capital and technology know no national boundaries; and customers world-wide demand the best value, often regardless of the providers' country of origin.

Obviously, firms are also social agents in addition to its economic role in the society. As such they bear tremendous social responsibility to their country of origin and to the communities where they draw their resources from and sell their products to. Social responsibility and economic profit are often not exactly compatible, yet better performing firms are, however, often those that have better social image and identity. Because it makes good business sense to behave in ways acceptable to people which not only are customers but also employees, citizens, and members of the community.

The Nobel Laureates in Economics Milton Friedman would argue that the only social responsibility of business firms is to create profit and shareholder value. I would argue instead that the only socially responsible thing for a firm to do is to create constellation of advantage and win. A firm owes to its stakeholders to win, its employees, its customers, and its community. For without winning, there is likely no survival, especially in the competitive global market. And all the talk about social responsibility becomes impractical and meaningless.

IMPLICATIONS FOR STRATEGISTS

Regardless of a firm's specific endowment, venturing in businesses activities where it has the best possibility for creating unique customer value generates comparative advantage. Fighting a losing war in businesses where a firm has not even the slightest chance of winning is a disservice both to the firm and society. Should more firms subscribe to such a winning philosophy, there will be more winning opportunities for the greatest number of firms. Consequently, the allocation and utilization of our limited social economical resources will likely, it just might, be more effective and efficient.

Don't misunderstand. Winning, by definition, is context-specific. Should a firm be able to create the best value to its immediate customer base in its business eco-systems, it is then a winner, however large that eco-systems may be. It does not have to beat everyone in its industry. In fact, due to limitation of the firm's constellation of advantage and often the bleak future in changing it, some firms are bound for long time to be only niche players. If they step out of their league, disasters ensue. For instance, a good local restaurant chain could be a sure winner in its region because of its rich cultural linkage with the region but often a disappointment if trying to make it national, messing-up or even losing its entire advantage constellation. That is, some winners are bound to be a big fish in a small pound.

The ultimate winners, however, win it all—at the highest level and to the largest scope possible, e.g., Coca-Cola's dominance in the worldwide soft drink industry. They define industry standard. They dominate market share. They are the synonym of their industry in minds of the customers. Both types of winners, big or small, I believe, will benefit from better understanding of their constellation of advantage should they apply the analytical tools provided in this book.

For firms that are satisfied with just being a dog's head instead of a lion's tail—which is still possible in some business at certain time—this book will still be of help. It advises them on how to select rivals and avoid lions, and, in one word, achieve comparative advantage in their respective niches.

What the advantage-based view really helps, however, are those who intend to be the biggest fish in the biggest pond, to be better than the best. For the advantage-based view treats the firm as a vehicle for winning. Winning in creating the best customer value to the widest extent possible.

    Winning inspires employees.

    Winning better creates customer value.

    Winning justifies the firm's existence.

    Winning validates the firm's worth.

    So strive to win.

    Win all the way.

    Conquer the world market.

Bibliography

Aaker, D. A., 1996, *Building Strong Brands*, New York, NY: The Free Press.

Aaker, D. A., 1991, *Managing Brand Equity*, New York, NY: The Free Press.

Abell, D. F., 1980, *Defining the Business*, Englewood Cliffs, NJ: Prentice Hall.

Amit, R., and Schoemaker, P. J. H., 1993, Strategic assets and organizational rent, *Strategic Management Journal*, 14 (1), 33—46.

Ansoff H. I. 1965. *Corporate Strategy: An Analytic Approach to Business Policy for Growth and Expansion*. New York, NY: McGraw-Hill.

Axelrod, R. 1984. *The Evolution of Cooperation*. New York: Basic Books, Inc.

Bailey, E. E., 1997, *Integrating Policy Trends into Dynamic Advantage*, In Day, G. S. And Reibstein, D. J. (Eds.) 1997, *Wharton on Dynamic Competitive Strategy*. New York, NY: John Wiley & Sons, Inc.

Bain, J., 1956, *Barriers to new competition*, Cambridge, MA: Harvard University Press.

Barnard, C.I., 1938, *The Function of Executives*, Cambridge, MA: Harvard University Press.

Barney, J. B. and Zajac, E. J., 1994, Competitive organizational behavior: toward an organizationally-based theory of competitive advantage, *Strategic Management Journal*, Winter Special Issue, 15: 5—10.

Barney, J. B., 1989, Assets stocks and sustained competitive advantage, *Management Science*, 35 (12), 1511—1513.

Barney, J. B., 1986a, Strategic Factor Markets: Expectations, Luck, And Business Strategy, *Management Science*, 32: 1231—1241.

Barney, J. B., 1986b, Organization Culture: Can It Be A Source Of Competitive Advantage? *Academy Of Management Review*, 11: 656—665.

Barney, J. B., 1991, Firm Resources And Sustained Competitive Advantage, *Journal of Management*, 17: 99—120.

Barney, J. B., 2002, *Gaining And Sustaining Competitive Advantage* (2nd ed.), NJ: Prentice Hall.

Barney, J. B., 1997, *Gaining And Sustaining Competitive Advantage*, Reading, Ma: Addison-Wesley.

Barney, 1994, *The golden time of strategy research*, Panel Discussion, Academy of Management Annual Meetings, Dallas, TX.

Baron, D. 1995. Integrated strategy: Market and nonmarket components. *California Management Review*, 37(3): 47—65.

Baron, D. P., 1995, Integrating market and nonmarket strategies, *California Management Review*, 37 (2), 47—65.

Bartlett, C. A. and Mohammed, A., 1995, 3M: Profile of an Innovating Company, *Harvard Business School Publishing*, 9-395-016.

Bartlett, C. A., 1985, Caterpillar Tractor Co., *Harvard Business School Publishing*, 9-385-276.

Bennis, W. and Biederman, P. W., 1997, *Organizing Genius*, Reading, MA: Addison-Wesley Publishing Company, Inc.

Biggadike, E. R. 1981. "The contributions of marketing to strategic management," *Academy of Management Review*. 6 (October): 621—632.

Boston Consulting Group, 1972, *Perspectives on Experience*, Boston, MA: BCG.

Bower, J. and Hout, T. M., 1988, Fast-Cycle Capability For Competitive Power, *Harvard Business Review*, November-December: 2—9.

Bower, J. L. and J. Dial., 1994, Jack Welch: General Electric's Revolutionary, *Harvard Business School Publishing*, case #9-394-065.

Bower, J. L., 1986, *Managing the Resource Allocation Process*, Boston, MA: Harvard Business School Press.

Brandenburger, A. and B. Nalebuff, 1996, *Coopetition*, New York, NY: Currency/Doubleday.

Burgelman, R. A., 1983a, A Process Model of Internal Corporate Venturing in the Diversified Major Firm, *Administrative Science Quarterly*, 28: 223—244.

Burgelman, R. A., 1983b, A Model of the Interaction of Strategic Behavior, Corporate Context, and the Concept of Strategy, *Academy of Management Review*, 8, 1: 61—70.

Business Week, 1996a, *Lift off*, April 22: 136—147.

Business Week, 1996b, *Inside Microsoft*, July 15: 56—70.

Business Week, 2004, *Can Michael Eisner Hold the Fort*? March 22: p.96.

Business Week, 1997, *Cover Story: The Economics of a TV Supershow And What IT Means For NBC and The Industry*, June 2: 116—121.

Camerer, C., 1991, Does strategy research need game theory? *Strategic Management Journal*, 12 (Winter Special Issue): 137—152.

Caves, R. E. and Ghemawat, P., 1992, Identifying Mobility Barriers, *Strategic Management Journal*, 13: 1—12.

Caves, R. E., 1984, Economic Analysis And The Quest For Competitive Advantage, *American Economic Review*, 74: 127—132.

Chance, A., Cooper, W. W., Lewin, A., and Seiford, L. M., 1994, *Data envelopment analysis: theory, methodology, and applications*, Boston, MA: Kluwer.

Chandler, A. D. Jr., 1990, *Scale and Scope: The Dynamics of Industrial Capitalism*, Cambridge, MA: The Belknap Press of Harvard University Press.

Chandler, A. D. Jr., 1962, *Strategy and Structure*, Cambridge, MA: MIT Press.

Chandler, A. D. Jr., 1977, *The Visible Hand: The Managerial Revolution in American Business*, Cambridge, MA: The Belknap Press of Harvard University Press.

Chen, M.-J. and MacMillan, I. C., 1992, Nonresponse and delayed response to competitive moves: The roles of competitor dependence and action irreversibility, *Academy of Management Journal*, 35: 539—570.

Chen, M.-J. and Miller, D., 1994, Competitive Attack, Retaliation and Performance: An expectancy-valence framework, *Strategic Management Journal*, 15: 85—102.

Chen, M.-J., 1996, Competitor analysis and interfirm rivalry: toward a theoretical integration, *Academy of Management Review*, 21: 100—134.

Chesbrough, H. W. and Teece, D. J., 1996, When virtual virtuous? Organizing for innovation, *Harvard Business Review*, January-February: 65—73.

Child, J., 1972, Organizational Structure, Environment and Performance: The Role of Strategic Choice, *Sociology*, 6 (January): 2—22.

Coase, R., 1937, The nature of the firm, *Economica*, 4: 386—406.

Collins, J. C. and Porras, J. I., 1996, Building your company's vision, *Harvard Business Review*, September-October: 65—77.

Collins, J. C., 2001, *Good to Great: Why Some Companies Make the Leap and Others Don't*, New York, NY: Harper Business.

Collis, D. J. and Montgomery, C. A., 1997, *Corporate Strategy: Resources And The Scope Of The Firm*, Chicago, IL: Irwin.

Collis, D. J., 1994, How Valuable Are Organizational Capabilities? *Strategic Management Journal*, Special Issue, Winter: 143—152.

Contractor, F. J. and Lorange, P., 1988, *Cooperative Strategies In International Business*, Lexington Books.

Cooper, R., 1997, Sony Corporation: The Walkman Line, *Harvard Business School Publishing*, Case #9-195-076.

D'Aveni, R., 1994, *Hypercompetition*, New York, NY: The Free Press.

Day, G. S. and Reibstein, D. J., 1997, *Wharton on Dynamic Competitive Strategy*, New York, NY: John Wiley & Sons, Inc.

Deal, T. E. and Kennedy, A. A., 1982, *Corporate Cultures*, Reading, MA: Addison-Wesley.

Demsetz, H., 1973, Industry structure, market rivalry, and public policy, *Journal of Law and Economics*, 16: 1—9.

Dierickx, I. and K. Cool, 1989, Asset Stock Accumulation And Sustainability Of Competitive Advantage, *Management Science*, 35: 1504—1511.

Doh, J. P., 2000, *Entrepreneurial privatization strategies: Order of entry and local partner collaboration as sources of competitive advantage*, Academy of Management Review, 25, 3: 551—572.

Drucker, P. F., 1954, *The Practice of Management*, New York, NY: Harper & Row.

Dyer, J. H. and Singh, H., 1998, The Relational View: Cooperative Strategy and source of Interorganizational Competitive Advantage, *Academy of Management Review*, 23, 4: 660—679.

Eccles, R. G. and Nohria, N., 1992, *Beyond The Hype: Rediscovering The Essence Of Management*, Boston, MA: Harvard Business School Press.

Egelhoff, W. G., 1988, *Organizing the multinational enterprise: An information processing perspective*, Cambridge, MA: Ballinger Publishing.

Eisenhardt, K. M., and Brown, S. L., 1998, *Competing on the edge: Strategy as structured chaos*, Boston, MA: Harvard Business School Press.

Evans, P. B. and Wurster, T. S., 1997, Strategy and the new economics of information, *Harvard Business Review*, September-October: 70—83.

Farh, J. L., Tsui, A. S., Xin, K., and Cheng, B. S., 1998, The influence of relational demography and guanxi: The Chinese case, *Organization Science*, 9, 4: 471—488.

Fast, N and Berg, N., 1983, The Lincoln Electric Company, *Harvard Business School Publishing*, case #9-376-028.

Fiegenbaum, A., Hart, S., and Schendel, D., 1996, Strategic reference point theory, *Strategic Management Journal*, 17 (3), 219—235.

Follett, M. P., 1941, *Dynamic Administration*, New York, NY: Harper & Row.

Forbes, 1997a, *Format Wars*, July 7.

Forbes, 1997b, *Encirclement*, December 1: 145.

Forbes, 1984, *General Electric-Going with the Winners*, March 26: 106.

Forbes, 1998, *Star Bucks: Top 40 Entertainers*, September 21: 220.

Ford, H., 1923, *My Life And Work*, New York, NY: Doubleday, Page, & Co.

Fortune, 1997a, *Fortune 500 Largest U. S. Corporations*, April 26: 189—207 and F1-F42.

Fortune, 1995a, *Open season on banks*, August 21: 42—52.

Fortune, 1996a, *The brand's the thing*, March 4: 72—86.

Fortune, 1995b, *Competition: Nike vs. Reebok*, September 18: 90—106.

Fortune, 1996b, *The Fortune 500*, April 29: 260—276 and F1-F42.

Fortune, 1997b, *Tiger!* May 12: 73—84.

Fortune, 1994, *Can The Limited fix itself?* October 17: 161—172.

Fortune, 1995c, *Cover Story: How We Did It*, October 2: 69—86.

Fortune, 1997c, *Cover Story: Inside Microsoft's Brain*, December 8: 84—98.

Fortune, 1996c, *Gates and Grove: Mr. Software and Mr. Hardware Brainstorm Computing's Future*, July 8: 42—58.

Fortune, 1985, *Sony*, April 15.

Fortune, 1998, *Why Wall Street's buying Wal-Mart again*, 92—4.

Freeman, R. E. 1984. *Strategic Management: A Stakeholder Approach.* Boston, MA: Pitman Publishing, Inc.

Gates, W. III., 1995, *The Road Ahead*, New York, NY: Viking Penguin.

Ghemawat, P., 1991, *Commitment: The Dynamics Of Strategy*, New York: The Free Press.

Ghemawat, P., 1986, Sustainable Advantage, *Harvard Business Review*, September-October, 64: 53—58.

Ghoshal, S. and Bartlett, C. A., 1997, *Individualized Corporation: A Fundamentally New Approach to Management*, New York, NY: Harper Business.

Ghoshal, S. and Bartlett, C. A., 1992, *Kao Corporation*, INSEAD Case.

Ghoshal, S. and Bartlett, C.A., 1988, Matsushita Electric Industrial (MEI) In 1987, *Harvard Business School Publishing*, 9-388-144.

Ghoshal, S., 1992, *Canon: Competing On Capabilities*, INSEAD Case.

Gimeno, J., and Woo, C. Y., 1996, Hypercompetition in a multimarket environment: The role of strategic similarity and multimarket contact on competitive de-escalation, *Organization Science*: 7, 322—341.

Gomes-Casseres, B., 1994, Group versus Group: How Alliance Networks Compete, *Harvard Business Review*, July-August: 4—11.

Goold, M. Campbell, A. and Alexander, M. 1995. Corporate Strategy: The Quest for Parenting Advantage, *Harvard Business Review*, March-April: 120—132.

Grant, R. M., 1991, A Resource Based Perspective Of Competitive Advantage, *California Management Review*, 33 (Spring): 114—135.

Grant, R. M., 1996, *Contemporary Strategy Analysis* (2nd Ed.), Cambridge, MA: Blackwell Publisher.

Grant, R. M., 1998, *Contemporary strategy analysis* (3rd Ed.), Malden, MA: Blackwell Publishers.

Griffin, N. and Masters, K., 1996, *Hit & Run: How Jon Peters and Peter Guber Took Sony For A Ride In Hollywood*, New York, NY: Simon & Schuster.

Grimm, C. M. and Smith, K. G., 1997, *Strategy as Action: Industry Rivalry and Coordination*, Cincinnati, OH: Southwestern Publishing.

Grove, A., 1996, *Only the Paranoid Survive*, New York, NY: DoubleDay.

Gulati, R., 1998, Networks and Alliances, *Strategic Management Journal*, 19, 293—318.

Gulati, R., Nohria, N., 1992, Mutually assured alliances, *Academy of Management Best Papers Proceedings*, 1992: 17—21.

Gupta, A. K. and Govindarajan, V., 2001, Converting Global Presence Into Global Competitive Advantage, *Academy Of Management Executive*, 15, 2: 45—58.

Gupta, A. K. and Govindarajan, V., 1991, Knowledge flows and the structure of control within multinational corporations, *Academy of Management Review*, 16: 768—792.

Hall, R., 1992, The Strategic Analysis Of Intangible Resources, *Strategic Management Journal*, 13, 2: 135—144.

Hambrick, D., 1982, Environmental Scanning And Organizational Strategy, *Strategic Management Journal*, 3: 159—174.

Hamel, G. and Prahalad, C. K., 1994, *Competing For The Future*, Boston, MA: Harvard Business School Press.

Hamel, G. and Prahalad, C. K., 1989, Strategic Intent, *Harvard Business Review*, May-June: 63—76.

Hamel, G., Doz, Y and Prahalad, C. K., 1989, Collaborate With Your Competitors And Win, *Harvard Business Review*, 67: 133—139.

Hannan, M. and Freeman, J., 1977, The population ecology of organizations, *American Journal of Sociology*, 72: 267—272.

Hansen, G and Wenerfelt, B., 1989, Determinants of firm performance: The relative importance of economic and organizational factors, *Strategic Management Journal*, 10: 399—411.

Harvard Business Review on Strategic Alliances, 2002, Harvard Business School Publishing Co.

Harvey, M. G., Novicevic, M. M., Buckley, M. R. and Ferris, G. R., 2001, A historic perspective on organizational ignorance, *Journal of Managerial Psychology*, 16: 449—469.

Haspeslagh, P. C. and Jemison, D. B., 1991, *Managing Acquisitions: Creating Value Through Corporate Renewal*, New York, NY: The Free Press.

Hayes, R. H., Pisano, G. P., Upton, D. M. and Wheelwright, S. C. 2004. *Operations, Strategy, and Technology: Pursuing the Competitive Edge.* Indianapolis, Ind.: John Wiley & Sons, Inc.

Henderson, B. D., 1989, The origin of strategy, *Harvard Business Review*, November-December: 2—5.

Henderson, B., 1979, *Henderson on Corporate Strategy*, Cambridge, MA: Abt Books.

Henderson, B., 1984, *The Logic of Business Strategy*, Cambridge, MA: Ballinger Publishing Company.

Henderson, H., 1996, *Building A Win-Win World: Life Beyond Global Warfare*, San Francisco, CA: Berrett-Koehler Publishers, Inc.

Hill, C. W. L. and Jones, G., 1996, *Strategic Management* (3rd ed.), Boston, MA: Houghton Mifflin.

Hill, C. W. L., 1997, Establishing a standard: Competitive strategy and technological standards in winner-take-all industries, *The Academy of Management Executive*, 11, 2: 7—25.

Hitt, M.A., Ireland, R. D., Camp, S. M. and Sexton, D. L., 2001, Strategic entrepreneurship: entrepreneurial strategies for wealth creation, *Strategic Management Journal*, 22, 6—7: 479—491.

Hofer, C. W. and Schendel, D., 1978, *Strategy Formulation: Analytical Concepts*, St. Paul, MN: West.

Itami, H., 1987, *Mobilizing Intangible Assets*, Boston, MA: Harvard University Press.

Jacobson, R., 1992, The "Austrian" school of strategy, *Academy of Management Review*, 17: 782—807.

Jacobson, R., 1988, The persistence of abnormal returns, *Strategic Management Journal*, 9: 41—58.

Jemison, D., 1981, The importance of an integrative approach to strategic management research, *Academy of Management Review*, 6: 601—608.

Johnson, B., 1997, IBM moves back to Intel Co-op deal, *Advertising Age*, March 10: 4.

Kang, T. W., 1989, *Is Korea The Next Japan*? New York, NY: The Free Press.

Katz, D., 1994, *Just Do It: The Nike Spirit in the Corporate World*, Holbrook, MA: Adams Media Corporation.

Kelly, G., 1976, Seducing the Elites: The Politics of Decision Making and Innovation in Organizational Networks, *Academy of Management Review*, 1: 66—74.

Kim, W. C. and Mauborgne, R. 2005. *Blue Ocean Strategy*. Harvard Business School Press.

Kim, W. C. and Mauborgne, R., 1997, Value Innovation: The Strategic Logic of High Growth, *Harvard Business Review*, January-February: 103—112.

Kissinger, H. A., 1994, *Diplomacy*, New York, NY: Simon & Schuster.

Klein, A., 1990, Phil Knight: CEO at Nike, *Harvard Business School Publishing*, 9-390-038.

Kogut, B. and Singh, H., 1988, The effect of national culture on the choice of entry mode, *Journal of International Business Studies*, 19: 411—432.

Kogut, B., 1988, Joint Ventures: Theoretical and Empirical Perspectives, *Strategic Management Journal*, 9, 319—332.

Kotter, J. P., 1997, *Matsushita Leadership: Lessons From The 20th Century's Most Remarkable Entrepreneur*, New York, NY: The Free Press.

Kuhn, T. S., 1962, *The structure of scientific revolutions*, Chicago: University of Chicago Press.

Lado, A. A., Boyd, N. G., and Hanlon, S. C., 1997, Competition, Cooperation, and the Search for Economic Rents: A Syncretic Model, *Academy of Management Review*, 22, 1: 110—141.

Landis, B., 1997, License-plate lowdown: R.I. has 27 No. 1's, *Providence Sunday Journal*, September 28: A1, A15.

Learned, E. P., Christensen, C. R., Andrews, K. R. and Guth, W., 1965, *Business Policy: Text and Cases*, Homewood, IL: Richard Irwin.

Lebrecht, N., 1994, *The Maestro Myth: Great Conductors in Pursuit of Power*, Seacaucus, NJ: Carol Publishing.

Ledford, G. E. Jr. and Lawler, E. E. III., 1994, Dialog: research on employee participation: beating the dead horses? *Academy of Management Review*, 19 (4), 633—636.

Leonard-Barton, D., 1992, Core capabilities and core rigidities: a paradox in managing new product development, *Strategic Management Journal*, 13 (Summer Special Issue), 111—125.

Levitt, T., 1983, The globalization of markets, *Harvard Business Review*, 61, 3: 92—102.

Lieberman, M. and Montgomery, D., 1988, First Mover Advantages, *Strategic Management*

Journal, 9: 41—58.

Lippman, S. and R. Rumelt., 1982, Uncertain Imitability: An Analysis Of Interfirm Difference In Efficiency Under Competition, *Bell Journal Of Economics*, 16: 418—438.

Luo, Y. and Peng, M. W., 1998, First mover advantages in investing in transitional economies, *Thunderbird International Business Review*, 40(2): 141—163.

Luo, Y., 1998, Timing of investment and international performance in China, *Journal of International Business Studies*, 29: 391—408.

Ma, H., 1999, Anatomy of Competitive Advantage: A SELECT Framework, *Management Decision*, 37, 9: 709—718.

Ma, H., 2000, Competitive Advantage and Firm Performance, *Competitiveness Review*, 10, 2: 15—32.

Ma, H., 1997, Constellation of Competitive Advantage and Persistent Superior Performance, Paper presented at the Academy of Management Annual Meetings, Boston, MA.

Ma, H., 1999, Constellation of Competitive Advantage: Components and Dynamics, *Management Decision*, 37, 4: 348—355.

Ma, H., 1999, Creation and Preemption for Competitive Advantage, *Management Decision*, 37, 3: 259—266.

Ma, H., Karri, R. and Chittipeddi, K., 2004, The Paradox of Managerial Tyranny, *Business Horizons*, July, In Press.

Ma, H., 1998, Mutual Forbearance in International Business, *The Journal of International Management*, 4, 2: 129—147.

Ma, H., 2000, Of Competitive Advantage: Kinetic and Positional, *Business Horizons*, 43, 1: 53—64.

Ma, H., 2000, Toward an Advantage Based View of the Firm, *Advances in Competitiveness Research*, 8,1: 34—59.

Ma, H., 2003, What's Luck Got to Do With It? *Management Decision*.

Mahoney, J. T. and Pandian, J. R., 1992, The Resource-Based View Within The Conversation Of Strategic Management, *Strategic Management Journal*, 13: 363—380.

Mancke, R. B., 1974, Causes of interfirm profitability differences: A new interpretation of the evidence, *Quarterly Journal of Economics*, 88 (May), 181—93.

Marcus, B., Blank, A., and Andelman, B., 1999, *Built from Scratch: How a Couple of Regular Guys Grew the Home Depot from Nothing to $ 30 Billion*, New York: Crown Business.

McGahan, A. M., 1991, Philips Compact Disc Introduction (Case Series), *Harvard Business School Publishing*.

Meyer, A. D., 1982, Adapting to environmental jolts, *Administrative Science Quarterly*, 27 (4), 515—538.

Micklethwait, J. and Wooldridge, A., 1996, *The Witch Doctors: Making Sense Of The Management Gurus*, New York, NY: Times Books.

Miles, R. E. and Snow, C. C., 1978, *Organizational strategy, structure, and process*, New

York, NY: McGraw-Hill.

Miles, R. H., 1982, *Coffin Nails And Corporate Strategy*, Engelwood Cliffs, NJ: Prentice Hall.

Miller, A., 1993, The U. S. Athletic Shoe Industry, In Dess, G and Miller, A., *Strategic Management*, New York, NY: McGraw-Hill.

Mintzberg, H., 1978, Patterns in Strategy Formation, *Management Science*, 24, 9: 934—949.

Mintzberg, H., 1996, The Honda effect revisited (a series of articles), *California Management Review*, 38, 4: 78—79, 92—93, 96—99.

Moore, J. F., 1996, *The Death Of Competition: Leadership & Strategy In The Age Of Business Ecosystems*, New York, NY: Harper Business.

Nanda, A. and Bartlett, C. A., 1994, Intel Corporation—Leveraging Capabilities for Strategic Renewal, *Harvard Business School Publishing*, case #9-394-141.

Nelson, R. and Winter, S., 1982, *An Evolutionary Theory Of Economic Change*, Cambridge, MA: Harvard University Press.

Nohria, N. and Gulati, R., 1996, Is Slack Good Or Bad For Innovation? *Academy Of Management Journal*, 39, 5: 1245—1264.

Nonaka, I., 1991, The Knowledge-Creating Company, *Harvard Business Review*, November-December: 2—9.

Ohmae, K., 1988, Getting back to strategy, *Harvard Business Review*, November-December: 149—156.

Ohmae, K., 2000, *The Invisible Continent: Four Strategic Imperatives of the New Economy*, London: Nicholas Brealey.

Ohmae, K., 1982, *The Mind of Strategist*, New York, NY: McGraw-Hill.

Oliver, C., 1997, Sustainable Competitive Advantage: Combining Institutional and Resource-Based Views, *Strategic Management Journal*, 18: 697—713.

O'Shea, J. and Madigan, C., 1997, *Dangerous Company*, New York: Times Business.

Pan, Y., and Chi, P. S. K., 1999, Financial performance and survival of multinational corporations in China, *Strategic Management Journal*, 20: 359—374.

Pan, Y., Li, S., and Tse, D. K., 1999, The impact of order of entry and mode of market entry on profitability and market share, *Journal of International Business Studies*, 30: 81—104.

Pascale, R. T., 1984, Perspectives On Strategy: The Real Story Behind Honda's Success, *California Management Review*, 26, 3: 47—72.

Penrose, E., 1959, *The Theory Of The Growth Of The Firm*, Oxford, England: Blackwell.

Peteraf, M. A., 1993, The Cornerstones Of Competitive Advantage: A Resource-Based View, *Strategic Management Journal*, 14: 179—191.

Peters, T. and Waterman, R., 1982, *In Search Of Excellence*, New York, NY: Harper & Row.

Pfeffer, J., 1994, *Competitive Advantage Though People*, Boston, MA: Harvard Business School Press.

Porter, M. E., 1985, *Competitive Advantage*, New York: The Free Press.

Porter, M. E., 1990, *Competitive Advantage Of Nations*, New York: The Free Press.

Porter, M. E., 1980, *Competitive Strategy*, New York: The Free Press.

Porter, M. E., 1984, Strategic Interaction: some lessons from industry histories for theory and antitrust policy, In Lamb, R. (Ed.), *Competitive Strategic Management*: 415—445, Englewood Cliffs, NJ: Prentice Hall.

Porter, M. E., 1981, The contribution of industrial organization to strategic management, *Academy of Management Review*, 6: 609—620.

Porter, M. E., 1991, Towards A Dynamic Theory Of Strategy, *Strategic Management Journal*, 12 (Winter Special Issue): 95—118.

Porter, M. E., 1996, What Is Strategy? *Harvard Business Review*, November-December: 61—78.

Powell. T. C., 2001, Competitive Advantage: Logical and Philosophical Considerations, *Strategic Management Journal*, 22: 875—888.

Powell, T. C., 1992, Strategic Planning As Competitive Advantage, *Strategic Management Journal*, 13: 551—558.

Prahalad, C. K. and Hamel, G., 1990, The Core Competence Of Corporations, *Harvard Business Review*, May-June: 79—91.

Prahalad, C. K., Lieberthal, K. 2003. The End of Corporate Imperialism. *Harvard Business Review*, August: 109—117.

Quinn, J. B., 1980, *Strategies For Change: Logical Incrementalism*, Homewood, Il: Irwin.

Reichheld, F. F., 1996, *The Loyalty Effect: The Hidden Force Behind Growth, Profits, and Lasting Value*, Boston, MA: Harvard Business School Publishing.

Reich, R. B. and Mankin, E. D., 1986, Joint Ventures with Japan Give Away Our Future, *Harvard Business Review*, March-April: 78—85.

Roddick, A., 1991, *Body and Soul: Profits with Principles—The Amazing Story of Anita Roddick and the Body Shop*, New York, NY: Crown Publishers.

Rogers, D. J., 1987, *Waging Business Warfare: Lessons From The Military Masters in Achieving Corporate Superiority*, New York, NY: Charles Scribner's Sons.

Rosenzweig, P. M., 1991, Bill Gates and the Management of Microsoft, *Harvard Business School Publishing*, 9-392-019.

Rumelt, R. P., 1991, How Much Does Industry Matter? *Strategic Management Journal*, 12: 167—185.

Rumelt, R. P., Schendel, D. E., and Teece, D. J., 1991, Strategic management and economics, *Strategic Management Journal*, 12 (Winter Special Issue): 5—29.

Rumelt, R. P., 1974, *Strategy, structure, and economic performance*, Boston: Harvard University Press, 1974.

Rumelt, R. P., 1996, The Many Faces Of Honda, *California Management Review*, 38, 4: 103—111.

Rumelt, R. P., 1987, Theory, Strategy, and Entrepreneurship, In Teece, D. (Ed.), *The Competitive Challenge*: 137—158, Cambridge, Mass: Ballinger.

Rumelt, R. P., 1984, Toward A Strategic Theory Of Firm, In Lamb, R. (Ed.), *Competitive Strategic Management*: 556—570, Englewood Cliffs: Prentice Hall.

Saloner, G., 1991, Modeling, game theory, and strategic management, *Strategic Management Journal*, 12 (Winter Special Issue): 119—136.

Sanchez, R., 1993, Strategic flexibility, firm organization, and managerial work in dynamic markets: A strategic-options perspective, In Shrivastava, P., Huff, A. S., and Dutton, J. E. (Eds.), *Advances in Strategic Management*, 9: 251—291, Greenwich, CT: JAI Press, Inc.

Sanchez, R., 1995, Strategic Flexibility in Product Competition, *Strategic Management Journal*, 16 (Summer Special Issue): 135—159.

Schoemaker, P., 1990, Strategy, Complexity, And Economic Rent, *Management Science*, 36: 1178—1192.

Schumpeter, J. A., 1950, *Capitalism, Socialism, and Democracy*, New York: Harper & Row.

Schumpeter, J. A., 1934, *The Theory Of Economic Development*, Cambridge, MA: Harvard University Press.

Selznick, P., 1957, *Leadership in Administration*, New York: Harper & Row.

Senge, P. M., 1990, *The Fifth Discipline: The Art and Practice of The Learning Organization*, New York, NY: Double Day/Currency.

Shrivastava, P. 1996. *Greening Business: Profiting the Corporation and the Environment.* Cincinnati, Ohio: Thompson Executive Press.

Simon, H. A., 1947, *Administrative Behavior*, New York, NY: The Free Press.

Smith, K. G., Grimm, C. M., Gannon, M. J., 1992, *Dynamics of competitive strategy*, Newbury Park, CA: Sage Publications.

Stalk, G. and Hout, T., 1990, *Competing Against Time: How Time-Based Competition Is Reshaping Global Markets*, New York, NY: The Free Press.

Stalk, G., Evans, P., and Shulman, L. E., 1992, Competing On Capabilities, *Harvard Business Review*, March-April: 57—69.

Stalk, G., 1990, Time—The Next Source Of Competitive Advantage, *Harvard Business Review*, July-August: 41—51.

Stewart. T. A, 1997, *Intellectual Capital: The New Wealth of Organizations*, New York, NY: Doubleday/Currency.

Stigler, G., 1968, *The Organization of Industry*, Chicago, IL: University of Chicago Press.

Tan, J. J., 2001, Innovation and risk taking in a transitional economy: A comparative study of Chinese managers and entrepreneurs, *Journal of Business Venturing*, 16, 359—376.

Teece, D. J., 1990, Contributions and impediments of economic analysis to the study of strategic management, In Fredrickson, J. W. (Ed.), *Perspectives on Strategic Management*, 39—80, New York: Harper Business.

Teece, D. J., Pisano, G. and Shuen, A., 1997, Dynamic Capabilities and Strategic Management, *Strategic Management Journal*, 18: 509—533.

Time, 1994, *They Are Back*! July 18: 52—55.

Ulrich, D. and Lake, D., 1990, *Organizational Capability: Competing From the Inside Out*, New York, NY: John Wiley.

Ulrich, D., 1997, *Human Resource Champions*, Boston, MA: Harvard Business School Publishing.

Ungson, G. R., Steers, R. M., and Park, S. H., 1997, *Korean Enterprise, The Quest For Globalization*, Boston, MA: Harvard Business School Press.

Vogel, E. F., 1985, *Comeback*, New York, NY: Simon & Schuster.

Wall Street Journal, 1997, *Computer Firms Tell of Microsoft's Tough Tactics*, Oct. 23: A3 and A6.

Wall Street Journal, 1996, *Don't hate me because I'm beautiful*, December 31: 7.

Wall Street Journal, 1998, *Manager's Journal: A Match Made in Heaven? Find Out Before You Merge*, Nov. 30.

Wall Street Journal, 1993, *Tweeter's Customers Told: Your Check is in the Mail*, August 17.

Walton, S., 1992, *Made In America: My Story*, New York, NY: Doubleday.

Wernerfelt, B., and Montgomery, C. A., 1986, What is an attractive industry? *Management Science*, 32, 1223—1230.

Wernerfelt, B., 1984, A resource-based view of the Firm, *Strategic Management Journal*, 5: 171—180.

Wernerfelt, B., 1995, The resource-based view of the firm: ten years after, *Strategic Management Journal*, 16: 171—174.

Wheelen, T. L. and Hunger, J. D., 1997, *Strategic Management and Business Policy: Entering 21st Century Global Society*, Reading, MA: Addison-Wesley.

Williamson, O. E., 1975, *Markets and Hierarchies: Analysis and Antitrust Implications*, New York: The Free Press.

Williamson, O. E., 1991, Strategizing, Economizing, And Economic Organization, *Strategic Management Journal*, 12 (Winter Special Issue): 75—94.

Wind, J., 1997, *Preemptive Strategies*, In Day, G. S. and Reibstein, D. J., 1997 (Ed.), *Wharton on Dynamic Competitive Strategy*, New York, NY: John Wiley & Sons, Inc.

Winter, S., 1987, Knowledge And Competence As Strategic Assets, In D. Teece (Ed.), *The Competitive Challenge*: 159—184, New York, NY: Harper & Row.

Yan, A., 1998, Structural stability and reconfiguration of international joint ventures, *Journal of International Business Studies*, 29: 773—796.

Yip, G., 1995, *Total Global Strategy: Managing for Worldwide Competitive Advantage*, Englewood, Cliffs, NJ: Prentice Hall.

Yoffie, D. and Cusumano, M. A., 1999, Judo strategy: the competitive dynamics of Internet time, *Harvard Business Review*, 77 (1), 70—82.

Yoffie, D., 1990, The World VCR Industry, *Harvard Business School Publishing*, 9-387-098.

Zajac, E., 1992, Relating economic and behavioral perspectives in strategy research, In Dutton, J., Huff, A., and Shrivastava, P. (Eds.), *Advances in Strategic Management*, Greenwich, CT: JAI Press Inc.

Zeng, M. and Williamson, P. J., 2003, The Hidden Dragons, *Harvard Business Review*, October: 92—99.

图书在版编目(CIP)数据

竞争优势:解剖与集合(Competitive Advantage: Anatomy and Constellation)/马浩著. —北京:北京大学出版社,2004.9
(北京大学中国经济研究中心研究系列)
ISBN 7-301-07774-2

Ⅰ.竞… Ⅱ.马… Ⅲ.企业-市场竞争-研究-英文 Ⅳ.F270

中国版本图书馆 CIP 数据核字(2004)第 087135 号

书　　　　名:	竞争优势:解剖与集合(Competitive Advantage: Anatomy and Constellation)
著作责任者:	马　浩　著
责 任 编 辑:	张　燕
标 准 书 号:	ISBN 7-301-07774-2/F·0919
出 版 发 行:	北京大学出版社
地　　　　址:	北京市海淀区成府路 205 号　100871
网　　　　址:	http://cbs.pku.edu.cn　电子信箱:em@pup.pku.edu.cn
电　　　　话:	邮购部 62752015　发行部 62750672　编辑部 62752926
排　版　者:	北京高新特打字服务社　82350640
印　刷　者:	三河市新世纪印务有限公司
经　销　者:	新华书店

650 毫米×980 毫米　16 开本　19 印张　245 千字
2004 年 9 月第 1 版　2004 年 9 月第 1 次印刷
2006 年 2 月第 2 次印刷

国 内 定 价:30.00 元
International Price: US $ 30.00

未经许可,不得以任何方式复制或抄袭本书之部分或全部内容。
版权所有,翻版必究